I0127783

Living Sexuality

Teaching Gender

Series Editor

Patricia Leavy (*USA*)

International Editorial Board

Tony E. Adams (*Bradley University, USA*)
Paula Banerjee (*University of Calcutta, India*)
Nitza Berkovitch (*Ben Gurion University, Israel*)
Robin Boylorn (*University of Alabama, USA*)
Máiréad Dunne (*University of Sussex, UK*)
Mary Holmes (*University of Edinburgh, UK*)
Laurel Richardson (*Ohio State University (Emerita), USA*)
Sophie Tamas (*Carleton University, Ottawa, Canada*)

Scope

Teaching Gender publishes monographs, anthologies and reference books that deal centrally with gender and/or sexuality. The books are intended to be used in undergraduate and graduate classes across the disciplines. The series aims to promote social justice with an emphasis on feminist, multicultural and critical perspectives.

Please consult www.patricialeavy.com for submission requirements (click the book series tab).

VOLUME 14

Living Sexuality

Stories of LGBTQ Relationships,
Identities, and Desires

By

Keith Berry, Catherine M. Gillotti and Tony E. Adams

BRILL
SENSE

LEIDEN | BOSTON

All chapters in this book have undergone peer review.

The Library of Congress Cataloging-in-Publication Data is available online at http://catalog.loc.gov

ISSN 2542-9205
ISBN 978-90-04-41877-6 (paperback)
ISBN 978-90-04-41878-3 (hardback)
ISBN 978-90-04-41879-0 (e-book)

Copyright 2020 by Koninklijke Brill NV, Leiden, The Netherlands, except where stated otherwise.
Koninklijke Brill NV incorporates the imprints Brill, Brill Hes & De Graaf, Brill Nijhoff, Brill Rodopi, Brill Sense, Hotei Publishing, mentis Verlag, Verlag Ferdinand Schöningh and Wilhelm Fink Verlag.
All rights reserved. No part of this publication may be reproduced, translated, stored in a retrieval system, or transmitted in any form or by any means, electronic, mechanical, photocopying, recording or otherwise, without prior written permission from the publisher.
Authorization to photocopy items for internal or personal use is granted by Koninklijke Brill NV provided that the appropriate fees are paid directly to The Copyright Clearance Center, 222 Rosewood Drive, Suite 910, Danvers, MA 01923, USA. Fees are subject to change.

This book is printed on acid-free paper and produced in a sustainable manner.

ADVANCE PRAISE FOR
LIVING SEXUALITY: STORIES OF LGBTQ RELATIONSHIPS, IDENTITIES, AND DESIRES

"*Living Sexuality* explores the diverse ways that people who identify as LGBTQ experience and live their sexualities. The authors show how sexualities are constructed, changed, and understood, and how desires and relationships with family, friends, and partners are animated in day-to-day social practices. Unique in its attention to everyday details, embodiment, and emotional vulnerability, the autoethnographic stories add both a personal and conceptual dimension to our understanding of sexuality, evoking a rich and textured experience of the complexities, fears, joys, and sorrows of living LGBTQ lives. Discussions at the end of each chapter will stimulate lively and introspective discussions in classrooms, particularly those focused on human sexuality, queer studies, and gender. This is an important and welcome addition to the literature on LGBTQ issues."
– **Carolyn Ellis, Distinguished Professor Emerita, Department of Communication, University of South Florida**

"*Living Sexuality* makes good on its claim that engaging stories provide valuable insight into the lived experience of desire, identity, and communication. Berry, Gillotti, and Adams (with welcome trans cameos from their colleague Billy Huff) exhibit their diverse and complementary strengths in personal narrative and authoethnography. Through the LGBQ(T) stories they tell across ably disposed chapters, and across the arcs of their lives to date, we understand better how relational communication matters in complex contexts of friendship, family, mentorship, religion, sexual liaison, partnership, and more. They offer much to reflexively contemplate as we strive as queer people to communicate better with those who share the sexuality of our daily lives."
– **Charles E. Morris III, Professor and Chair, Department of Communication and Rhetorical Studies, Syracuse University, co-editor of *QED: A Journal in GLBTQ Worldmaking***

"Demonstrating that sexualities should be more naturalized and less subject to ideological critique, *Living Sexuality* weaves the deeply personal, sometimes painful, and often joyful experiences of authors Keith Berry, Catherine M. Gillotti, and Tony E. Adams into a thinking/feeling experience not soon forgotten. Whether celebrating *The Golden Girls* or musing about monogamy, the authors offer meaningful, productive, and candid accounts of their sexual being. This book is a must for my next Sexuality & Communication seminar."
– **Jimmie Manning, Chair and Professor, Communication Studies, University of Nevada**

CONTENTS

ACKNOWLEDGMENTS

We are grateful to Patricia Leavy and Shalen Lowell for the opportunity to publish in this series—without them, this book would not exist. We also would like to thank the Brill | Sense staff for their support, especially John Bennett, Jolanda Karada, and Paul Chambers. Also, our thanks to Dr. Billy Huff (Lecturer, Department of Communication, University of Illinois, Urbana/Champaign, and Researcher, Unit for Institutional Change and Social Justice at the University of Free State in South Africa) for allowing us to include his stories in our book.

Keith: I feel like the ways in which I've lived sexuality have led me to experience the highest of highs, and the lowest of lows. This includes researching and writing on these issues, such as writing this book. I've tried to live through these experiences as fully as possible, awake, and able to learn from them. This practice has not always been successful; I've tried to learn from the unsuccessful moments, too. I am thankful for my amazing co-authors, Cathy and Tony, for their part in this process, and our collaboration here, and the many family members, dear friends, colleagues, and students who have helped to make my life better. I'm grateful, and lucky. Peace.

Cathy: I am deeply grateful to Keith and Tony for the opportunity to join my voice with theirs in telling our stories. It has been a privilege to collaborate with you. For all the women who accompanied me on this journey, I am grateful for the time we spent together and the lessons I learned by knowing and loving you. And for my family (of origin and of choice), thank you for always believing in me. Your unwavering love has shaped me into the person I am, and continue to aspire to be.

Tony: I am grateful for my esteemed co-authors, Keith and Cathy, as well as for the many others who have made my writing life possible, especially Mitch Allen, Bernard Brommel, Derek Bolen, Robin Boylorn, Marcy Chvasta, Norman K. Denzin, Andrew Herrmann, Stacy Holman Jones, Lenore Langsdorf, Jimmie Manning, Ron Pelias, Sandy Pensoneau-Conway, Jillian Tullis, and Jonathan Wyatt; my former colleagues at Northeastern Illinois University and current colleagues at Bradley University; my mother, Sharon Rome; my mentors, Art Bochner and Carolyn Ellis; and my patient and loving partner, Jerry Moreno.

INTRODUCTION

What does it mean to relate with others, and ourselves, in terms of sexuality, particularly for people who identify as Lesbian, Gay, Bisexual, and Queer (LGBQ)? How do LGBQ identities inform and, in turn, how are they informed by people's social interactions and relationships? In what ways do we come to understand ourselves, others, and our worlds when communicating sexuality? What restrictions, freedoms, challenges, and opportunities comprise such relating and being? In *Living Sexuality: Stories of LGBTQ Relationships, Identities, and Desires* we explore these questions. We do so with the intent to cultivate meaningful conversation, debate, and novel ways of understanding the concept and experience of sexuality.

Several assumptions inform and complicate the study of communication, sexuality, and identity. We have written this book assuming:

(1) sexuality is a persistent and consequential dimension in people's everyday lives;

(2) sexuality is reflected in, and created through, communication, including relational communication;

(3) issues concerning LGBQ identities interrelate with concerns about relationships and desires, and with issues of sex/gender (e.g., transgender), and other cultural standpoints;

(4) research that demonstrates a first-hand understanding of the meaningfulness of relating and identities is invaluable;

(5) autoethnography and personal narrative provide such an understanding by boldly and intimately accounting for the promise and peril affecting LGBQ bodies and beings.

Understanding these issues, we contend, entails focusing on the diverse ways in which people are actually *living sexuality* within communication, together, and the meaningfulness of these experiences. Let us elaborate.

The relational communication approach we use in this book entails exploring the ongoing, everyday mundane social practices that comprise and make possible LGBQ lives. Relational communication is a co-constitutive, or jointly accomplished, dialogical process in which conversation partners use linguistic and embodied messages to symbolically create, share, interpret, and use meaning within social interaction (Gergen, 2009; Wilmot, 1995; Wood, 2000). Partners function interdependently when interacting; each person participates from the unique vantage point of their lived experience, and each contributes to the meanings created and used within interactions. Thus, social interaction is also often a tensional process fueled by different and contradictory understandings, interests, and needs (Baxter & Montgomery, 1996). Overall, relational communication is dynamic and complex, subject to multiple interpretations, and, thus, inherently uncertain.

A relational approach entails working to better understand the relevance of relationships in LGBQ lives. Wilmot (1995) writes,

> For most of us, our personal relationships with family, friends, work colleagues, and romantic partners sometimes flow and sometimes trip us up—they are among the most fulfilling and frustrating events of our lives ... Our personal relationships ebb and flow throughout our entire life span, yet our knowledge about them is often not equal to the challenges they bring us. (p. 1)

Although the relationships we keep and nurture (or don't) are subject to the "ebb and flow" of time and experience, these bonds are a constant and influential presence in our lives and, consequently, in the stories we convey in this book. With Bochner and Ellis (1995), we orient to our stories by assuming that relationships are socially constructed phenomena:

> [R]elationship life is an intersubjective world; we not only live in the same world as our partner but also participate in each other's existence. To a certain extent we must not only understand each other's views of the world but also be able to make them our own. In the course of performing and negotiating our views of the world within a close relationship, we mediate and modify each other's views. Thus we are linked by an ongoing conversation that forges a mutual identification in the face of sinister threats of competing definitions of reality that may be encountered. (pp. 204–205)

Relating requires conversation partners to try to reconcile the outcomes created by the mutual influence inherent to relationships. Different types of relationships appear throughout *Living Sexuality* including parents and children, siblings, grandparents, extended family members, "chosen" family, teacher/student, classmates, neighbors, community members, strangers, and workplace colleagues. The ways communicators relate to themselves are also of considerable interest. In what ways do relationships influence LGBQ lives, and to whose benefit and at whose expense?

Examining LGBQ lives also means emphasizing the relevance and significance of these identities. At the very least, the study of identity entails asking questions about self-understanding and the constitution of subjectivity. Although identity formation is certainly informed by one's biology or genetics, we focus primarily on identity as a co-constitutive process socially enacted with others. Put differently, people symbolically develop identities, and we come to understand ourselves, and others, within interactions and relationships. Identities are contested cultural phenomena (Martin & Nakayama, 2013), formative processes enacted under social constraints (e.g., power) and sometimes duress (see, for example, Adams, 2011; Berry, 2016).

Emphasizing the ways people live as LGBQ also entails exploring communication and identity as it occurs within specific contexts. *Living Sexuality* hones in on relating as it happens within a diverse number of contexts including families, romantic relationships, friendships, religion, media (e.g., television, film, social media, dating and hookup apps), schools, workplaces, and public situations. The cultural contexts in which relating occurs shape the meanings displayed through this communication. As a result, LGBQ communication and identities are not universal or generalized processes, but rather contingent, particularized, and local.

The climate of the relationships matters as well. The stories in this book show bonds in which people demonstrate a wide array of (often competing) climates including: intimate and cold, supportive and defensive, inclusive and exclusionary, peaceful and violent, accepting and judgmental, open and secretive, confrontational and avoidant, narcissistic and codependent, loving and cruel, objectifying and affirming, close and distanced, and freeing and suffocating. In addition, the stories show pivotal relational moments occurring in one's life, such as coming out as LGBQ and T[1]; staying with and leaving religion; living "open" intimate relationships; finding a sitcom whose characters and storylines resonate deeply; coming to terms with and reconciling one's stigmatized identity; forgiving others (or not); moments when others evolve from being adversaries to advocates; and coming to accept and love ourselves within our difference. In this way, the climates at play influence relating, and, in turn, relating influences these climates. Taken together, these qualities and critical moments shape conversation partners and relationships in big and small ways. They also further illustrate the fundamental interconnectedness that exists between people, and the personal and consequential nature of relational bonds.

Living Sexuality offers perspectives on cultural problems that inform and sometimes govern the lives and well-being of communicators. The stories offer insights into life-shaping issues like inclusive and epithetical uses of language, homophobia, heteronormativity, transphobia, transitioning, queerness, sex, monogamy, hyper- and hegemonic masculinity, embodiment, the closet, coming out as LGBQ, gender fluidity, authenticity, being "normal," sexual masochism, codependency, HIV/AIDS, bullying, resilience, pride, estrangement, "unlearning," and forgiveness. The problems appearing in our stories are often thorny and confounding. They are also deeply personal. Yet, although the stories we tell are ours, we also hope that they resonate with readers and their experiences. Nevertheless, by telling our stories, the relationship between cultural problems and the ways people can(not) relate and self-identify come into view.

How have we gone about the process of telling these stories? Primarily through the use of autoethnography. Autoethnography is an approach to research and writing that entails researchers reflexively drawing upon personal lived experience to describe and examine culture. The approach is known for its diversity in concept and form (Ellis & Bochner, 2000), and for the inclusion of stories and issues commonly overlooked, if not altogether dismissed or ignored, by normative academic research (Ellis, Adams, & Bochner, 2011; Holman-Jones, Adams, & Ellis, 2013). In this way, the approach provides a welcoming space for the telling of novel accounts of lived experience. The center of autoethnography is comprised of intimate stories that show heavy description, vulnerability, emotion, and evocative detail to demonstrate the uniqueness and commonality of experiences comprising the human condition (Bochner & Ellis, 2016).

Personal stories are ideal tools for understanding the relational experiences of sexuality, and good stories are about more than just the storyteller. Bochner (2012) writes,

> The truths of autoethnography exist *between* storyteller and story listener; they dwell in the listeners' and readers' engagement with the writer's engagement with adversity; the heartbreaking feelings of stigma and marginalization; the resistance to the authority to canonical discourses; the therapeutic desire to live up to the challenges of life and to emerge with greater self-knowledge, the opposition to the repression of the body, the difficulty of finding words to make bodily dysfunction

meaningful, the desire for self-expression, and the urge to speak to and assist a community of fellow sufferers. The call of these stories is for engagement from within and between, and not from without. (p. 161, emphasis in original)

Stories operate as communicative texts that reach out to readers, enabling them to consider the ways that the stories being told resonate with their experiences (Berry & Patti, 2015; Bochner & Ellis, 2016). Stories also allow researchers to trouble or disrupt normative conceptualizations of identities and experiences, reveal truths that had previously been concealed, and question and (re)imagine taken-for-granted assumptions and practices (Boylorn & Orbe, 2014; Holman Jones & Adams, 2010). In turn, stories enable researchers to identify and advocate for a multiplicity of meanings and truths inherent to relating and being. Moreover, working with stories allows us to address the contested nature of stories and storytellers' lives. As Allison (1996) writes, "Behind the story I tell is the one I don't. Behind the story you hear is the one I wish I could make you hear" (p. 39).

We've written and organized *Living Sexuality* so that readers may engage with the book in at least four main ways. First, organized conceptually, each story offers a distinct account of one of us conveying their lived experience with a significant issue, or series of issues.

Second, many of the stories relate to and complement each other. For example, Keith offers two stories about similar relational issues (Chapter 1 and Chapter 8), but from a different perspective. Cathy's stories demonstrate the ways in which her relating and being with respect to sexuality has evolved over time, enticing readers to trace her movements across her five accounts. Also, Tony's detailing of "the closet" (Chapter 2) can be used as a way to understand Cathy's story about coming out, and Keith's lack of awareness or ability to recognize gayness in his youth (see Chapter 1 and Chapter 8).

Third, the book's design allows readers to confront the same issue from multiple and sometimes dramatically different vantage points. Take, for instance, the ways some of Cathy's and Tony's stories disparately reconcile issues of religion.

Fourth, all of the stories in the book appear together as a collective story that speaks to the complexities and contingencies inherent to the pursuit of living, being, and relating with regard to sexuality.

Each of us come to this project and the writing of our stories with distinct and shared academic backgrounds. Much of Keith's work has been rooted in autoethnographic and ethnographic approaches to studying relational communication, and communication and culture, more generally. His research interests have primarily focused on how communicators perform and use identities within communication processes. Cathy's training is in interpersonal and health communication. While much of her scholarship is in health communication, her teaching style is grounded in storytelling and focused on the examination of the "light" and "dark" sides of interpersonal relationships. Tony uses qualitative research methods, most often ethnography and autoethnography, to explore interpersonal and family communication, sexuality, and queer theory.

Each of us also emerges from this research and writing process having learned a great deal about the relational and existential conditions that inform living sexuality. In particular, we have learned about ourselves and the relational partners we keep (or don't) in our lives.

In my (Keith's) stories, I primarily focus on the bonds that were important in my youth and those that are vital in my life today. In "Ode to the Boys" (Chapter 1), I explore the close personal friendships I had with two boys, Cody and Kyle, when I was in high school. These connections enabled me to feel more at ease in a time in my life when I couldn't recognize I was gay, and when pursuing friendships with most boys, especially hyper-masculine boys, was the last thing I wanted to do. Similarly, in "Relational Gifts" (Chapter 8), I catalogue the innumerous bonds I've maintained with girls and women in my youth, and women in my adulthood, and the meaningfulness of these connections in regards to my identity and well-being. Telling this story has allowed me to realize, for the first time with such clarity, just how vital these girls and women were/are to my survival and happiness. In "Things I Don't Have to Do" (Chapter 5) and "Things I Must Still Do" (Chapter 15), I use a reflexive and descriptive "notes" representational style to describe and make sense of the social practices that I don't have to do as a result of being gay, as well as the practices I still must enact, and the problems I must still face, because I'm gay. In "The Resilient You" (Chapter 17), I describe the ways of performing I relied on in my youth as a means of being resilient in the face of being bullied. Conveying this story has allowed me to revisit how I worked to keep myself well, and to demonstrate that subjectivity (e.g., victim subjectivity) is more complex than folk wisdom on the bullying problem might otherwise suggest.

My (Cathy's) stories invite readers to accompany me on a journey that begins in elementary school when I insist on taking gymnastics with the boys instead of the girls and ends in the present. "Mental Gymnastics" (Chapter 3) explores my earliest feminist ideals while simultaneously revealing my body image issues. My stories chronicle my struggles with acceptance, self-love, and loving others. The next two chapters, "True Companion" (Chapter 7) and "Rumination (Chapter 11) demonstrate the passion and risks of coming out, first love, first love lost, and reconciling my religious beliefs with my sexual identity. While sometimes painful to recount, sharing these stories makes me all the more grateful for the experiences. For "True Companion," I interviewed my first love (Emily) to provide a more balanced recollection of our history. This conversation and co-construction of our past was a gift as important as, if not more important than, the relationship itself. In "The Joy" (Chapter 14), I explore the codependent—narcissistic continuum by documenting times when I have been the co-dependent and the narcissist in previous relationships. The story demonstrates the dynamic interplay of relating, the complexities of these behavioral tendencies, and the light and dark sides of us all. Finally, in "Refrain" (Chapter 16), I write to myself 20 years in the past to share the words of wisdom (refrains of love) from my beloved family and friends that have shaped who I am today.

Across my (Tony's) chapters, I discuss prominent concepts and issues associated with sexuality, as well as describe how sexuality has informed my relationships with partners, friends, and family. In "The Closet" (Chapter 2), I describe characteristics of "coming out of the closet," a type of self-disclosure in which a person reveals same-sex/gender attraction to others. In "Language Matters" (Chapter 10), I identify terms and assumptions related to sexuality and language and demonstrate the importance of being accurate, inclusive, and respectful with our words. In "Queer Duck" (Chapter 6), I describe some of my experiences with being the first, and still only, openly self-identified queer person in my family—to borrow Kath Weston's (1991) phrase, a (queer) duck residing in a family of (heterosexual) swans (p. 75). In "Monogamy" (Chapter 13), I venture into the concept of monogamy by exploring what it means to me and why I reject the idea. I conclude with "Estrangement ⇔ Pride ⇔ Forgiveness" (Chapter 18), where I explore how LGBQ persons can use the interrelated concepts of "estrangement," "pride," and "forgiveness" to address and remedy past harms, overcome adversity, and cultivate self-love.

In "The Girls" (Chapter 9), we (Keith & Tony) describe the relationship between gay men and the 80s/90s hit television sitcom *The Golden Girls*. We use a dialogue format to reflect on the intimate and enduring bonds we have formed and sustained with characters on the show, and the program in general. For us, *The Golden Girls* are inseparable from any discussion that seeks to understand how we live sexuality.

We are honored to include two stories on living as trans written by our colleague Dr. Billy Huff. In "Walls" (Chapter 4), Billy focuses on his trans body and desires, looking at the relationships between bodies, identities, pleasures, desires, recognition, and social expectations. In search for an outlet for his authenticity, he confronts pervasive sex negativity with the force of a desiring trans body. In "The Sexual Relationship" (Chapter 12), Billy continues to convey barriers that exist between self and others, using Jacques Lacan's notion that "there's no such thing as a sexual relationship" to explore a sexual relationship in transition. He reflects on what a sustained sexual relationship during gender transition taught him about sexual relationships in general.

Boundaries inform and confound all inquiry, such as the stories we include in the book. Our accounts demonstrate the position that all stories are "partial, partisan, and problematic" (Goodall, 2000, p. 55). That is, stories are incomplete, perspectival, and subject to multiple interpretations, disagreement, and debate. In this way, we are mindful that not all stories relevant to the LGBQ issues appear in the book. We hope this book inspires readers to convey their stories using autoethnography, or a similar approach that is committed to the sort of understanding that can gained from first-hand, candid, and vivid accounts of lived experience. May these future stories serve to verify and challenge our stories, and spark dialogue, advocacy, and action taking concerning LGBQ lives and social justice, more generally.

We also hope readers move through the book by remembering the powerful nature of stories in people's lives. According to Yoshino (2007),

> We all have a story we must repeat until we get it right, a story whose conveniences must be corrected and whose simplifications must be seen through before we are done with it, or it is done with us. Each time I tell my story, I am released, yet there is also the story from which I yearn to be released. (p. 50)

Conveying our stories has provided us with the opportunity to examine the ways in which LGBQ (and trans) identities shape and sometimes harm relational and cultural lives, and, in turn, how communicating relationally and culturally informs and puts at risk these identities. Our stories complicate the "conveniences" and "simplifications" that, if we're not careful, can and do prevail in contexts of difference. Too much is at stake to allow stories to remain untold and for simplistic stories to go unchallenged. We emerge from the process of telling our stories feeling "released." But we also are aware, yet again, that there are stories from which we, and others, still "yearn to be released." May this storytelling and the liberation it enables resonate, inspire, and create the conditions for greater self-awareness, and the awareness of others, for living sexuality at relational, cultural, intercultural and societal levels.

NOTE

[1] Throughout this book, we use "lesbian," "gay," "bisexual," and "queer" (LGBQ) when referencing identities tied to same-sex/gender attraction. Although "trans" (T) identities often share similar issues and struggles as LGBQ identities, T identities are tied to sex/gender, not sexual desire or attraction; a person who is trans can be trans *and* heterosexual, trans *and* queer, trans *and* gay (see Adams, 2017; Meadow, 2018).

REFERENCES

Adams, T. E. (2011). *Narrating the closet: An autoethnography of same-sex attraction*. Walnut Creek, CA: Left Coast Press.

Adams, T. E. (2017). GLBT communication studies. In M. Allen (Ed.), *The Sage encyclopedia of communication research methods* (pp. 624–626). Thousand Oaks, CA: Sage. doi:10.4135/9781483381411.n221

Allison, D. (1996). *Two or three things I know for sure*. New York: Plume.

Baxter L. A., & Montgomery, B. M. (1996). *Relating: Dialogues & dialectics*. New York: Guilford Press.

Berry, K. (2016). *Bullied: Tales of torment, identity, and youth*. New York: Routledge.

Berry, K., & Patti, C. J. (2015). Lost in narration: Applying autoethnography. *Journal of Applied Communication Research, 43*, 263–268. https://doi.org/10.1080/00909882.2015.1019548

Bochner, A. P. (2012). On first-person narrative scholarship: Autoethnography as acts of meaning. *Narrative Inquiry, 22*, 156–164. Doi: 10.1075/ni.22.1.10boc

Bochner, A. P., & Ellis, C. (1995). Telling and living: Narrative co-construction and the practices of interpersonal relationships. In W. Leeds-Hurwitz (Ed.), *Social approaches to communication*. New York: Guilford Press.

Bochner, A., & Ellis, C. (2016). *Evocative autoethnography: Writing lives & telling stories*. New York: Routledge.

Boylorn, R., & Orbe, M. (2014). *Critical autoethnography: Intersecting cultural identities in everyday life*. New York: Routledge.

Ellis, C., & Bochner, A. P. (2000). Autoethnography, personal narrative, reflexivity: Researcher as subject. In N. K. Denzin & Y. S. Lincoln (Eds.), *The handbook of qualitative research* (2nd ed., pp. 733–768). Thousand Oaks, CA: Sage.

Ellis, C., Adams, T. E., & Bochner, A. P. (2011). Autoethnography: An overview. *Forum: Qualitative Social Research, 12*, http://dx.doi.org/10.17169/fqs-12.1.1589

Gergen, K. J. (2009). *Relational being: Beyond self and community*. New York: Oxford University Press.

Goodall, H. L. (2000). *Writing the new ethnography*. Lanham MA: AltaMira Press.

Holman Jones, S. & Adams, T. E. (2010). Autoethnography and queer theory: Making possibilities. In N. K. Denzin & M. G. Giardini (Eds.), *Qualitative inquiry and human rights* (pp. 136–157). Walnut Creek, CA: Left Coast Press.

Holman Jones, S., Adams, T. E., & Ellis, C. (2013). *Handbook of autoethnography*. New York: Routledge.

Martin, J. N., & Nakayama, T. K. (2013). *Intercultural communication in contexts*. New York: McGraw-Hill.

Meadow, T. (2018). *Trans kids: Being gendered in the twenty-first century.* Berkeley, CA: University of California Press.

Weston, K. (1991). *Families we choose: Lesbians, gays, kinship.* New York: Columbia University Press.

Wilmot, W. W. (1995). *Relational communication.* New York: McGraw-Hill.

Wood, J. T. (2000). *Relational communication: Continuity and change in personal relationships* (2nd ed.). Belmont, CA: Wadsworth.

Yoshino, K. (2007). *Covering: The hidden assault on our civil rights.* New York: Random House.

ODE TO THE BOYS

Keith Berry

I have come to understand myself and others, and the changing and complex world in which we live, by performing in ways that are directly related to the people with whom I interact on a regular basis. Put differently, who I am, and who I am not, is the sum total of all of the symbolic interactions with others from my lived experience (Blumer, 1986). This includes the bonds I've experienced with LGBQ and heterosexual friends. These friendships have been instrumental in making fun times more joyful and difficult ones more manageable. For instance, my LGBQ friends comprise an invaluable network of relationships, and I consider some of them to be "chosen family." I shudder when trying to think about what life would look like without my co-authors Tony and Cathy, whom I've been lucky enough to know and be close to since 2002 and 1997, respectively. In addition, I would not be who I am today, and possibly not even alive, without the love and support given to me by the girls and women with whom I have been friends (see Chapter 8; Berry, 2016). Yet, girls were not the only friends who mattered to me in this way in my youth. I also benefited from friendships with guys who related to me in ways that allowed me to stay well, or at least well enough. They were special boys. These boys saved me.

In this chapter I tell the story of my friendships with two influential boys, Cody and Kyle. I return to important memories of salient interactional moments from our lived experience together to better understand how my bonds with these boys helped me. I focus on the ways in which Cody and Kyle performed, and didn't perform, and how their ways of relating with me, in effect, enabled me to relate in ways that resonated with how I felt, and not how I "should have" felt as a boy. I owe much to these boys. Thus, I also use this story as a way to acknowledge the care demonstrated within these relationships, and in the spirit of my gratitude.

© KONINKLIJKE BRILL NV, LEIDEN, 2020 | DOI:10.1163/9789004418790_001

CODY

I meet Cody during my first year of high school. I attend a private, Roman Catholic, college preparatory school in the south suburbs of Chicago, near where I live with my mom, dad, older brother, and younger sister. I am a short, dark brown haired, somewhat chubby boy who likes to spend a lot of time watching television, playing with neighbors, and talking with my friends' mothers in their kitchens, or while sitting with them sipping iced tea on their front porches. Unlike so many of the other boys I know, I am not very athletic, nor am I interested in sports, or girls. Since most of my close friends attend the public high school near where I live, I am having trouble adjusting and making friends in my new school. I am flourishing academically and am well in many ways in my life. Yet, a lingering and difficult-to-name dis-ease is shaping my life (see Berry, 2016).

"I feel … bleh," I often say to my mother.

"What is it? How are you feeling bleh?" She says in response, searching for answers so that she and my dad can help.

"I don't know, I just feel … different … weird." Not being able to give my mom a clear answer adds to my dis-ease. I can tell she so badly wants to help me, and to see me happier. She continues to probe, and eventually arrives at an answer.

"What's one way you feel different, honey?" Her tenderness is helpful in opening me up and allowing me to speak about my feelings.

I try to put my feelings into words. "I feel different from the other boys." For as long as I can remember, I've always felt different, and I have been aware of this difference. My feelings and awareness ignited when I started middle school, but were especially acute by the time I graduated.

"I don't like the same things most kids like."

"I know, honey, you're a special boy." Mom often tells me I'm special. Even if we are not able to leave situations, or conversations about issues, with definitive answers, she reminds me I'm special. She will go on to do so throughout my youth and twenties. "Also, who says you have to like the same things or be the same person?" She rarely fails to comfort me in ways that allow me to move forward.

In spite of the helpfulness of our talk in the moment, I continue feeling dis-ease. To help, my mom arranges for me to assist with the spring play at Heritage, the middle school from which I graduated. She teaches in the school district and knows the play's director.

"I don't want to go back to that school," I say. "I graduated and I'm now in high school. It wouldn't be normal for me to be back there so much."

"You are normal, honey," she says. "Plus, you loved being in the play when you were at Heritage, and if you do this, you'll be part of the play's orchestra. You love playing the piano. You love plays."

I do love to play the piano, and sometimes spend hours downstairs by myself riffing. It is therapeutic, and fun. Also, going back to that school and now being older than those students may feel good. I could be the "cool kid" who comes back "older" and "more mature."

"Okay, I'll do it."

"Goooood! I know you'll have fun."

My mom is correct. I not only enjoy myself, but assisting with the play also allows me to meet one of the most influential boys I have ever met.

***

Cody is a short, thin, seventh grader who has wavy brown-blonde hair, and whose bright smile lights up dark school hallways. He and his mom, dad, older sister, and younger brother live a few blocks away from me and my family, but he and I have never met, and my family doesn't know his family. Cody is a stereotypically attractive kind of boy to whom others seem to be immediately attracted. "Cody is so cute." "Isn't Cody adorable?!" "Cody, I love your jeans." "You are so good in your part (of the play)." Girls flirt with him, and he reciprocates. Yet, their fawning over him doesn't lead him to be arrogant. Instead, he is humble, unassuming, and kind. Additionally, Cody moves through the world in soft and gentle ways that distinguish him from most of the boys I know at my school. Even more, he is a "play kid" who is invested in drama and the arts, and disinterested in the usual "boy stuff" like sports and roughhousing. Cody's ways of performing lead me to feel easily attracted to him on an interpersonal level. He and I become close friends.

Over the next several months, several times a week I go directly from my high school to play practice. This routine gives Cody and me plenty of opportunities to interact, whether while we are on break, or just before and after practices. Each time I look forward to being around him, even if only for a few minutes. When together, Cody laughs at my jokes, and I laugh at his. The more outlandish our jokes are, the better. We make sure we greet each other when arriving and say goodbye when we leave practice and go home. Absent in these interactions, and our relationship, generally, are combative comments that pit us against each other. Also, we don't interact with anyone around us in that manner either. We relate through shared jargon and other styles of relating, and an intimate way of understanding what they mean and how we are using them. I notice others noticing the bond we have. They see I have a close friend, a friend who's a popular guy, someone who puts a smile on my face and allows me to feel more at ease. Knowing they feel this way makes me feel more comfortable.

The closeness of my bond with Cody sometimes makes it difficult for me to navigate the interactions and relationships I have with other friends and peers, especially with "typical" and "normal" boys. For instance, I go from interactions with Cody that entail our exchanging confirming messages that allow us to be ourselves and to feel supported and appreciated, and, thus, valued and safe, to interactions filled with disconfirming messages that are filled with others' critique and dismissal. Granted, these other boys may not mean to be hurtful. Also, relating in this way may show a distinct mode of bonding that, for these conversation partners, distinctively conveys intimacy. Regardless, I don't identify with that style. It makes me uneasy. In addition, the more I switch from interacting positively with Cody, to awkwardly with others, serves to stress and underscore the intimacy and trust that I value and prefer with Cody, and the mistrust and distance that I feel when I am around other kids. Although being with Cody allows me to feel better about myself, it also immerses me in jarring relational performances that lack stability, and increase my uncertainty, and distressing feelings.

Cody and I relate in these ways—intimate, affirming, fun, freeing—throughout the entire play season. On the last night of the production, when the play director debriefs with us that night's performance, and our performance season overall, he and I decide to sit together. While the director extolls great praise for our performances, her voice drifts to the background of my attention when I look over at Cody and realize this is the last time we will see each other. So far, he and I are only together during play-related activities at the school. I don't feel comfortable asking him to hang out once play season ends. I don't want to be that creepy high school kid hanging out with a seventh grader. Also, I don't even know if he wants to be friends now that the play season has ended. Maybe he doesn't see me in that way. When the director finishes her speech, Cody and I hug and say goodbye to each other.

"See ya' later, alligator," he says, as he smiles and winks at me in a smooth and cool manner.

"Later alligator," I say. I try to mimic his winking in ways that sync with my words, but fumble, making my winking clumsy. I quickly try to cover my awkwardness, by pulling him into me again to give him another and longer hug.

"Have a good summer, my friend," I say, as I start to walk to the door.

"You too, my friend," he says, walking back into the rehearsal room to gather his backpack. I already miss him.

Cody and I do not keep in touch for the next academic year. I feel a little better that year, more confident and sure of myself, but my dis-ease remains. At the end of the year, Cody is, again, cast in the play, and I return again to assist. Unlike last year, however, I am eager to be back at Heritage. I return to be around the drama kids. More importantly, I return to be around Cody on a regular basis. Just knowing that I'll be seeing him soon makes me happy.

When I walk through the large metal and glass front doors and into the school the first day of practice, I see Cody talking with his other guy friends. Facing the doorway, he spots me immediately. Although it has been almost a year since he and I have seen each other, we instantly return to the same rapport we used last year.

"Keith Berry, you're back … oh no!" he says in a teasing voice, his smile beaming.

"I know," I say, "I'm back. I guess I couldn't help myself. Here comes trouble." I am smiling widely, knowing he hears the sarcasm in my response.

"It's good to see you friend."

"Same here, it is good to see you."

"You ready for another play run? For more rehearsals and memorizing? More jokes and shtick?"

"Oh yeah, I'm definitely ready!"

Although it has been many months, our time apart feels like a couple of weeks. Now back around Cody again, the ways I can sometimes feel unsure of myself and others feel less important. With Cody I feel that special feeling of confidence he seems to draw out of me, or at least, allows me to draw out of myself. In returning to our friendship, we've returned to the shared language and meanings, and the care we infuse and rely on when interacting. Back with Cody, I feel at home and at peace.

Cody and I spend this new play season in much the same way as we did last year. Our conversations continue to be easy and enjoyable. Our time together is wonderful. New this year is his bragging about me in front of others. Rarely does a rehearsal go by when he does not say kind things about me.

"How's bigtime high school life going, Keith Berry?" He loves to use my first and last name together. "Are the classes hard?" "I'm sure you're the cool kid in school!"

"Classes are hard," I say, "but I'm doing well." "I don't know how cool I am. Not as cool as you." I do not feel "cool," nor do I think others see me in that way.

"I'm sure Keith Berry is the 'cool cat at school.'"

I might not believe that I am cool, even when hearing Cody say those words. But hearing him say them warms my heart. Being around him makes me feel happy, alive even, in new and welcomed ways. Maybe I am not that different. Or if I am different, maybe that's fine.

Cody and I become closer friends during the second play season, so much so that when we are approaching another end to the season, the thought of saying goodbye makes me feel sad. Cody will soon graduate and move on to the public high school nearby, and not mine. Feeling more confident this year, I build up the nerve to ask him to make plans to get together socially.

"Hey, friend, when the play is done, we should hang out and do stuff." "Wanna play tennis sometime?" Exhale. Done. I asked him.

"Sure, I love tennis, let's do it," he says.

I don't like to play tennis that much, but I heard him mention that he plays with some of his other friends at a rehearsal last week. I figured playing with him would be a way for us to see each other again. I had secured a way to prolong my happy feelings.

Cody and I play tennis together, just the two of us, each Saturday morning for the next three weeks. The relational magic that inspired so many of our laughs and moments of good will from over the two past play seasons continues, and grows. He and I perform the same shtick, as well as develop new jokes, and try to outdo each other in creativity and timing. We create nicknames for each other and use them when talking. We "high five" each other after a great match in support and celebration. I rarely high five other boys. Usually when boys want to do so, it's physical and rough, and sometimes the harder the better, so as to validate one's toughness. When I high five Cody, it's still enthusiastic and definitely makes a loud clapping noise, but it is not aggressive. I can feel Cody's kindness as our hands make contact, and suspect he feels the same. I am a little clumsy at first, as I don't have much practice. Yet, I am also comfortable. I don't feel awkward when doing it, as if I am trying to be someone I am not through a forced display of hyper-masculinity.

Cody and I soon join a tennis league together at the local YMCA, and have fun playing competitively each Saturday for almost a full year. A few weeks after our league ends, he meets a girl who quickly becomes his girlfriend. They stay together for a few months. Yet, his new life in high school, again, not the one I attend, results in infrequent visits. Once again I miss him, but this time, these feelings feel different than they had in the past when he and I parted ways after play seasons ended. Now, we stay in touch and hang out still, but not as frequently. When we do get together, the play, rapport, and care we enact are still there for me. I still love being around him. This time something is different, and like in the past, I am not able to name and express my feelings clearly.

One night a few weeks after I had last spent time with Cody, my mom comes into the kitchen from our family room, only to find me sitting at the kitchen table with the lights off, my head folded into my arms and resting on the table.

"Honey, what are you doing in here with the lights off," she asks in a confused and concerned voice. After turning on the light, she sits down on a chair to my left, and begins to gently rub my back. I remain crouched down with my head buried in my hands.

"Honey?" "Talk to me …" She pauses for a good ten seconds, as if to figure out what she wants to say or ask, and more likely, to figure out how she will say what she wants to express. Her silence leads me to lift up my head, ever so slowly, and to sit upright in my chair, while still looking only at my hands on the table.

"What's bothering you?" She is now speaking more emphatically.

"I don't know, mom. I'm not feeling well. My stomach aches. I can't think straight." We pause in our conversation for another ten seconds, which feels like it is more like sixty seconds. I suspect it also feels that way for my mom, who now looks worried.

"Is this about Cody?"

Her last question surprises me. It is not the response I would expect in this situation. I respond by saying nothing. Yet, I look at her distressed.

"Hang in there baby doll, and come watch TV with your father and me in the family room. *Dynasty* is on and I know you love that show. You're going to be okay sweetie; you're a very special boy." She kisses me on the forehead, grabs a drink from the refrigerator, and walks out of the kitchen and sits on her favorite spot on the sofa.

***

As I write this story today, re-visiting and re-thinking these experiences almost thirty years later, I am still "with" that boy who is working to reconcile his difference and dis-ease. I feel the ways my body opens with happiness and acceptance when I remember how positively Cody influenced me. Yet, I also feel the pain of the boy trying to think his way through how confusing and difficult unknowns can feel. The kitchen interaction with my mom stands out as particularly significant, and resists easy answers. What was going on? What meanings can I give to that painful experience in the here and now?

It is possible I respond in this way because I truly don't know why I am anxious. My response brings to the surface, and to our interaction, the physical pangs of a dis-ease that feels vague and unclear. In this sense, my silence speaks to my ignorance and the resulting uncertainty and numbness. Yet, it is also possible I am responding to her in this way because I don't want to allow myself to feel the emotions I am feeling. Maybe I feel ashamed for missing Cody so much. Boys need to be tougher in handling (i.e., not acknowledging and expressing) feelings. Actually, boys should not feel these emotions for other male friends, and they probably should not express these sorts of feelings for friends who are girls, unless they're romantic ones. Maybe I am feeling shame because these emotions feel more intimate than feelings someone would ordinarily have for a friend, but boys should not have those feelings, nor should we fathom having such bonds. Each of these interpretations feels plausible.

Cody and I stay friends until my junior year in high school. We see each other occasionally, but slowly fall out of touch and eventually do not talk to each other again. Surprisingly, I do not feel much of a loss. I'm betting he doesn't either. We must like different things. Plus, I have other, closer friends, with whom I spend my time. However, I will always remember his kindness and the ways he opened his arms to me.

KYLE

I am standing at the front register at Oakwood Pharmacy, the drugstore where I work beginning my sophomore year of high school. I will work at Oakwood until the summer of my second year of college. It's a slow night and, having completed my work stocking the shelves with candy bars and magazines, I am reading a magazine and observing customers as they enter the store. After a long gap between customers, I see a familiar face walk through the doorway. Kyle is a guy from school I have known since we were both in the fourth grade. He's wearing a brown aviator leather jacket, just like the one Tom Cruise wears in *Top Gun*. As he works his way into the middle of the store he falls out of my view. I return to reading.

A few minutes later, Kyle walks up to the register and plops a bunch of groceries down onto the counter. Many families send their kids to Oakwood after school to purchase last minute food to use as ingredients in that evening's dinner. He and I say "hey" to each other by nodding our heads and I begin ringing up his purchases.

"You're Mrs. Berry's son, Keith, right?" he says.

"Yep, that's me," I respond, dramatically waving my hands in the air.

"Your mom is awesome. She was my teacher a long time ago."

"Thanks, a lot of people I meet here say the same thing. That's nice. You're … Kyle … and you work at the arcade, right?"

"Yep, that's me," he responds, smiling but without my dramatic flourish. He pays for his purchases and begins to exit. "Okay, thanks, I'll see ya around."

"See ya, enjoy that dinner." I point to the spaghetti and jar of Ragu in his hand.

As Kyle walks out of the store and to his vehicle, I look through the windows and notice him getting in a jeep. Moments later he soars out of the parking lot with the jeep's top down, blasting the radio and bobbing his head to the beats of the music.

I see Kyle again at the drugstore several times over the next couple of weeks. Each time we see each other, we chat for a few seconds, mainly small talk, as he purchases his goods. Each conversation lasts a bit longer, and each seems more personal. He's easy to talk with, and seems to enjoy chatting with me.

One day when Kyle checks out with me at the register, our chat gets even friendlier. "Hey we should hang out sometime," he says. "Maybe we can hangout at the arcade where I work, or go to the movies?"

"Okay, that would be cool." I pause a bit after responding, mainly because I'm surprised Kyle wants to socialize with me. It's not that I don't have plenty of friends, or that I see myself as not friend worthy. I pause because he is the sort of guy who others think is cool and good looking, attributes I don't always believe others would use to describe me. Also, I feel like I'm not the "guy's guy" who I thought Kyle might be, and many guys my age are. I'm thrilled he's asked and would like to be his friend.

"That sounds awesome." Kyle and I exchange telephone numbers, hang out that weekend, and each weekend to follow. We soon become best friends.

Developing this friendship with Kyle couldn't happen at a better time. My life in high school continues to be difficult. The school's Roman Catholic mission often suffocates and bullies me (see Berry, 2016). Most of my friends still attend the public school near where I live, where Kyle attends, and I don't feel inclined to make new friends at my school. Consequently, I often feel divided and perform "split" selves: the "academic me" when I am at school and the "social me" when I am away from school. At school I continue to excel academically. I try out for and make it onto the school's marching band, and am placed on the drum line. I last for only one semester before quitting. Maybe there is something about my short and petite body toppling over while trying to march with my bass drum that makes marching band unattractive. Away from school I have a small group of good guy friends with whom I do a lot of fun things, like going to the movies, swimming, bowling, or hanging out at one of our houses. "Social me" feels happiest when I am with Kyle. As a result, I try to spend as much time with him as possible.

Kyle is tall, thin, and has feathered dark brown hair. Like many boys at this time in the 1980s, including me, his hair is styled in layers and somewhat wavy. He lives with his mom, dad, and two brothers and sister in a subdivision about two miles from where my family lives. His family is tightly-knit and often bonds around, and proudly raves about, their Irish and German heritages. They love that I, too, come from a mixed Irish and German background. His father, a wonderful man whom Kyle reveres, loves to speak in an Irish brogue. Almost immediately after Kyle and I become friends, his family includes me in their activities. "Don't cha know," his dad says in an animated voice, "you must come to our annual St. Patty's Day festivities, young man." Also, his parents talk in such endearing relational terms. "You're an honorary member of this family," his dad frequently says. "You're like one of our own," his mom tells me. "I agree," I say. "You're my 'bonus family.'" Similar to his parents and siblings, Kyle moves through the world with kindness and peace, and he is endlessly supportive of me. He's also sensitive about things, including his physical appearance. He is the sort of boy who routinely tries to gain weight. Yet, no matter how hard he tries, much to his chagrin, his physique remains toned but thin. He and I are opposites in this way; whereas, I spend most of my time trying to stay fit and thin, he wants "muscle mass" to "bulk up."

Kyle and I enjoy doing many different things when we are together. Our favorite: driving around town with the top down in his family's jeep, listening to music and talking. In these times his influence on me is most significant.

"Dude ride is on, get in, my dude!" Kyle says to me, as I enter the passenger side of his jeep and begin to fasten my seatbelt.

"I'm in, dude, let's hit the streets!"

Bill and Ted's Excellent Adventure is a hit movie in U.S. culture this summer. The storyline is inane, but the movie is important to our relationship. Bill and Ted are best friends who build a time machine to help them complete a history project in high school, which they are working feverishly to finish at the last minute. The two embody a stereotypical White Southern California beach attitude, constantly repeating words like "dude" and "most excellent" when interacting with each other, and everyone else. Although we are different from them in most ways, Bill and Ted's ways of being shape how Kyle and I spend time together. For example, our "dude rides" are filled with "most excellent stops" at the arcade or at fast food restaurants, where he and I "secure and consume most excellent morsels (of food)" that we eat while we drive. I make cassette tapes filled with our favorite "dude songs," the "excellent tune-age" that also provides a soundtrack for our cruising. I think Bill and Ted are so appealing to me and Kyle because of the funny and outlandish ways they act; indeed, they are arguably role models for how not to perform. I also love them because they are constantly together and, in the end, care about and love each other, and openly demonstrate such feelings.

On dude rides, Kyle and I perform in stereotypically masculine and heterosexual boy ways. With the wind blowing in our faces and through our hair, we sing out loud, sometimes in unison, lyrics from our favorite pop rock groups, like The Cars, Def Leppard, INXS, and ZZ Top. We sing the choruses to songs, and aren't afraid to perform an occasional "air guitar" or "air drums" in tandem during guitar and drum solos. We sing as if our hearts are pouring out with the group's male singers, whose words frequently crave sexy female bodies and lament lost female love. Yet, while we sing in unison, the connection Kyle and I embody concerning the song's stories are distinct in important ways. Kyle has had a girlfriend throughout much of high school. I have never had a girlfriend, nor, as I share above, do I feel attracted to them in the ways I see Kyle, and most boys, feeling. I am not aware of my same-sex attraction and desire at this time in my youth. It's possible (likely?) I am repressing these feelings, but, if this is the case, doing so falls outside of my immediate awareness. Nonetheless, what I know for sure is that the ways in which we sing are different, and emanate from different places, existentially speaking.

"Have any girls caught your attention at school?" he says, turning down the music, so we can more easily talk.

"Nah, Kyle, not really. Maybe they're all too religious for me," I say sarcastically. The relevance of girls in my life in terms of attraction, dating, and relationships matters only a few times when Kyle and I are best friends. He witnesses me attend "Turnabout" at my high school, the annual dance for which a girl asks a guy to be her date, with a platonic female friend as my date. I am not romantically interested in her. If she is interested in me, she doesn't mention it, or I am oblivious to her signals. A few years later I go to the Prom at Kyle's high school with another platonic female friend, Kyle and his girlfriend, and another close guy friend and his girlfriend. It is well known that my date and I are attending the dance as friends. A year and a half later, he'll observe me go on a date with his girlfriend's friend (see Chapter 8). "How did it go?" he asks me enthusiastically the next day. "She's great and super sweet. She's just not my type," I say. Kyle nods his head in response and doesn't ask any more questions.

Kyle's ways of responding to me, as well as the ways he chooses to not respond, are curious. I think about what is missing from these interactions, and our relationship. He doesn't pressure me to tell him more details about the Turnabout dance, or my failed date. There's no questioning about whether or not we "went to third base" or if I "got lucky." In addition, he does not try to persuade, or even urge, me to pursue other girls, or to talk about girls that I like. Thankfully, I never feel like he's going to broach the subject. Also absent is the hyper-masculine jocular razzing that I've seen many boys and men perform. Instead he simply witnesses what's going on, or not going on, and on this one occasion asks me about the date, and then lets the topic go. Because of the cultural conditions at this time, and given that Kyle is heterosexual, I would imagine that he must wonder about my lack of interest and activity with girls. Again, he doesn't see me dating. I rarely talk about girls, and when I do, it doesn't concern my desiring them. I give him short and pithy responses when he questions me. Nevertheless, the presence of this issue is negligible in our relationship. Also missing from our relating are homophobic comments; neither of us labels each other as "fag" or "fairy." We don't ever use those terms, or epithets, generally.

These absences are helpful. Not being required to perform in normative ways in terms of sexuality and gender allows me (and Kyle, too) to experiment more comfortably with who I want to be. To be sure, I am still signaling normative conventions and expectations when it comes to some of our banter. I'm thinking here of the "dude ride" and our ways of performing "Bill and Ted." Kyle and I are not performing Liberace, the famous pianist in the 1970s and 1980s who was admired by many, but also a closeted and beautifully graceful gay man, whom people mocked in vicious and homophobic ways. We're "dudes" to each other, and living up masculinity, embodying stereotypes, and bonding through the process.

I cherish the bond Kyle and I have developed, which continues to grow as we graduate from high school and attend the same university, Illinois State University (ISU), to pursue our bachelor's degrees. We room together in one of the campus dorms. I love having him by my side during this first year at ISU. I feel safer having a familiar face, my best friend, around me. I no longer get homesick when away from my family and regular routine, like I used to in middle school and early in high school. In addition, I can tell he appreciates that I'm by his side. He's able to vent about professors, talk through the challenges he's facing at school, and share the ups and downs he experiences with his girlfriend.

Kyle decides to stop attending college before the start of the second semester. Although he's smart and an outstanding student, he doesn't enjoy school and wants to become an electrician. The news affects me hard. Suddenly my best friend, my sidekick, Bill, won't be around on a regular basis. Yet, I also understand his decision and am happy for him. That next year I develop new friendships at school. Kyle and I remain best friends, often seeing each other on summer and winter breaks.

During my next few years in college I begin to actively explore my sexuality. At this point I am aware that I am attracted to men, not women. Yet, I am also not yet ready to identify as gay, and I figure I'm bisexual. I keep up this façade for several years, denying it to myself, and then once accepting I was gay, keeping it from others out of fear of horrible conflict and rejection. Each time I ruminate about disclosing my gay identity to family and close friends feels scary and worrisome. Yet each time my disclosure ends well, and far better than my rumination would allow me to imagine. The anticipation of disclosing to Kyle, however, is especially painful. By the time I am ready to tell him, he is engaged to be married, and I have agreed to be his best man. I'm thrilled to participate in this way. Yet I spend many nights ruminating that my "coming out" to him will be disastrous. How will he respond? Does he know? Will he hate me and want to stop being friends? Will he no longer want me to be his best man? That would crush me. I lose much sleep rehearsing my coming out to Kyle. On an almost nightly basis, I visualize myself sneaking into the church and hiding while I watch Kyle get married to Becky from the back of the church. My fears have an incapacitating grip on me. Yet the rumination feels necessary, as I'm afraid I'm about to lose a dear friendship.

"What time is the pizza gonna be ready?" I say to Kyle. I am about to come out to him, and I am so nervous my bones feel like they're trembling. We're at his new apartment. He only recently signed a lease and has not yet moved in. We're christening his new home by eating our favorite pizza—deep dish, pineapple and Canadian bacon, extra sauce—for dinner.

"15 minutes … why, you have a hot date or somethin'?" The wide grin tells me he's only joking. He knows I don't have a date.

"You're funny, but no, I don't have a hot date. I want to tell you something." My voice is shaking as I gesture for us to sit on the floor.

"What's up?" He has a concerned look on his face.

"Umm, I've wanted … and, umm, to tell you something for a long time. I'm nervous to say it. Fuck, I shouldn't be nervous, because there's nothing wrong with what I have to tell you. This is crazy, I'm shaking." I try to catch my breath and not let my nervousness overtake me. He's waiting patiently, still smiling, but his face now looks nervous. I wonder if he thinks I'm about to tell him I have cancer, or some deadly disease, or that my parents are getting divorced.

"I need … and want … to tell you that I'm gay." I exhale and wait for his response.

"Oh, okay." He looks relieved. "No big deal. I mean, I wish you would have told me sooner. But I am definitely glad you told me now." He gets up off of the floor and extends his hand to help me up. Once I'm standing, he gives me a long hug. I feel tears well up in the back of my eyes.

"Thank you. I love you." I feel like the weight of the world has been lifted off of my shoulders.

"Love you too, but you already know that. Let's go, we need to pick up our pizza."

We don't say much as we walk to his car. Once we are inside and before we both have a chance to even buckle our seat belts, Kyle leans over, grins, and says, "So, does this mean there'll be no stripper at my bachelor party?" I appreciate his efforts to disarm me and the situation.

Kyle and I stay best friends, and I remain an honorary member of his family, for many years after I come out to him. I don't know many better people than him. Kyle and Becky marry and go on to have two beautiful sons. Their boys are lucky to benefit from the deep love and wisdom they show as parents. I am still friends with Kyle. Although we don't talk often, the moment one of us calls the other, we pick back up with our bond, and stories, like we never have missed a day of communication.

ENDINGS/BEGINNINGS

"Can I ask you something about your "Ode" chapter?" Cathy (co-author, nickname "Gilly") is sitting across from me, working on her stories for this book on her laptop at my dining room table. It is the morning of the last day of her week-long visit to Tampa. We are immersed in a writing retreat, feverishly working to complete the book. She and I have been talking about our stories as we both write, and this one piqued her curiosity.

"Sure," I say.

"Let me see if I can find the right words."

"Go for it." Gilly has a knack for identifying viable central ideas or "thematizing" stories of lived experience, so I'm eager to hear what she's thinking about this story.

"How is it that these two boys made you? Do you have a clear sense yet?" Prior to finishing this story, I have been talking with Gilly and Tony (co-author) about the positive effects some boys have had on my identity. I've used "made" to mark identity formation as a co-constitutive process of making and remaking of selves relationally and culturally.

"I do have a clear sense, and it feels powerful. In fact, I woke up today thinking about their influence on my identity, and on my ways of being, more generally."

"Great, so what's your sense?"

"Here goes ..." I am clearing clutter off of the island in my kitchen, which is the perfect way, for me, to debrief, because it will keep me from overthinking things. "I'll just talk it out."

"First, being friends with these boys created a space for me to interact with them more freely. This is because of who they were, and were not, in terms of their identity and ways of communicating. With them, I didn't need to try to be something I didn't feel I was. I didn't have to talk about or act "tough," in the normative sense of the word (i.e., physically strong). So, I didn't have to perform hyper-masculinity."

"You could be yourself," she says.

"Yes, they allowed me to be my version of me, rather than others' version of me."

"I like the way you say that. Makes me think of my own stories and the ways others have made me."

"My friendships with Cody and Kyle allowed me to be a teenager who could experiment with my identity in open and safe ways. By being close to them, and their gentleness, I was spared some of the frustrations that I would have experienced had I been friends with boys who more so personified toxic masculinity, and who over-talked about girls and sex. With Cody and Kyle, and especially Kyle, I could explore and play with who I was … or who I wanted to be."

"Also, being able to have these boys as friends meant that I didn't have to be confined only to a socialization in my youth that was conditioned, and sometimes governed, by heterosexuality and heteronormativity." I may not have known what these terms and social problems were at that time in my life, but they certainly shaped how I lived.

"It's not that heteronormativity 'went away' when I spent time with these friends. Heterosexual assumptions and expectations were persistently influential, similar to how those structures are still here today. Instead, spending time with these boys, and bonding in the ways that we did, allowed me to play with my own responses to these pressures, to see what my ways of performing mean to me, and might mean to others. Bonds like these have alleviated some—and sometimes many—pressures in my life."

"Sometimes when I spent time with Kyle I worked to pass as being 'straight.' I wasn't being true to myself, or to him, because I was scared to be myself. With Kyle even those moments of passing now seem, to me, like a 'gentler' type of passing. I felt relieved by the lack of pressure he exhibited, especially when it came to the absence of our talking about girls, dating, and sex." I pause to catch a breath and because the look on Gilly's face tells me she has something to say.

"Your story makes me think about not only who you were in these friendships, but who these boys were. They're a different type of boys, and that made a difference for you."

"That is what I'm beginning to understand by writing this story. Cody and Kyle transcended rigid social categories and expectations that informed, and often legislated, what 'normal boys' are, and should be. They blurred the categories, so to speak, and in doing so made way for a welcomed and different way of thinking and feeling. Even more, the types of boys they were, and were not, allowed us to relate in ways that, in effect, disrupted these myopic ideologies and ways of performing."

"Good point," Gilly says, prompting me by nodding her head and gesturing with her hand to continue working through my ideas.

"No matter how far we've come in terms of progressive orientations to sexuality and gender, I still hear people talk about friendship in highly normative ways. While my friendships with Cody and Kyle did show stereotypical behaviors, for instance, we bonded in part through shared activities, we also bonded through the sharing of feelings, and through dialogue. In this way, my boys remind me/us that alternative ways of performing boy-boy friendships exist. I've lived a different story with these boys, and our story changed me.

"They made you, my brother," Gilly says enthusiastically. She often names me "my brother" when we talk. I don't remember exactly when she began to use this form of address, but I know it was around the time that her dear brother Steve tragically died of cancer. I take her naming me "brother" as a badge of honor, and love. She tells me that she considers me among her closest friends who constitute her chosen family.

"At the same time they were also saving me from having to endure the challenges, and the related pain and suffering, from participating more fully in hyper-masculine friendships."

"That could be a subtext to this story, "Ode to the Boys *who saved me*."

"Yes!"

"But from whom, or what, did they save you?"

"They saved me from being suffocated by the gross limitations of society in terms of sexuality and gender, conditions that persist today, and again, from having to socialize and try to rely on hyper-masculine straight boys. They saved me by helping me cope with a harsh world. Also, they saved me from myself. Without them, I don't know if I would have survived. They helped me relate to myself in different and more relaxed ways." Gilly again looks like she has something to add.

"Also, I think there's a way in which you saved Cody and Kyle," she says. "By relating with you, they were spared from that same toxic masculinity. You helped them."

"That's a lovely point. Also, it wasn't only Cody and Kyle who saved me. There's also Nick (Apostolopolous), whom I've been friends with since the early 1990s. There's also Jay (Brower) at the top of this list. The grace and fluidity he has brought to our relationship as best friends has been invaluable. I love witnessing him perform in similar ways with his partner Lynette (Adams) and their daughter Roma (Adams-Brower)."

"I'm sure Nick shows the same care and ease with his wife and their two sons, too," Gilly says.

"Yes, those boys have an outstanding model of what it means to be a good man. Also, let's add Chris (Patti), my dear friend and collaborator in mindfulness, to this list."

"I was just about to mention dear Chris."

"Keeping these types of wonderful men around me—heterosexual men whose ways of being affirm and celebrate my life, friends whom I can trust, and with whom I identify and am at peace around—has mattered to me in deep and crucial ways for as long as I can remember."

"We need more boys and men like Cody, Kyle, Nick, Jay, and Chris, guys who are confident in themselves and help to build up the confidence of others, especially others who occupy spaces of difference."

"I will be eternally grateful to all of these boys and men."

DISCUSSION QUESTIONS

1. How have the close friendships in your life shaped your identities?
2. What ways of communicating are "present" and "absent" when you relate with close friends? Same-sex/gender friends? Friends of different sexes/genders?
3. In what ways have your friends "saved" you?
4. Do you have an "honorary" family, or "chosen" siblings, in your life? What role have they played in shaping your identity?

REFERENCES

Berry, K. (2016). *Bullied: Tales of torment, identity, and youth*. New York, NY: Routledge.
Blumer, H. (1986). *Symbolic interactionism: Perspective and method*. Berkeley, CA: University of California Press.

CHAPTER 2

THE CLOSET

Tony E. Adams

Much of my research has been about the metaphorical closet, referenced in the phrase "coming out of the closet." "Coming out" still attracts much attention and concern: this celebrity came out; this sport has never had an "out" athlete; so-and-so was fired for coming out. Some researchers also suggest that the closet no longer exists or is an inadequate metaphor for discussing sexuality (see Kampler & Connell, 2018). I disagree: Coming out of the closet is a kind of self-disclosure: the revealing of personal information about oneself, or in the case of the closet, disclosing one's sexuality. As long as self-disclosure exists, as long as we use language to tell others about our desires, as long as we reveal (and conceal) information with words, then the closet will maintain its importance. Granted, those who suggest the closet no longer exists often suggest that there are fewer ramifications for revealing same-sex/gender attraction—an argument with which I generally agree, at least as it applies to the United States. Yet the phrase "coming out" is still in widespread use, and in its most basic form, may only be a reference to someone sharing—disclosing—their sexuality to others.[1]

***

In general use, the closet refers to a space for hiding private objects from public view. According to the *Oxford English Dictionary* (OED), a closet can be a "room for privacy," an "inner chamber," a "private repository of valuables," or the "den or lair of a wild beast." A person may also have a "skeleton in the closet"—a "private or concealed trouble in one's circumstances, ever present, and ever liable to come into view." Origins of the phrase "coming out of the closet" in reference to sexuality date back to the 1930s and 1940s, when coming out marked a LGBQ person's entry into LGBQ society, e.g., first attending a drag ball. At this time, secrecy about same-sex/gender attraction was not the essence of coming out (Chauncey, 1994).

© KONINKLIJKE BRILL NV, LEIDEN, 2020 | DOI:10.1163/9789004418790_002

The phrase morphed into the revealing of sexuality in the United States particularly when others began to police same-sex attraction, when the attraction came to mark or designate a particular kind of person (e.g., "queer," "lesbian"), when this attraction became something to hide, not discuss, and act otherwise (i.e., "heterosexual"). This transition in meaning made the act of coming out possible. To come out means to make hidden, private, and possibly valuable information public; to reveal one's "inner chamber" to others; to expose the living quarters of a "wild beast" or a concealed, troubling "skeleton"; or to "admit (something) openly, to cease to conceal" information, especially same-sex attraction ("homosexuality"). The person who does not disclose same-sex attraction may risk being considered a "closet queen" (a person who only comes out to other queer people yet avoids association with these people out of a fear of stigmatization) or a "closet case" (a slang term for "a homosexual who conceals or denies his or her sexuality"; Oxford English Dictionary, n.d.). Although these definitions offer a sense of the closet and coming out, there are five additional characteristics of the metaphor and its relationship to sexuality, particularly to same sex/gender attraction (Adams, 2011).

First, the closet is applicable to, and coming out is necessary in, contexts in which a person's same-sex/gender attraction is hidden, unknown, and/or assumed to be otherwise (e.g., heterosexual). In these contexts, a person must disclose their same-sex/gender attraction, often by saying something (e.g., "I am queer") but sometimes by engaging in an intimate same-sex/gender act (e.g., kissing someone of the same sex/gender; see Crimp, 1993). A few years ago, a Facebook friend posted a link to a press release titled, "Queen Latifah Comes Out of the Closet (Finally)" (Rose, 2012). Alex, another friend, posted "No she didn't [come out] … She says nothing in the press release about being gay." Janice, another friend, posted, "Queen Latifah isn't a lesbian?" Alex replied: "I'm not saying she's not [a lesbian] … I'm just saying, she hasn't come out."

The article's title and the brief Facebook exchange illustrate a key assumption about coming out. Even if people assume that Queen Latifah is a lesbian or has same-sex/gender attraction, Queen Latifah must somehow validate this assumption; I could say she is a lesbian, but that does not mean that she identifies as a lesbian or has same-sex/gender attraction. Consequently, coming out requires confirmation in discourse or some other action. The need for confirmation is noted not only by the assumption that Queen Latifah (finally) came out in the press release, but also in Alex's second comment that Queen Latifah has not yet come out; that is, she has not done anything to confirm her lesbian identity or same-sex/gender attraction. Queen Latifah's out-ness is not unique either—similar ambiguous coming-out moments have occurred with Jodie Foster's cryptic speech at the 2013 Golden Globes (James, 2013), and Taron Egerton's Instagram account (2018), when he commented "Cutie. My boy ❤" on the image of a male friend (Henderson, 2018).

Second, the closet is a relational construct; it exists and is meaningful in relation to other people, particularly what others know and do not know about a person's same-sex/gender attraction. For example, a brother may not know about his sister's same-sex/gender attraction, which may make her "closeted" in relation to him. An employee may assume that the boss does not know about his same-sex/gender attraction and may thus feel closeted in relation to the boss. A woman may be out to her cousin, but not out to her mother; out to coworkers, but not out to the server at a restaurant; and out to her therapist but not to her dentist. In these situations, the closet exists not as something that is totalizing or essentializing but based on contextual information that has not been revealed in particular relationships. The closet also could exist when others deny or pretend to not know about a person's same-sex/gender attraction, even though the person has told these others about their same-sex/gender attraction several times (see Adams, 2011, pp. 125–126).

Third, the relevance of same-sex/gender attraction—and, correspondingly, the closet—depends on whether the attraction is considered to be important information for a relationship. A mother may ask her son if he finds a particular woman attractive intimately and sexually. The mother may even try to get this son to marry the woman and encourage the (heterosexual) couple to (biologically) reproduce in order to "carry on the [patriarchal] family name." But if the son does not find women attractive or does not want to marry a woman, and instead finds men attractive and may even desire a man to marry, then his concealed (closeted) same-sex/gender attraction would be relevant information to his mother/their relationship. If the son could disclose (come out) to his mother, she may no longer have such expectations about her son and may not pressure him into a relationship that he does not find to be satisfying or important. Should the son happen (that is, feel forced) to marry the woman, his same-sex/gender attraction would be important to that relationship as well, especially if the woman assumes that the son is heterosexual and that he desires her intimately and sexually.

Fourth, coming out can be risky and dangerous, as a person might reveal information others will condemn. There are many accounts of parents

21

reacting negatively to their children's coming out (see Barton, 2012), and some colleges and employers can dismiss a student or employee for disclosing same-sex attraction. In some places (e.g., Russia, Uganda), a person can be fined, imprisoned, or even killed because of same-sex attraction (Cowell, 2014; Kramer, 2013). As such, a person who comes out can lose access to important resources and may experience emotional stress and physical harm; a person who stays closeted may maintain safety and protection, at least in relation to others. However, as many queer activists have argued, coming out is important for recognition, pride, and honesty; even though it may be risky and dangerous, not coming out can perpetuate the assumption that same-sex/gender attraction is unimportant, inappropriate, or abnormal.

Fifth, for a person with same-sex/gender attraction, the closet can be an enduring construct, as coming out can become a perpetual, lifelong process (Sedgwick, 1990). If coming out means to reveal private or concealed information to others, then a person may be closeted when immersed in new contexts with unfamiliar others, contexts in which the person's attraction is hidden, unknown, or assumed to be otherwise (e.g., heterosexual). Every new work environment, every trip to the grocery store, every new encounter on social media, every new venture into social life—the closet does not simply disappear with one act or utterance; new audiences make for new times to disclose.

***

The significance of the closet will exist as long as sexuality is a topic we/others care about, and as long as coming out is understood to be an act that reveals information about which others might perceive as inappropriate and taboo. Thus, I conclude with four insights about the closet and ways to navigate the act of disclosing same-sex/gender attraction.

Contrary to those who dismiss the prevalence of the closet, coming out still matters as long as same-sex/gender attraction continues to be hidden, unknown, stigmatized, or erroneously assumed by others; given that coming out is a kind of self-disclosure, there is no "post-closet" world as long as self-disclosure exists. Granted, the value and evaluation of the disclosed information can change and the disclosure of same-sex/gender attraction may receive fewer hateful responses from others. Nevertheless, disclosing sexuality will always be necessary, again, because every new audience introduces new moments to disclose. Others might make assumptions about my likes and attractions, but only until I convey this information to others do I confirm or challenge these assumptions.

Second, my experience has taught me that the immediate moments of coming out—those first few seconds, minutes, and days—are often formative and memorable for the person who comes out (Adams, 2011, pp. 100–101).[2] For audiences of the coming-out disclosure, I encourage them to be mindful about their immediate reactions, however difficult this might be. Conversely, for LGBQ persons who come out, I encourage them to lessen the importance of those first few moments, as difficult as it might be. It may take years for a LGBQ persons to come to terms with their sexuality; when disclosing the sexuality to others, these others should have some time to reflect on the disclosure. As LGBQ persons, I note that we might only remember and recall the first few moments of coming out, not later moments of contentment and bliss we might experience with others post coming out, especially others who, at the moment of coming out, may have responded in unsupportive ways.

Third, in addition to being freeing, honest, and dangerous, there are political reasons for coming out. Coming out makes LGBQ persons identifiable targets of discrimination and hate, but also makes their sexuality known to others who may have never known or cared about LGBQ issues or people. When people do not know about, or are not familiar with, queer people, then it can be easy to enact prejudice against them. Yet, for some, enacting prejudice toward someone they regard positively might be more difficult. (This assumption is the essence of Allport's [1954] "intergroup contact hypothesis.") Although some researchers have cautioned against this assumption (e.g., Meadow, 2018), for some people, knowing a familiar and likable LGBQ person can contribute to queer support.

Fourth, LGBQ persons should put less pressure on themselves for (not) coming out and others should put less pressure on when and how the person comes out.[3] Coming out can create a "damned-if-we-do, damned-if-we-don't" situation. Some people criticize LGBQ persons for coming out "too soon," or "not soon enough." Some people criticize LGBQ persons not for their revelation of same-sex/gender attraction, the essence of coming out, but because of when (e.g., at 20 or 45 years old) and how they came out (e.g., in person, on social media), and who else may have known first (e.g., friend, parent, co-worker). There is often never a right time to disclose, and, as LGBQ persons, thinking about coming out can be easy and unplanned, or a strategic and exhausting calculation about when and how to disclose their sexuality.

DISCUSSION QUESTIONS

1. To what other situations might coming out/the closet apply? Although "the closet" and "coming out of the closet" are constructs describing the disclosure of same-sex/gender attraction, these constructs also can be used to understand disclosures of hidden and possibly taboo information.
2. Coming out can be freeing, honest, healthy, and politically important, yet also dangerous. If a person is out, they may feel anxious, content, and proud. If a person is not out, they may feel anxious, safe, and deceptive. Some people might not want to come out to a new person for a few weeks, months, or never at all; others might want the LGBQ person to come out immediately upon meeting others. Given these complexities of coming out, what is your advice for people who come out? How might you respond to an acquaintance who reveals same-sex/gender attraction immediately or after a few months? In what contexts does the revealing of same-sex/ gender attraction still pose risk?
3. Sometimes coming out is perceived to be a key part of LGBQ experience. But coming out does not solve all problems and there may be new problems that emerge after the disclosure. Identify struggles a LGBQ person may have to deal with post coming out, after the person has disclosed their same-sex/gender attraction to others.

NOTES

[1] Parts of this chapter have been adapted from Adams (2016).
[2] Kenji Yoshino (2007) writes, "Nothing has convinced me of the power of words as much as the experience of coming out the first few times—one ends the sentence a different person" (p. 13).
[3] One exception: A closeted person (e.g., politician) who enacts prejudice against LGBQ persons should be criticized for not coming out and should even outed by others, especially if the person engages in hypocritical and harmful acts against LGBQ persons.

REFERENCES

Adams, T. E. (2011). *Narrating the closet: An autoethnography of same-sex attraction.* Walnut Creek, CA: Left Coast Press.
Adams, T. E. (2016). The closet. In A. Goldberg (Ed.), *The Sage encyclopedia of LGBTQ studies* (p. 235). Thousand Oaks, CA: Sage.
Allport, G. W. (1954). *The nature of prejudice.* Reading, MA: Addison-Wesley.
Barton, B. (2012). *Pray the gay away: The extraordinary lives of Bible Belt gays.* New York, NY: New York University Press.

Chauncey, G. (1994). *Gay New York, NY: Gender, urban culture, and the making of the gay male world, 1890–1940.* New York, NY: Basic Books.

Cowell, A. (2014, February 24). Uganda's President signs antigay Bill. *The New York Times.* Retrieved October 1, 2014, from http://www.nytimes.com/2014/02/25/world/africa/ugandan-president-to-sign-antigay-law.html

Crimp, D. (1993). Right on, girlfriend! In M. Warner (Ed.), *Fear of a queer planet: Queer politics and social theory* (pp. 300–320). Minneapolis, MN: University of Minnesota Press.

Henderson, T. (2018, October 30). Rocketman's Taron Egerton may have just come out. *www.pride.com.* Retrieved December 28, 2018, from https://www.pride.com/comingout/2018/10/30/rocketmans-taron-egerton-may-have-just-come-out

James, S. D. (2013, January 14). LGBT activists cringe and praise Jodie Foster coming out. *ABC News.* Retrieved February 1, 2019, from https://abcnews.go.com/Entertainment/lgbt-advocates-applaud-cringe-jodie-foster-coming/story?id=18211672

Kampler, B., & Connell, C. (2018). The post-gay debates: Competing visions of the future of homosexualities. *Sociology Compass, 12,* 1–12. https://doi.org/10.1111/soc4.12646

Kramer, A. E. (2013, June 11). Russia passes bill targeting some discussions of homosexuality. *The New York Times.* Retrieved October 1, 2014, from http://www.nytimes.com/2013/06/12/world/europe/russia-passes-bill-targeting-some-discussions-of-homosexuality.html

Meadow, T. (2018). *Trans kids: Being gendered in the twenty-first century.* Berkeley, CA: University of California Press.

Oxford English Dictionary. (n.d.). *Closet.* Retrieved July 20, 2014, from http://www.oed.com

Rose, S. (2012, May 4). Queen Latifah comes out of the closet (finally). *Sandrarose.com.* Retrieved February 28, 2019, from http://sandrarose.com/2012/05/queen-latifah-comes-out-of-the-closet-finally/

Sedgwick, E. K. (1990). *Epistemology of the closet.* Berkeley, CA: University of California Press.

Yoshino, K. (2007). *Covering: The hidden assault on our civil rights.* New York, NY: Random House.

CHAPTER 3

MENTAL GYMNASTICS

Catherine M. Gillotti

I once did an exercise when teaching my interpersonal communication class that I "borrowed" from an episode of the daytime television talk show *Dr. Phil*, where you create a timeline for your life. You are supposed to start with your earliest childhood memory. Above the timeline, you document the events and people in your life that you view as positive. The exercise aims to give people an overall perception of their life. Below the line you document the negative events and people. Given that I was in my 30s, I decided going back to my earliest childhood memory would take too long. Instead, I decided to start with the age of 10 when my parents decided we should move. Our neighborhood was beginning to deteriorate with drug deals happening on the street in the middle of the day, and neighbors' houses being robbed in broad daylight. Although we hated to move, we also knew we had to as it was just not a safe place to live anymore. So on my timeline, I listed age 10 – moved – both above and below the line.

The next August, after the move, I found myself enrolled in fifth grade at Holy Angels Elementary School. I had 21 classmates. Holy Angels seemed like it would be a good place to go, and while I was nervous to make new friends and meet new teachers, I knew I had my older brothers, Mike and Steve, with me. The transition to Holy Angels was the worst for Mike, as he was entering eighth grade. Eighth grade was a particularly difficult year to switch schools. He was losing his peers not only for his last year of elementary school, but also for high school since most of his classmates from our old school attended a different high school.

I had the best chance of the three of us to be fully integrated and make a smooth transition because I had more time to cultivate friendships. I liked my new classmates, although I always felt a little out of place because I did not have their shared history. I was the new kid in a class of 22 students, a little chubby, a tomboy, and an easy target for bullying.

One of my classmates welcomed me to the school during that first year by pulling my chair out from underneath me as I went to sit down. I went

© KONINKLIJKE BRILL NV, LEIDEN, 2020 | DOI:10.1163/9789004418790_003

from standing to a hard landing on the linoleum floor. Whatever I weighed then was enough to break my tailbone. I then had the humiliation of sitting on a donut for months until I could tolerate the normal seats. I also stood out because I was the first girl in my class to get her period. My body had betrayed me. I was 10, but had the reproductive organs of a teenager. As a result, I was incredibly self-conscious. Thankfully, wearing a uniform everyday helped ease some of the natural social comparisons that people make since we essentially all looked the same in our Catholic plaid.

My family was comfortably middle class; however, we had moved into a neighborhood of upper middle-class residents. It was not that we felt inferior to anyone, but there was always this underlying vibration that our family was different. For example, one day one of our neighbors, who also happened to be one of my classmate's mom, came to the door to offer my mom her daughter's hand-me-down designer clothes. Even though we wore uniforms at school, our wardrobe was not immune to critique. Although this person may have had good intentions, it is something my mom and I have never forgotten. It was as if others' evaluation became a part of my shadow. "Welcome to the neighborhood and here are some designer label clothes, so your daughter fits in better" was the subtext. I think both my mom and I were embarrassed and insulted.

Being in a new neighborhood with new socio-economic expectations, a new school, new buses, new friends, new sports teams was almost too much to bear. Years later my family members and I shared that we each secretly cried ourselves to sleep the night we moved, and many nights in that first year.

One of the best parts of my new school came in the form of gym class. It seemed like children either hated gym or loved it. It all depended upon how athletic they were. I loved gym class, for the most part, because I had been playing soccer since I was six and was fairly athletic and competitive. While I loathed labeling, I was sporty, so gym class was definitely in my comfort zone. While some children practically have nervous breakdowns at the thought of running laps, climbing ropes, or being picked last for a team, I was comfortable knowing that I could excel in gym.

One peculiar thing about my new school was that we did not have a gymnasium for gym class. As luck would have it, the University of Dayton was one block away. Since the state required that all children participate in gym, the school arranged for us to have gym class in the university facilities.

Instead of playing dodgeball in the school parking lot, we learned sports from the university students majoring in physical education. We were not just running off excess energy for an hour, we learned the fundamentals of each game or sport they covered. We took archery, track and field, racquetball, tennis, swimming, and gymnastics. We got to use the locker rooms in the field house, and our gym instructors—the college students—were a lot more fun than our regular teachers. All of us were so excited to take part in this arrangement.

The best part of gym was the class time itself. The worst part of gym was changing in and out of our gym clothes. I was self-conscious and modest as a child. Growing up with two older brothers, I had the luxury of my own room and was raised to be modest. I was terribly uncomfortable with the inevitable social comparison that happens within a school locker room. Although, the more I excelled at the sport we were covering that week, the less self-conscious I was. It was merely five minutes of the fastest undressing and dressing one could humanly do. However, there were two activities I dreaded the most: swimming and gymnastics. I was terrified that I would have my period during the weeks we covered swimming. I also felt like a stuffed sausage in my bathing suit while all of my classmates were thin and from my perspective beautiful. While I could swim, it was not my strongest sport. My inner monologue was ruthless in its own social comparison. Everyone else was thin and I was "fatty Cathy." Thankfully, the swimming unit came and went without too much difficulty, save for the embarrassment of the full strip down to get in and out of my swimsuit, which I did in the bathroom stall.

Our next event was the gymnastics unit. My anxiety rose as I thought about the humiliation I would suffer from hanging from the uneven bars with my stomach fat pressed against the top bar and my short legs swinging to find footing on the bottom bar. I could not do it. I also abhorred the ideas of the floor routine, and the balance beam. There would be fatty Cathy tumbling across the mat without an ounce of grace, or wobbling on the balance beam that I imagined would only accentuate how wide my body was in comparison to the width of the beam. I did not want to learn gymnastics on the female apparatus. The notion of gender-specific events in a sport smacked in the face of my young, feminist sensibility. Anything a boy could do, I could do. After all, I had been playing soccer since I was six. So, I made a decision to learn gymnastics with the boys. My first consciously feminist act was committed at age 10. By the reactions of the adults, you would have thought I had sent a bomb threat to the school.

"What do you mean you want to participate in gym class with the boys?"

"What do you mean you want to learn the rings, parallel bars, and pommel horse? That equipment is for the boys."

"Wouldn't you rather be with your friends learning the balance beam, uneven bars, and floor exercises?" My answer was "no." The boys were my friends too.

Conversations happened, people were consulted, and for all I knew the university legal counsel was brought in to approve the request. Finally the school granted my request. I was able to learn the gymnastics unit with the boys. Instead of having my body compared in terms of height, weight, and grace, I could be admired for my sheer determination to complete each apparatus as well as any of my male classmates. I was ecstatic to learn the "robin's nest" move on the rings. In this move, you hook both your hands and feet in each ring and turn yourself inside out. I felt like I was flying. In a week's time, I was able to do it just like the boys. Instead of gymnastics being about my size (my perceived weakness), it became about my strength.

Before feminists hail my gymnastic gender protest as a step forward for women's rights, it is important to convey my underlying motivation. I look back now and see the importance of that protest as a feminist performance. However, at the time, it really boiled down to a 10-year-old's tainted body image. I could only see an overweight, unattractive child. I could only see my breasts, which were huge for my age. Cooley's (1983) "looking glass self" was, for me, a fun house mirror—completely distorted. I knew I was different from the other girls, and they were wishing their breasts would develop. In the meantime, my parents, especially my father, were insistent that I take dance class, specifically ballet class. I defiantly resisted.

A few years earlier, my parents and I had gotten into an argument over ballet classes. Mom and dad were seated around the table in the breakfast nook. I was standing in the archway between the nook and the kitchen, crying and stomping my feet that I did not want to take ballet. My dad asked, "Don't you want to be graceful?" Grace had nothing to do with it. For me it was again about how I felt about my body. Did I want to be graceful? Yes, but I also did not want to wear a stupid, pink leotard. I did not want to be the heaviest child in ballet class. It would have been like standing before the class naked—exposed. I think my parents also knew I was different. They wanted me to be strong, independent and my own person, but also to conform and perform traditional gender roles. I look back and wonder if they knew I was gay, and erroneously conflated sexual orientation with gender identity. If I were just interested in dancing, dolls, make-up, and dress-up, they would be able to steer me from the treacherous waters of homosexuality. Feminine meant straight and straight was the only option in the 1970s as a Catholic, Italian, German, Irish, English family. We knew that I did not move through the world in normatively "feminine" ways. I was the consummate tomboy. While I had and played with my Barbie dolls, I also played "Kick the Can" with all the other children in the neighborhood, mostly boys. My favorite game was "office" not "dress up" or "dolls." Our biggest issue always seemed centered around how I dressed.

I did not feel comfortable in dresses. Dressing "like a girl," taking dance classes to be more graceful, which is code for feminine, felt like taking part in Halloween year-round. Dresses, patent leather shoes, later on make-up, and high heels were costumes—not clothes. Maybe this is why I dislike Halloween to this day. It seemed like it was time to pretend, and to pretend meant that I was not okay as I was.

Dad and I had many arguments over the subject of high heels. "I would like to see you in a higher heel." "Why don't you wear a dress instead of slacks?" "You know your grandmother would want to see you in patent leather shoes." I shed many tears during my adolescent years because I felt that I was not good enough, and I was in a constant battle with my parents. I am sure they saw me as blatantly contrary. I resisted society's expectations for how I was supposed to perform feminine, even though I also really wished I could be just like all the other girls. I wanted to just blend in so that I would have everyone's approval.

I did not have the maturity or self-awareness about my sexual identity to give voice to the issue of conflating gender identity and sexual orientation. My story is not unique here in that many people confuse the two constructs. I know plenty of lesbians who are feminine; they are sometimes upset when no one knows they are lesbians. Like everyone else, they want to be seen for who they are, but once again society teaches us that the gender continuum and the sexual orientation continuum are synonymous. If you are "butch," then you must be a lesbian. If you wear makeup, dresses, and high heels then you must be straight. It is confusing given that many lesbians do perform more stereotypical masculine behaviors, and many "lipstick lesbians" embody stereotypical femininity. Those of us who are tomboys, also called "chapstick lesbians," will fall somewhere in between. One day we might wear make-up and a dress, and the next a baseball cap and jeans.

Crawley (2002) powerfully discussed the complicated intersection between gender and sexual identity, and how her distaste for wearing dresses represented being feminine, and being feminine in traditional, heteronormative ways represented being disabled. "For me, the appearance of femininity signals the appearance of disability. However … dresses are not perceived as disabling by all women (my sister in particular), which establishes a particular complexity to interaction" (p. 78). Similar to Crawley,

I felt out of place wearing dresses, and that my gender had nothing to do with me ability to do any particular task. However, unlike Crawley, I would not feel comfortable in a tuxedo either.

Jeffrey Weeks (1991) described sexual identity as a strange thing in that it is non-static and fluid. Why does the gender of one's relationship partner have to concretely define one's sexual orientation, and to whose benefit and at whose expense? In terms of gender, we might best understand the lack of concreteness by considering Butler's (1989) explanation of gender as a series of performative acts: "… [G]ender is in no way a stable identity or locus agency from which various acts proceed; rather, it is an identity tenuously constituted in time—an identity, instituted through a *stylized repetition of acts*" (p. 270, emphasis in original).

The human tendency to "ossify" (Blumstein, 1991) our gender, sexual orientation, and sexual identity makes these identities seem simple and predictable. Perhaps it is, for some, the human's psychological need to reduce uncertainty? Perhaps, it is the human's need to find more similarity to oneself than difference? Perhaps, for some, it is an innate fear of difference? Whatever the reason, it is easier to fit neatly into defined gender roles and sexual orientation and sexual identity than to create risks for oneself. It is certainly easier to be perceived as a girl if one dresses like a girl, acts like a girl, and takes gymnastic classes with the girls. But who said life was supposed to be easy and predictable?

DISCUSSION QUESTIONS

1. How was Cathy socialized to perform feminine?
2. How do you perceive Cathy's self-image shifted throughout her childhood and adolescence? How has your identity evolved over time?
3. How were you socialized to perform your gender identity in childhood?
4. What is the intersection between sexual and gender identity?

REFERENCES

Blumstein, P. (1991). The production of selves in personal relationships. In J. Howard & P. Callero (Eds.), *The self-society dynamic* (pp. 305–322). New York, NY: Cambridge University Press.

Butler, J. (1989). Performative acts and gender constitution: An essay in phenomenology and feminist theory. In S. E. Case (Ed.), *Feminist critical theory and theatre* (pp. 270–282). Baltimore, MD: Johns Hopkins University Press.

Cooley, C. H. (1983). *Human nature and the social self.* New Brunswick, NJ: Transaction Publishers.

Crawley, S. L. (2002). "They still don't understand why I hate wearing dresses!" An autoethnographic rant on dresses, boats, and butchness. *Critical Studies ⇔ Critical Methodologies, 2,* 69–92. https://doi.org/10.1177/153270860200200110

Weeks, J. (1991). *Against nature: Essays on history, sexuality, and identity.* London: Rivers Oram Press.

CHAPTER 4

WALLS

Billy Huff

I am sitting in the waiting room outside my therapist's office. I'm thirty nine years old, and I've never been through therapy before. I'm only here now because I want to transition. I was diagnosed female at birth, and I desire to begin testosterone to develop masculine secondary sex characteristics. In order to be treated by an endocrinologist, I have to first secure a diagnosis of "gender dysphoria" from a mental health therapist. I have never met her before. In fact, I found her on Google, and I chose her because of her master's degree from Brown and her doctorate from Columbia. I know she's smart, but I hope she's also open-minded and kind. As I sit here, I rehearse the lines that are promised to convince her I'm transsexual. "I've always felt male inside." "I was born in the wrong body." "I just need to change my body to be more in line with my soul." "I always liked playing with the boys when I was young." "I gravitated more to trucks than dolls." "I hated dancing ballet." "I hate my body." "I never masturbate." "I can't bring myself to take my pants off when I have sex." "I don't even like sex." I've always been terrible at lying, but this time my life depends on it.

I practiced these lines in the mirror at home for hours. I scrutinized my face. Do I look believable? Will she know I'm lying? I studied for this appointment more than I studied for my doctoral comprehensive exams. Am I ready? The therapist calls me in, and I instantly begin to doubt myself. I know she notices the sweat on my right palm when we shake hands. She is small and awkward, but she seems nice. Her desk displays pictures of her grandchildren, undoubtedly grandchildren born from a son or daughter who is not transsexual.

"How can I help you?" she begins.

"After years of thought, I have realized that I'm transsexual," I reply. Despite the number of times I have practiced this introduction, it comes out shaky and unsure. I've never actually said these words to another person before. My face flushes and I can feel sweat marks appearing on the armpits of my blue, button-down shirt, a shirt that is secured with my

© KONINKLIJKE BRILL NV, LEIDEN, 2020 | DOI:10.1163/9789004418790_004

most masculine-looking tie. I make it through my first session and the three months of weekly sessions that would follow. I was prepared to scale the wall of any psychological and medical regulatory regimes that stood in my way. I knew its contours by heart. My toes easily found the surest foothold with every question. I scaled the wall with precision and dove head first off of the other side, but I didn't get over the wall unscathed. I had to leave a major part of myself behind. I got my diagnosis and began testosterone.

***

I am sitting in the back seat of my mom's new Honda Civic. My mom, stepdad, and I are on our way home from visiting my stepdad's father in a nursing home in Greenville, South Carolina. It's the week before Christmas, and I'm home for the break. We have a two hour drive ahead of us. My stepfather is silent in the driver's seat. He is no doubt contemplating the degeneration of his father, a man who was the esteemed reverend of Mauldin First Baptist Church in a small town in South Carolina for more than thirty years, but can now barely remember his own name. My mother is listening to Christmas music and intermittently singing along. She loves Christmas. I am in the back seat trying to find a way to pry open my lips and let the breath come out that will carry the words I know will break her heart. A trans friend of mine told me before I started injecting testosterone that I should be prepared to lose the relationships with everyone. I think that's something hard to fathom until it actually happens.

"I am transsexual," I blurt out and then immediately brace for impact. I repeat the phrase "hold it together" over and over in my head. My mom is best characterized as a Southern belle. She was born and raised in Georgia, and she raised me with the mantra, "anyone can be a woman, but you have to earn the right to be called a lady." She was heavily invested in the fantasies she invented for who I would be. She envisioned weddings, baby showers, and ladies' luncheons. She has never found the words to call me her gay daughter, and here I am asking her to call me her son.

I was prepared for the litany of questions that would follow. "How can you do this to me? Did we not give you enough attention growing up? How could you tell us this way? You've ruined Christmas!" I entered this conversation knowing that it would not go well. "Hold it together. Hold it together. Hold it together." I have to distance myself from their words. My body is in the back seat of the car, but my mind roams through painful memories. I remember my favorite uncle's funeral. He lost a long fight and died from AIDS-related complications. He contracted it in a bathhouse, but my family insisted he contracted HIV in a mugging (that I'm convinced was a gay bashing). I remember deciding that the only thing that could assuage my mom's despair at the funeral was to wear one of her dresses. I remember her pushing me up against the wall at the church and forcing lipstick on my lips as she cried out through her tear-streaked face, "How can you do this to me?" I've heard these words before.

I didn't prepare for this conversation like I prepared for therapy. Every time I tried to script my words, I was overcome with anxiety. The truth is, I don't know what to say. My mom knows that I didn't always feel like a man inside. I didn't always hate being a girl. She knows how much I loved my Cabbage Patch Kid, Louie Ken, and how much I reveled in dancing ballet. She was with me when I tried on hundreds of prom dresses until I found the perfect one. "I just can't live as a woman anymore" is all I can say. These words build an indestructible wall. My mom has cancelled Christmas for the past two years. We hardly speak, and when we do, we don't talk "about that."

***

It's the first day of my first semester teaching at University of South Florida, and I'm standing in front of my Communication, Gender, and Identity class. I've taught this class many times before, but this is the first time since my transness became readable to others. I've been on testosterone for almost two years now, but I don't feel like I've changed that much. I have a shaved head from the hair loss caused by testosterone (I am a middle-aged transman after all), and I have seven bristly whiskers trying their hardest to push their way through the skin on my upper lip. My face is dotted with acne, another unfortunate side-effect of the testosterone. I'm forty years old now, but I'm at the beginning of male puberty. I'm standing in front of a group of students at the end of their adolescence. It's August and the weather is terribly hot and humid, but I am nonetheless wearing my best dress pants, button-up shirt, and tie.

Immediately before the class starts it strikes me that teaching this class will be different this time. I'm now positioned as a man. I'm transitioning into a place of privilege, and it didn't even occur to me that, as someone who aims to teach reflexively, this would and should affect my teaching of this subject. A wave of anxiety washes over my already nervous body. I look out over the room full of strangers who have most likely never thought much about gender. I've never felt so nauseous on the first day of school. The syllabus I hold is audibly rattling from the shaky hands that I'm unable to still.

I take a deep breath and begin. "I'm Dr. Billy Huff, and I'll be your instructor this semester. We're here to think critically about gender. You might have thought you would be learning the differences in the ways that men and women communicate in this class, but that is not what we will do. Instead, we're going to look at the ways that we use communication to construct our identities and the identities of others. We'll look at the different ways that we do gender and the ways that our performances of gender are constrained. We're going to think through the ways that our social institutions construct and police our ideas of gender and the ways that we move through the world."

I take another deep breath. "There is probably nobody better to teach this class right now than me, because I'm transsexual. Not only do I study gender, but I spend more time than most thinking about it in my own life. I want you to all feel comfortable to ask me any questions you have about me. I look forward to some challenging and productive discussions." The students look at me with wide eyes, they look at each other, and then they look back at me. Silence. I don't know what to do. They've no doubt heard about Caitlyn Jenner and Jazz Jennings. Is this what they're thinking about me right now? I don't know what they're wondering because no one has said a word. Do I explain myself? They probably haven't yet learned the language about gender they will need to come close to understanding that I don't really identify as a woman or a man. I give up on the first day. I quickly go over the syllabus and let the students go. I have a lot to think about before I see them again in two days.

The semester was terrible. The wondrous discussions I wanted never happened. Students seemed too afraid they would offend me if they said the wrong thing. I was, after all, still assigning grades at the end of the semester. I felt like a zoo animal. I made my best case for the social construction of gender, but all the while I felt like I was running full speed down a road that was always painted on a wall. I posed questions in my head to fill their silence. "If gender is socially constructed and a mere repetitive, performative citation of norms, why do you feel the need to change your body so drastically?" I have no answer. "If you're not born a man or a woman, but you learn it from your culture, how did you end up this way?" No answer. "How did you know you were trans?" "What is trans?" I have no answers—no answers that I can tell them anyway.

***

I'm sitting in front of my computer at Starbucks writing this story. This is the same Starbucks where the baristas hand me coffees with the name "Milly" emblazoned across them in Sharpie black. I pronounce the "B" that begins my name with enthusiasm, but it never helps. This is the same Starbucks where a woman recently asked me what kind of cancer I was fighting. I guess the shaved head makes me look more like a sick woman than a man coming to terms with baldness. I whispered "testicular cancer" under my breath and chuckled to myself. My laptop screen stares back at me and reminds me of my therapist's eyes, my parents' eyes, my students' eyes, and the eyes of countless others I've looked into since I declared myself trans and found myself constantly compelled to account for myself.

It has become common among many academics and activists to critique the pathologization of trans. Many have called upon trans people to come out as trans, resist narratives of normalization, and tell our *true* stories. Many have noted the insufficiency of the gendered categories available to us. What I find lacking, however, is an interrogation of the walls that crush trans folks like me under their weight. Every time I am asked to explain myself, even when asked by those who genuinely want to understand, I am faced with the simple fact that sex, fantasy and pleasure are not considered appropriate topics for sustained discussion. In the words of Gayle Rubin (1999), "This culture always treats sex with suspicion. It construes and judges almost any sexual practice in terms of its worst possible expression. Sex is presumed guilty until proven innocent" (p. 150). What if I can't think about myself without recourse to fantasy? What if none of us can?

If you're reading this story, then you are about to join a cadre of casual Grindr hookups who (sadly) know me more intimately than even most people who are closest to me. As long as I can remember I fantasized about being on the receiving end of punishment from men. In these fantasies I was always a boy. The fantasies did not begin as sexual fantasies. I didn't even know what sex was when I started having them. I did somehow know, however, that they were fantasies about which I should feel ashamed. I have vivid memories of playing "house" or "school" with other neighborhood children. These were some of my favorite childhood moments, because I was allowed to freely play out my fantasies. No one thought it was weird that I wanted to be the little boy, and the game was more fun for everyone when I was mischievous. I always provoked the older boys to punish me for my transgressions.

As I entered puberty, the fantasies took on a more sexual hue. They became secrets. I was too old to play "house." I started dating, but I could never figure out a way to ask my boyfriends to do *that* to me. They were, after all, taught to never hit a girl. I knew I would never keep a "straight" boyfriend long, if he knew I imagined myself as a boy when we were fucking. The gay men in my life were uninterested in my feminine body. I learned to separate my fantasies from my sense of identity, my relationships, and my life in general. As a result, I suffered almost twenty years of unfulfilling relationships. I went bar hopping in gay neighborhoods for years. I stood abandoned outside bathhouses with my face pressed against the black glass walls that my female body was not allowed through. I finally decided I could do it no more. As I neared the age of forty I decided I couldn't wait any longer to make my fantasies come true. I could be the boy I saw in my dreams. I could have the amazing sex with gay men I always wanted. I just couldn't tell anyone.

I could not say any of this to my therapist. A satisfactory diagnosis of gender dysphoria requires that one is not trans for sexual reasons. Indeed, sexual masochism is still considered a pathology in the *Diagnostic and Statistical Manual V*. I could not say any of this to my parents. Sex is considered a "private good" and one too shameful to talk about with close family members. I could not say any of this to my students. I am a non-tenure track faculty member who recognizes limits to academic freedom. The wall rises in my face every time I am asked to speak to a community organization or speak to a class about what it means to be trans. It knocks me down every time I encounter an old friend who expects an explanation for why I now go by "Billy." They ask me how I chose my name, but I can't tell them that I wanted a "boyish" name for a very particular reason. The heavy wall buries me on the occasions when supporters offer me a rare opportunity to speak "authentically."

Being trans, for me, means making fantasies come true, but in many ways this makes me no different from anyone else. We are all born into families that preexist us and that have their own fantasies about who we will become. Most of us fail to live up to our prescribed roles. We all find our own places in our own unique fantasies (whether sexual or not) that tell us who we are, shape how we experience pleasure, and place us in relation to others. None of us really knows where these fantasies come from. They seem to invade us from the outside, even as it seems that nothing could be more intimate and personal. We have all even changed our bodies in various ways that allow us to honor our fantasies. Whether building bigger biceps in the gym or tweezing that one pesky hair that keeps sprouting out of a nipple, we are all indebted in some way to fantasies about who we are and who we desire to be with others.

After many years of struggle, I have discovered the blueprints to the walls that silence me. The cement blocks are made of sex negativity. Sex negativity is the pervasive idea that sex is somehow an inherently destructive force. It is treated as unimportant even while it is overburdened with significance. The cement blocks are held together by the cement of normativity. What is considered socially "normal" is treated with value, while the "deviant" is constantly demeaned and policed. I can't help but to wonder how many others are confined by this same wall. It stands steadfast and will continue to prevent me and others from any right to speak my own truth without significant consequence. I am not transsexual. Like all of us, I'm merely transitioning. I was not "born this way," and I will never be a "man." I am finally admitting that I transitioned for no other reason than sexual gratification. I can't be understood outside the fantasies that inhabit the core of my being. I can't be understood on the other side of the wall, the side on which you no longer stand.

DISCUSSION QUESTIONS

1. This chapter discusses the psychological regulatory regime as one of the walls Billy must ascend in order to have access to medical transition. Why do you think people who are trans- are required to articulate their stories in such limited terms?
2. As Billy moves from one context to another (therapist's office, in the car with family, in front of the classroom) he experiences barriers to sharing his authentic story. How are these barriers the same? How are they different?
3. In this chapter, Billy discusses the ways that he fails to live up to his parents' fantasy for who he would become. He suggests that this is true for us all. In what ways do your own particular ideas about yourself conform to social expectations? In what ways to they diverge?
4. How does Billy define sex negativity? In what ways is sex treated in our society as unimportant? In what ways is sex overburdened with significance?

REFERENCE

Rubin, G. S. (1999). Thinking sex: Notes for a radical theory of the politics of sexuality. In R. G. Parker & P. Aggleton (Eds.), *Culture, society and sexuality: A reader* (pp. 143–178). New York, NY: Psychology Press.

THINGS I DON'T HAVE TO DO

Keith Berry

For as long as I can remember, folk wisdom about the realities of LGBQ cultures has typically focused on the issues of discrimination, bigotry, and other modes of violence that inform, and sometimes govern, our lives. The most recent hate crimes perpetrated against persons who love, or seek pleasure, differently than the majority; anti-discrimination workplace policies and federal and local laws that are lacking, or at risk of being eliminated; and the stereotypical representation *du jour* of LGBQ "realities" on television and in films. Reminders about hardship pervade cultural and relational discourse. I also often travel in this discourse, as now more than ever we must fight for equal rights and greater inclusion. Yet, there are other dimensions to our lives than the hardship we face. I'm thinking of the more liberating social practices that are, in effect, enabled by self-identifying as LGBQ. These practices are, to me, far less discussed, if even discussed at all. As a result, they often dwell in our lived experience as "the socially standardized and standardizing, 'seen but unnoticed,' expected, background features of everyday [LGBQ] scenes" (Garfinkel, 1967, p. 36). These practices matter and merit our attention, not to downplay or trivialize the hardship, but to provide a more circumspect understanding of LGBQ cultures and identities.

Two main philosophies inform my interest in these social practices. First, my commitment to phenomenology requires me to resist certainty and dogmatism. These ways of understanding are problematic because they don't consider the perspectival and contingent nature of lived experience. There is almost always another way to interpret relating and being. Second, as someone who practices and teaches about mindfulness in everyday life, I am especially curious about what I and others are, and are not, noticing. A mindful orientation invites practitioners to expand our awareness and to curiously, openly, honestly, and even humorously attend to, and learn from, *all* of the possibilities in living. Taken together, these philosophies lead me to ask: What are other social practices present in our lives and how do

© KONINKLIJKE BRILL NV, LEIDEN, 2020 | DOI:10.1163/9789004418790_005

they matter? Asked differently, what other possibilities for living and sense making exist within LGBQ cultures and identities?

This chapter explores the "things I don't have to do" as a result of my being gay. These "things" are social practices that are not necessary, or at least not as important as they might be, if I were not gay. I represent these practices in the form of descriptive "notes" (see Berry & Adams, 2015; Sontag, 1964). Each note speaks to a distinct and recurring practice that is meaningful to me. Although I primarily focus on sexuality, these notes point to other dimensions of identity, especially sex/gender. In addition, I organize them topically, and not linearly, and their order is not meant to indicate interconnections between the notes. Overall, I aim for my notes to create a unique reflexive space in which to inventory and, thus, make explicit, personal and cultural realities that often remain unacknowledged and unthematized. May they expand our awareness and provoke dialogue.

THINGS I DON'T HAVE TO DO AS A GAY MAN

1. When I walk past men in public, especially strangers, I don't have to avert my eyes, or regulate the amount of time I sustain eye contact with them, out of fear that they will accuse me of being gay and making advances on them. I am gay, and I'm no longer afraid of being "outed." I regularly come across guys who will avoid eye contact with me, and I notice this pattern in other interactions between many men. I get that this awkwardness doesn't have to relate to attraction and desire. Other factors, such as introversion, may play a role. Still, not wanting to be seen as "gay" or as making an advance still matters in these interactions. Can't extended eye contact between men also indicate friendliness or a way of forging human connection? Then again, what if the eye contact *is* an indication of attraction and desire?

2. I don't have to be preoccupied about whether or not I am, to others, "masculine" or "tough." Being a gay man who usually performs gender more gracefully, and definitely not in rough and rugged hyper-masculine ways, and accepting and loving these qualities, has allowed me to understand that gender identity, like sexual identity, is fluid and multiple, and not fixed or static. I observe many men, including "straight-acting" gay men, who look like they exert way too much effort to perform in rough and rugged ways. Voices lowered. Chests puffed up. Walking with a swagger. It all looks exhausting! The moment in my life when I learned how to set aside and reject rigid conceptualizations of identity was also

the moment when I first learned how to fully exhale and let my chest soften to where it wanted to be.

3. I don't have to engage in sexual activity that morally aligns with the prurient interests of normative heterosexual sexual activity. As a gay man, rarely, if ever, do I pay attention to whether or not my ways of having sex are "dignified" and "respectable." Some of them don't even need to be "beautiful" and "loving." Although some people may continue to judge gay sex and gay love heteronormatively, I do not. Being gay allows me to engage with sex (and love) in fruitful and expansive ways. In addition, not needing to align gay sex with "straight" sex also means I don't feel like my sexual activity is any less important or exciting because it doesn't facilitate procreation. Being gay means I no longer need to feel shame for being different in these ways. Neither do the readers of these notes.

   Heterosexual sexual partners also do not have to engage in activity that aligns with the "moral majority." It just feels, to me, that the "perversion" tied to LGBQ sexual activities often carries more weight and consequences.

4. I don't have to worry about accidental pregnancy resulting from my sexual activity with men. I can revel in a sex life that is free from unwanted fatherhood. However, like other people LGBQ and otherwise, my sexual activity is not without complication or risk.

5. Being a cisgendered gay man, I don't have to survive everyday life feeling like I was born in the wrong body, and to be so maligned for feeling this way. I'm lucky. Oppression and physical violence against transgender folks persists, and little relief is in sight.

6. I don't have to obsess on whether others will deem certain colors of clothes I wear (e.g., pink, other pastels) as being "gay" (as in the epithet) or "faggy," while deeming other colors (e.g., blue, other darker colors) as being "straight" and "normal." I do not obsess on clothing generally. But when it matters, the choices I make, including those about colors, relate to what will make me feel good. They are not indicators of my sexuality. Besides, if my rainbow pride flag colored shorts signify to others I'm gay, then I will relish in that accurate assessment and am thankful for the compliment. Also, I will encourage them to buy a pair for themselves.

7. As an "out" and confident gay man, I don't have to ignore, or act like I didn't hear, the homophobic comments others make when they are in my presence, as I see other men do. I used to avoid these types of comments

in the past, before I was out. Ignoring them and burying my head in the sand was my way of avoiding detection and staying safe.

8. I no longer have to restrict my gait. Instead, I feel free to walk in ways that lead my hips to move, from left and right, in a swishing fashion whenever I want. Sometimes the swish is moderate; at other times, I move in "full swish." Normative prescriptions of sexuality and gender tend to code swishing as "gay," or at least "female" or "effeminate." Once I came out and learned to be more comfortable with who I am, and who I am not, "embracing the swish" quickly became a personal motto and practice of mine. When I swish I feel like I am being myself. It's fun, too. More (straight) men should embrace swish. I mean, if they can perform the "downward dog" pose while doing yoga, surely they can get a little swishy.

9. I don't have to say "no homo" after expressing intimacy or emotionally-laden messages to/with/around other men. If you listen closely to conversations held by some (many?) cisgendered and heterosexual men, especially teenagers and men in their twenties and thirties, there's a good chance you'll hear them utter these words. I'm sure some gay men say this phrase, too. "No homo" functions as a mode of impression management in the "presentation of self" to/with others (Goffman, 1959), of negotiating how one appears, in which speakers let listeners know that, although their words may "sound gay" (stereotypically speaking), as problematic as that phrase is, they are not gay. In this way, "no homo" talk suggests there's something wrong with being gay. So, it's also a mode of self-protection. (Don't even get me started on the uses and meanings of "bromance.")

10. I don't have to ask for my partner's father's "hand" in marriage, a tradition that is still practiced, and expected, in some heterosexual engagements and marriages. I understand some progressive women still opt to follow this tradition, and orient to the process as more of a gesture of love for one's father. There may now be LGBQ folk who engage in this process. However, the ritual also works in ways that demonstrate the sedimentation of past social and cultural practices that were/are patriarchal and limiting. Being gay allows me to escape from this limiting process and, consequently, to avoid intertwining the ways in which I love men with my being someone else's property. I do not feel like I need any person's permission to "give myself" to the person I love.

11. I don't have to grapple with the same presumptions and judgements from others claiming that I am "in denial" or "avoidant" of my sexuality

in the ways that bisexuals—those whom many people judge as being "in a phase"—must face. Sure, some people self-identify as "bi" until they are able to be comfortable with, and admit, to being gay. I self-identified as bisexual for a short time in my life. My denial was real. However, bisexuality, much like other sexualities, including pansexuality and asexuality, is real and merits respect.

12. I don't have to worry about whether or not I "carry down the family's name." For many people like me, being gay has typically led others to assume I will not become, or even want to become, a parent. As a result, I've been let off the hook with preserving "Berry." This is one less expectation-filled relational process that has preoccupied me. I do know a few LGBQ folks who are still pressured to have children. Also, the story is quite different for some gay friends and colleagues who are often pressured by family members to *not* be gay, so they can be with women, have children, and, thus, maintain the patriarchal family tree.

13. I don't have to label other men as being "flamboyant," as if that is negative. I won't "other" them in this way. I admit that I often enacted this practice when I was struggling to identify and be comfortable with my own gayness. Judging others distracted others, and me from my secret. It put the sunshine and heat on others, and kept me feeling safe in the existential shade, so to speak. Such judgements are cruel, consequential, and, frankly, unintelligent. Time and experience have led me to more mindfully understand that people should respect and cherish all performances of gender. What is "flamboyant" to one is "graceful" to others. Time and experience have also taught me about the ways in which graceful gay men are crucial to gay cultures and communities, and often serve as an enlivening way of embracing one's difference with/for others. Graceful gay men are fierce, and brave (see Savage, 1996).

14. As a gay man who will likely never rear children, I don't have to envision a life that requires me to worry about how my wife and daughter/s are being treated by others, especially by boys and men. I can only imagine how worrying in those ways feels. Yet, I do have to worry about the treatment of women and girls concerning issues of sexism, discrimination, sexual assault, and rape. I worry about this violence all of the time, as it pertains to girls and women, generally, but also the precious ones whom I know, love, and revere. I also worry about misogyny enacted by members of the LGBQ community.

15. I don't have to act like I am watching reruns of television shows like *Will & Grace* because "there's nothing else on." Similarly, I don't need

to feign an aversion to "chick flicks" and a love for action movies. It's assumed I will like them, and sometimes that assumption is stereotypical, and rooted in a belief that my consuming this media is a negative thing. "Of course you like those shows and films—you're gay." I watch these shows and movies because I enjoy them. I feel no shame, and no less of a man by doing so. I feel no threat to my sexuality nor my gender identity.

16. I don't have to worry that the many close personal relationships I maintain with women will lead them to think I am interested in anything else from them other than a close relationship. I don't worry about "mixed" and "ambiguous" messages. Hugging women for an extended period of time means I care about them, and not that I am romantically interested in them or want to have sex. My female friends tend to appreciate this type of intimacy, and I appreciate receiving it from them (see Chapter 8).

17. I don't have to tell stories about being pressured to get married. That pressure has never existed for me. For most of my adult life, getting married wasn't possible in the U.S. Curiously, even though marriage equality is (currently) legal, I still don't feel that pressure. I wonder if that will ever change? I know that those family and friends who love me want me to get married, if that's what I want. But even now that it's possible, I feel no pressure. Granted, I do know many LGBQ who do in fact get pressured by their families. Lucky them.

18. I don't have to abide by the same rules concerning the uses and meanings of epithetical words like "queer," "fag," "fairy," "queen." I'm thinking particularly about when these words are used in-community by LGBQ persons. I often witness others—usually folks who are not LGBQ—become confused, offended, angry, and sometimes even hostile, when they hear these words used in these situations. Many people respond in this way because they feel the words only carry harmful meanings. Some people respond in this way because they feel it's hypocritical, and express "if I cannot use these words, then neither can *they*!" Both types of responses suggest a belief that words carry universal meanings, or that these words have only one harmful meaning and thus should never be uttered. Yet, I orient to these terms as being culturally distinctive and not universal. In this way, they are cultural terms that carry communal meaning (Carbaugh, 1996). This social practice speaks to the re-appropriation, or co-opting of meaning, an empowering way of "taking back" the harmful meaning typically infused in some words when they are used as epithetical. In turn, using language in this communal way

allows LGBQ communicators to identify with each other and build community.

Also, I don't have to take others' epithets as epithets. I may be "gay," but I refuse to let that term carry the violence some might want it to entail.

***

I want the above notes to serve as the primary reflections for this chapter, and so will end by only offering four brief conclusions.

First, I feel I don't have to enact the noted social practices as a result of being a gay man. They resonate with the unique vantage point of my lived experience and, thus, are my own. Some of them will and will not resonate with others' experiences as gay men. I do not consider them universal or generalizable practices. I also do believe that each of the notes speaks to patterned ways of performing by gay men. Closer inspection and noting is necessary to identify the significance of those patterns.

Second, my own process of mindfully working through these overlooked or under-discussed practices makes me want to see the notes that would be created by people who are L, B, Q, and T. How are the social practices that resonate with their lived experiences similar and different?

Third, as I write this ending to the chapter, I'm unsure with what I want or need to do with these notes. I want the notes to provide a reflexive space that is instructive in its own right. Conveying them alone has been valuable for me in terms of being able to better understand the role of some of the more hidden understandings in LGBQ lives.

Fourth, as I've shown in several notes above, the "freedom" embodied in these social practices concerning sexuality, and gender, should not suggest that gay men, like LGBQ generally, are free from policing behavior. There are things that still must be done that require our attention (see Chapter 15).

DISCUSSION QUESTIONS

1. What do these notes lead you to think and feel about what it is like to be LGBQ? What have you learned about the challenges LGBQ (and T) must face?
2. What personal connections do you have with any of these notes? What notes would you add to this list? As an LGBQ person? An ally?
3. In terms of being your sexuality, what do you not need to do?

REFERENCES

Berry, K., & Adams, T. E. (2015). Notes on Cohen. In R. Silverman (Ed.), *The fantasy of reality: Critical essays on the Real Housewives* (pp. 175–189). New York, NY: Peter Lang.
Carbaugh, D. (1996). *Situating selves: The communication of social identities in American scenes*. New York, NY: SUNY Press.
Garfinkel, H. (1967). *Studies in ethnomethodology*. Cambridge MA: Prentice-Hall.
Goffman, E. (1959). *The presentation of self in everyday life*. New York, NY: Anchor Books.
Savage, D. (1996, December 13). The other love that dare not speak its name. *This American Life*. Retrieved February 28, 2019, https://www.thisamericanlife.org/46/sissies
Sontag, S. (1964). Notes on camp. *Partisan Review, 31*, 515–530.

QUEER DUCK

Tony E. Adams

Familial experiences of sexuality, especially lesbian, gay, bisexual, and queer (LGBQ) sexualities, often have unique characteristics that do not resemble the experiences of other identities such as gender, age, and ethnicity.[1] For example, families often consist of cisgender men and women of various ages; being female or male, or younger or older, is not necessarily deviant or inherently wrong, and there is an expectation that families will consist of cisgender men and women, old and young.[2] Family members, especially children, will often be exposed to different genders and ages by way of sisters and brothers, grand/fathers and grand/mothers, aunts and uncles. As such, many families operate in ways that suggest men and women exist, recognize that children did not choose to be male or female, and tend not to hate family members solely because of gender.[3]

Age functions similarly: Many families are comprised of various generations, and a child will typically learn that people have ages and, in turn, aging is expected. Within some families and cultural contexts, age and aging are celebrated, e.g., birthday parties, quinceañeras, Bar and Bat Mitzvahs, and anniversaries. As such, families tend to understand that different ages exist, recognize that children did not choose their ages, and tend to not hate family members solely because of age.

Familial experiences of ethnicity also display unique characteristics. Families often have one, or a few, ethnicities in common, and should two people reproduce biologically, the child will tend to share characteristics of these parents' ethnicities. Under circumstances of biological reproduction, I have never heard instances of parents not accepting their child solely because of the child's ethnicity. Further, the child may be exposed to the same (few) ethnicities throughout much of their early life, and a family might reject a child who befriends or dates others of different ethnicities.

At an early age, a child may come to an awareness about gender, age, and ethnicity but not necessarily about sexuality, especially LGBQ identities. Sexuality may be treated as a taboo topic, and "sex education" may be the primary, and

© KONINKLIJKE BRILL NV, LEIDEN, 2020 | DOI:10.1163/9789004418790_006

only, context in which sexuality is ever discussed. (Could we expect a child to have courses in "gender education," "age education," or "ethnicity education?") Further, family members may share, and celebrate, heterosexuality—that is, (cisgender) girls' attraction to (cisgender) boys and (cisgender) boys' attraction to (cisgender) girls, not necessarily a child's attraction to girls, boys, and to people who do not align with such rigid gender categories.

Children may not learn about sexuality and/or LGBQ experiences until later in life, especially if they were raised in heteronormative contexts— contexts that privilege different sexed/gendered attraction and frame persons as heterosexual until proven otherwise (Adams, 2011). As such, an LGBQ-identified child might be the only LGBQ-identified person in a family. As Weston (1991) remarks, "those who come out [as LGBQ] find themselves called upon to explain how it is that a duck could have come from a family of swans" (p. 75). Thus, the LGBQ child may assume the sole task/burden of not only introducing sexuality as a topic of conversation, but also having to explain what it even means to be LGBQ (while simultaneously learning what it means themselves). Further, the LGBQ child may encounter family members who do not accept same-sex/gender attraction, or who believe that it is the child's responsibility (fault) for choosing to be LGBQ, particularly if the child is the only LGBQ person in the family or that family members have ever known.[4]

In this chapter, I describe some of my experiences with being the first, and still only, openly self-identified queer person in my family—a (queer) duck in a family of (heterosexual) swans. I describe the estrangement I felt, and continue to feel, because of my sexuality, as well as the tension and sadness that have characterized my familial experiences for more than a decade. I conclude with questions about sexuality, LGBQ identity, and family life.

***

For my first twenty years (1979–1999), I lived in Danville, Illinois, an industrial town of approximately 25,000 people. My mother is an only child and my father has one sister, my aunt. My aunt and her husband, my uncle, have one child, my cousin; he is ten years older than me. Although I have a biological half-sister, I was raised as an only child. I have a few distant cousins, but my mother, father, aunt, uncle, and cousin are my primary family members.

Although my family is not religious, my parents perceived private Catholic schools as better than the public schools. As such, I attended Catholic school from age 5 until 18. There, I acquired limited, religious perspectives about sex and sexuality. I learned the sole purpose of sex was procreation (not pleasure);

marriage was an institution comprised of one woman and one man; all methods of birth control (condoms, pills) were sinful; and penis-vaginal sex occurring outside of marriage was sinful. I also did not learn how to masturbate until 2001; yet I knew masturbation was sinful—one shall not "waste his seed."

These lessons about sex and sexuality—sex only for reproduction, sex only within (cisgender) male-female marriage, and the dismissal of birth control and safe-sex practices—oriented me toward the ways in which I interacted with myself (e.g., no masturbation; repressing sexual desire) and with others (e.g., seeking marriage; appreciating unprotected penis-vagina sex; refusing sinful acts such as oral sex and same-sex sexual acts). Moreover, given that same-sex marriage was (is) not recognized in Catholicism, any attempt to marry someone of the same-sex would have been sinful, too.

***

Granted, pleasure was favored by most of my non-Catholic heterosexual friends and family members, though they strictly enforced heterosexual norms. There was the time when I acquired a "fake ID" (identification) that marked me as 21 (I was 18) so that one of my older friends could take me to 21-and-over erotic dancing clubs and buy me private dances with naked women. Or the time when my cousin paid his (female) friend who was a sex worker to come to my father's house to have sex with me. She arrived, undressed in the living room, and asked me to fuck her. "I'm nervous," I said and asked if she could put on her clothes. Or the time when an uncle promised to buy me a cake and have a celebration once I finally had (penis-vagina) sex with a woman. Or the time in Las Vegas when I attended an erotic dancing club with my father, the night before my grandmother underwent emergency heart surgery. Indeed, heterosexual sex was a common and explicit part of my environment, with lessons being taught by a variety of others who laboriously wanted me to be sexually intimate with a woman, others probably concerned about me being a bit queer.

I never knew a person who identified as lesbian, gay, bisexual, or queer when I lived in Danville, and those I heard about were shrouded in silence. "Jane has a 'friend'"—with an emphasis on friend, or a reference to a same-sex couple as "roommates," or stories about the lone queer kid in the area high school. It wasn't until I left Danville at the age of 19 that I met a self-identified LGBQ person. It wasn't until 22 when I began to consider myself to be queer.

***

To be fair to my friends and family, to better understand their lack of support, I need to acknowledge that I too contributed to the repressive, heterosexual contexts in which I was raised. Family members frequently discussed and celebrated heterosexuality, particularly (cisgender) men being sexually attracted to (cisgender) women and (cisgender) women being sexually attracted to (cisgender) men. Both of my parents have been (heterosexually) married multiple times. Before I came out, I willingly went to female strip clubs with my father. I suppose because of my "inadequate" enactment of masculinity, my cousin once referred to me as "the family faggot." This is the same cousin who hired his female friend to have sex with me. People regularly asked me about my sexual experiences with women; never did they ask about my sexual experiences with men.

I recently reviewed the only photograph album I ever assembled, probably in 2001, a few years before social media. The album includes photos of high school dances, excessive beer drinking, and kisses with women. There are photos from a trip with a male friend to Las Vegas. On the trip, he tried to rent us two female sex workers. I remember him saying the women first asked for $140/hour but he negotiated $70/hour. He told me about his plan in the lobby of the hotel as the women stood nearby. One of them waved at me. I refused the offer. He paid them both for one hour as I waited in the casino. I had never had sex before, did not understand sex work, and was ignorant, and cautious, about having sex with a sex worker.

Although the photographs represent interesting heterosexual moments from my life, they fail to capture my struggles with shame, same-sex/gender attraction, and learning to love myself. Had I publicly embraced my same-sex/gender attraction, I would have risked being ostracized in my rural community. I often expressed a desire to be a priest—a desire which quelled others' suspicions about my sexuality. When it became obvious that I wouldn't pursue the priesthood, I tried to have three serious, yet erratic, relationships with women, each of which lasted about six months. I was aggressively homophobic as well; I didn't want others to suspect my sexuality, and so I ridiculed gay men and lesbians as much as possible. These moments speak to why coming out was not only difficult for me, but also why, when it happened, my revelation of same-sex/gender attraction fractured many relationships.

***

In heteronormative situations—moments that assume or privilege discussions and expectations of heterosexuality—people can be hesitant to talk about same-sex/gender attraction. Sometimes I notice such hesitancy when a friend calls me a "homosexual" and then asks if it is okay to call me "gay" or "queer." Sometimes I notice this hesitancy when family members introduce my (male) partner of more than a decade as a "friend" rather than a "partner" or "husband." Sometimes I notice this hesitancy when people ask about my past sexual experiences with women. Sometimes I notice this hesitancy when a male relative talks about the size of his girlfriend's breasts and then asks if I find her breasts attractive. I remark that I am not attracted to breasts, at least as sexual objects, and feel guilty for perpetuating such a superficial and objectifying remark.

***

I was the first person in my family to identify as gay/queer. I told my mother—that is, "came out" to her—in 2001. In 2003, one month after my paternal grandmother's death, I told my father, aunt, uncle, and cousin (Adams, 2006).

After I came out, I did not receive much immediate support. Family members never asked about my relationships with men and, at best, I received lukewarm, seemingly-supportive responses, e.g., "I think you're too young to know if you are gay"; "I once knew a gay man; he was okay." My dad did not talk to me for six months and several relatives called my sexuality a "phase." Like me, I imagine that they too didn't know many queer people.

"At least your parents didn't physically harm or disown you," I heard from some friends, comments which suggested I should appreciate my family's lukewarm responses, stay quiet and feel lucky, and recognize that other queer kids have it much worse. I agree that others may experience more severe consequences after coming out, yet I also cannot dismiss the pain of my family's responses; their lack of support never felt good.

***

December 2006. I travel from Tampa, Florida, where I am pursuing my Ph.D., to my hometown with Tim, my then-boyfriend. Members of my family had not yet met Tim.[5]

Jane, my aunt and my father's sister, was one of my favorite relatives. She always supported me through difficult adolescent times. When I came out to Jane in 2002, she provided me with much needed affirmation and support. She encouraged me to tell other family members about my sexuality, and she phoned often, usually once every two weeks. I remember us even talking about the irrationality of homophobia. I never thought that her once-supportive stance would change.

"Hi, Jane!" I say on the phone. "Tim and I are driving through Atlanta. We should be in town tomorrow. We can't wait to see you and your new house!"

"Hi, Tony," she responds, unenthusiastically. "Have you told your dad where you are?"

"Yes," I answer. "He knows we'll arrive tomorrow. I can't wait to see you and your house—and I can't wait for you to meet Tim!"

Silence.

"Drive safely," she says. "I'm sure your dad will be glad to see you."

"Thanks," I reply. "I'm sure he will be glad to see us, too. Goodbye."

"Goodbye," she mumbles.

I think nothing of the awkward interaction until I arrive to town and talk with my father. He tells me that Jane and Mike, her husband, did not want Tim and me to visit them. They didn't approve of my "gay lifestyle" and did not want gay men in their house.

Although I perceived Jane as once accepting of me when I came out, my perception changed a few years later. Jane and I now only talk about twice a year and we have never been as close as we once were. The disclosure of my same-sex/gender attraction fractured our relationship in painful ways.

***

I am often nervous when I return to my hometown. I worry about those unexpected moments when my queer-present mixes with my less-queer-past. Every return is characterized by avoidance, discomfort, and paranoia, of being asked, by my high school best friend's father, to reconnect with this once best friend. I refuse to reconnect, as I do not want to navigate ignorance or hesitancy when talking about same-sex/gender attraction, my queer research, or the life I live with my (same-sex) partner. Should I reconnect and ignorant comments are made, I imagine disconnecting again, unable to deal with the comments. I might then feel guilty not only for disconnecting again, but also for not addressing the other's ignorance. So, by not returning, I have fewer chances to speak with the (former) best friend and others, fewer opportunities for ignorant statements and hesitancies. But I know the less I speak with her and others, I also avoid being able to speak about heteronormativity and queerness.

***

A few years after my aunt (Jane) refused a visit from me and Tim, I spent a week with her in a hospital where my father underwent surgery for colon cancer. During this time, she told me how family members, particularly her parents and brother (my dad), never approved of Jake, her husband (my uncle), and how she had to disregard their prejudices in order to marry him.

"Isn't it curious that family members may not approve of the people we love?" I said. "Others didn't approve of Jake for whatever reasons. Family members don't approve of my partner because he is male and because I am male. Like you, I frequently have to disregard others' prejudices and defend the person I love."

"It is curious," she replied and said nothing more. I never asked if she felt bad for refusing my visit or waiting six years to meet my partner.

***

In my book, *Narrating the Closet* (Adams, 2011), I described the ways in which my relationships were harmed because of my sexuality. I told the story of Jane, but in order to protect her privacy, I disguised her as a "cousin."

In 2014, immediately after reading this section of the book, my father called me.

"Which cousin wouldn't allow you to visit?" he asks.

"It wasn't a cousin," I reply, "it was your sister [my aunt]."

"She wouldn't allow you to visit?" he asks. "Why didn't you tell me?"

"Dad, you told me about their refusal years ago, when Tim and I visited. You and I didn't have the best relationship when the situation happened, and we did not talk about my sexuality. I felt especially uncomfortable reprimanding your sister."

"Don't live your life for her," he replies. "You have a great life and I am proud of you."

His comments indicate an evolved support for me and suggest that I should disregard his sister's actions—a suggestion that further estranges me from her, possibly estranges her from him, and draws me closer to him. Although his comment indicates the slow progress he and I have made in our relationship, it also demonstrates the ways in which my sexuality continues to fracture familial relationships.

***

After the June 2015 United States Supreme Court ruling in support of same-sex/gender marriage, I hope that I will experience supportive responses about the ruling from family members. However, my parents only neutrally comment about the case, and neither asks if I will marry my partner of (at that time) seven years—an avoidance that, at least to me, still indicates silence and rejection regarding my sexuality. Further, when I post praise about the ruling on Facebook, an online context in which these family members participate, none of them "like" my post—another silence that stands in stark contrast to the many other posts of mine they like.

***

After a cousin's wedding that I did not attend, an event that took place two weeks after the Supreme Court ruling, a wedding I avoided because I assumed that talk about, and the privileging of only heterosexuality would occur, my mother reported that the minister aggressively commented that marriage should be reserved only for a woman and a man. My mother was upset by the message and says that I made a good decision to not attend.

***

I began writing this chapter as my uncle Tony rests in a hospital. He's 89 and one of my closest relatives. I'm named after him. He will die in three weeks. One month later, a great aunt dies. And then a great uncle and the parents of a close family friend. I do not attend any of the funerals. I do not want to deal with others interrogating my sexuality or having to worry about justifying my relationship with a man.

I live increasingly separated from family members. I do not attend family events such as birthdays, anniversaries, or retirement celebrations, and I do not encourage family members to visit me. On the few times that I interact with them, I rarely bring my partner Jerry, because I do not want him to be treated differently because of our relationship, nor do I want him to witness ignorant remarks. After being out for nearly two decades, I am saddened to realize that, in order to protect myself and my relationship from uneasy silences and disparaging discourse, I refrain from fully participating in family life.

I continue to live as a duck among swans.

DISCUSSION QUESTIONS

1. I opened this chapter by describing potential differences between familial experiences of gender, age, ethnicity, and sexuality. Do you agree with these differences? Why (not)? How may familial experiences of gender, age, and ethnicity be similar to experiences of sexuality? When did you first learn about gender, age, ethnicity, and sexuality?
2. What advice do you have for people who are the only LGBQ-identified people in their family? How should they educate heterosexual family members about LGBQ experiences? How long should LGBQ-identified persons tolerate familial ignorance and prejudice toward their sexuality?
3. Do families need to approve who their children date or marry? How long are family members able to disapprove of a relationship? One year? Ten years? What if such disapproval never disappears, or only exists because of another person's gender, age, race, or sexuality?

NOTES

[1] Parts of this chapter have been revised from Adams (2017).
[2] I recognize that some families and cultures value cisgender men and women differently. I only stress that families often consist of men and women; biological, all-male and all-female families are difficult to sustain.
[3] These assumptions perpetuate the male-female gender binary and primarily apply to cisgender family members; they do not represent the experiences of families and family members who identify as genderqueer, transgender, or intersexed (see Dreger & Herndon, 2009; Meadow, 2018; Norwood & Lanutti, 2015).
[4] Some families have multiple LGBQ-identified persons. However, I assume that many families do not have an abundance of LGBQ-identified persons, at least when compared to family members who identify as heterosexual.
[5] This story has been revised from Adams (2014, pp. 64–65).

REFERENCES

Adams, T. E. (2006). Seeking father: Relationally reframing a troubled love story. *Qualitative Inquiry, 12*, 704–723. https://doi.org/10.1177/1077800406288607

Adams, T. E. (2011). *Narrating the closet: An autoethnography of same-sex attraction.* Walnut Creek, CA: Left Coast Press.

Adams, T. E. (2014). Post-coming out complications. In R. M. Boylorn & M. P. Orbe (Eds.), *Critical autoethnography: Intersecting cultural identities in everyday life* (pp. 50–61). Walnut Creek, CA: Left Coast Press.

Adams, T. E. (2017). Being a (gay) duck in a family of (heterosexual) swans. In P. Leavy (Ed.), *Privilege through the looking-glass: A text-reader on status characteristics in daily life*. Rotterdam, The Netherlands: Sense Publishers.

Dreger, A. D., & Herndon, A. M. (2009). Progress and politics in the intersex rights movement. *GLQ, 15*, 199–224. https://doi.org/10.1215/10642684-2008-134

Meadow, T. (2018). *Trans kids: Being gendered in the twenty-first century.* Berkeley, CA: University of California Press.

Norwood, K. M., & Lannutti, P. (2015). Families' experiences with transgender identity and transition: A family stress perspective. In L. G. Spencer & J. C. Capuzza (Eds.), *Transgender communication studies: Histories, trends, and trajectories* (pp. 51–68). Lanham, MD: Lexington.

Weston, K. (1991). *Families we choose: Lesbians, gays, kinship.* New York, NY: Columbia University Press.

TRUE COMPANION

Catherine M. Gillotti

It was our first substantive conversation about co-authoring this book. Keith, Tony, and I met during the annual conference of the National Communication Association in Las Vegas in a Starbucks to talk about the themes of the book and the structure and content of the chapters. I did not expect for either of them to say, we think you should include your "coming out" story. "Really?" "But this is not a coming out book," I said. Keith, more so than Tony, knew the intimate details of my coming out story because he had a front row seat to the process. He was one of the sane, empathetic voices for me in an insane time. With trepidation, I agreed to include my story because I felt that the lessons I learned from it might also resonate with others, and that it was actually more than a coming out story. It is a story about the power of a first love gained and lost, and the gift of an enduring friendship.

After the conference, I reached out to Emily by text message asking if I could talk with her about this book. She agreed to meet, and we set the date for us to go out for dinner and talk about our past. She was my first everything: girlfriend, true love, and devastating heartbreak. Essentially, Emily introduced me to my authentic self. For that I am always grateful.

I was nervous about having this conversation, as I knew it might open up positive and negative feelings. Yet, I also was willing to take that risk, especially since I knew that our friendship had survived more than twenty years. We went to dinner, which is where I originally planned to "collect data" for my story. I thought it would be interesting to co-construct our past together. We ate on the quaint patio at Bartlett's in Beverly Shores, Indiana, near the Indiana Dunes State Park. After dinner we decided to go to my house for more discussion since it was more private, and most importantly, there would be fewer mosquitoes biting us. The conversation was easy. It felt like putting on your favorite old sweatshirt—comfortable, familiar, and warm. I had to keep reminding myself that it was not a date. Emily and I don't see each other very often because even after 20 years our chemistry still smolders. I cannot explain it other than to say I am grateful I have

© KONINKLIJKE BRILL NV, LEIDEN, 2020 | DOI:10.1163/9789004418790_007

experienced that kind of passion. The account you will read below captures the essence of our conversation.

***

As we sat together on my enclosed patio, I began asking her to confirm the year we started to date, which was 1998. In 1996, I was a newly minted Ph.D., new to the university, and little did I know about to embark on a secondary adolescence. Emily was an undergraduate student in the department where I worked, although she never took my classes. She did, however, drop by my office regularly.

Over time Emily's visits during office hours became more frequent. I thought she was absolutely adorable. She was funny, petite, attractive, smart, and a good conversationalist. Of course, I meant this compliment in a purely platonic way. I even thought to myself how "lucky her boyfriend must be" to have such a smart, witty, cute girlfriend.

One day I asked her if she had a boyfriend. She laughed and told me she was a lesbian. I had no idea because my worldview was so heteronormative at the time. I still thought of myself as a straight woman who was simply waiting to meet the right guy so I could settle down and have children. Daniel Goleman (1985) would call this a "vital lie." Vital lies are lies we tell ourselves so often that we believe they are true. I am a straight woman, and I wanted children were two of my vital lies. These lies were the foundation of my internal argument for my parents' acceptance.

My relationship with Emily was about to shatter my vital lies. My unconscious mind was already laying the groundwork for coming out. By this time, I was having a recurring dream about my former hairstylist who had once come onto me. That moment of attraction stirred in me for years. In my recurring dream, I was forced to have sex with her. It was horrible and wonderful at the same time. It would not take a psychologist to do dream analysis here. My sexual attraction for women was surfacing, and my conscious self was not about to let that happen; hence, the rape fantasy of the dream. So, I married my work, earning tenure and being promoted, studying for my second-degree brown belt test in karate, and secretly pining everyday for Emily to visit. This courtship continued for two years; two years of hearing that laugh, seeing that smile, "innocently" embracing one another in hugs that lasted just a little too long to constitute friendship. The sexual tension was building.

In addition to Emily's regular visits to my office, we started to hang out socially. One night we went to a movie together. After returning to my apartment, she came in and we discussed the film. I wanted to touch her, to kiss her, but I was scared of what that meant about me and what that would do to our relationship, which might then move beyond friendship. The tension was palpable. She moved to leave and we shared yet another prolonged embrace. We held onto each other for several minutes. I remember thinking how well we physically "fit" together. Emily is a little taller than I am, and at the time was smaller than me. Hugging her was the epitome of two spoons nestled together. We both knew that we wanted more, but neither of us made the first move. She walked out the door. I closed it behind her, and laid my head on the inside of the door aching for her. She told me later that she was laying her head on the other side of my door wanting me as well. It was a foreshadowing. "You are killing me Emily" is what I told her often after that night. This disclosure was the chink in my heterosexual armor. I was on the edge and we both knew it.

Our chemistry was clear to everyone who saw us together. The mutual admiration, longing stares, smiling, and general giddiness between us must have looked comical to anyone who witnessed our interactions on campus. Several of my colleagues became concerned for me, not because it meant that I was gay, as they sensed that about me when I interviewed for the job, but rather what it might mean to get romantically involved with a student in the department.

My feelings for Emily grew every day. She was going through a difficult time. Her father was dying of liver cancer, and she and her girlfriend were breaking up. When her father died, I decided I should go to the wake for various reasons. I was raised Catholic and one of the corporal works of mercy is to bury the dead. I wanted to honor her and her father by attending the wake to support her. Our intimacy also was so strong that I felt like it would have been a betrayal not to go. It was that gesture of sympathy that pushed us closer together. My presence at the wake cemented our connection to one another.

Shortly after her father passed, we went on another movie outing. We were going to meet Keith to see *Analyze This* starring Billy Crystal. Emily first came to my apartment. We sat on the couch, turned toward each other, each with an arm draped over the back of the couch. We looked intently into each other's eyes. Our fingertips touched and then we held each other's hand. There was no stopping it; my vital lies fell away as our lips touched in what would be the best kiss of my life. Even Emily and I could never recreate the magic of that moment. There was no awkwardness, no wondering if it was right or how the other person felt about you. There were only the bright lights of the ecstasy of finally knowing why I never felt this way when I kissed a man. We kept kissing, touching each other, and feverishly embracing. Our hearts were pounding as we gasped for air. I wanted to cry because I never felt more alive and yet more afraid. I had crossed the line. I no longer just dreamed about my sexual attraction for women. I was living it. We finally pulled ourselves together after the most intense and satisfying make-out session of my life, and went to the theatre.

Once we arrived at the theater, I was certain Keith would take one look at us and know what we had done. My breath was shallow, my attention wildly moving around the theatre. *People will know. People will see us and just know.* I barely made it through the movie and could not tell you what it was about, because all I could concentrate on was those lips and tongue, and the warmth of her body. She was sitting next to me in the theater with our legs touching. The two-hour movie felt like an eternity, as all I wanted to do was be alone with her and kiss her again.

We came back to my place and spent the next eight hours making out. While technically we did not have sex, I did in my mind and heart. I was still scared and frankly felt like I had no idea how to sexually please another woman. While being physically intimate with a woman was unfamiliar, I also knew what felt good to me, so how hard could it be to pleasure her, right?

She courted me patiently for two years before that night, and finally we were together. Damn the consequences. Damn whether or not she and her girlfriend were really done with each other. Damn my family and what they thought. However, eight hours later when the sun rose to greet a new day, I rolled over, looked at her and said, "no offense, but I am not gay."

Emily laughed and said "okay." Her laugh told me she recognized the utter ridiculousness of my statement. Who spends eight hours making out with someone, practically making love, only to say, "whoops—I didn't mean to do that?" "No, I did not enjoy that." "No, I am not gay." We laughed again during our recent reminiscing conversation as we recounted this moment. She had such compassion for me then and knew I just wasn't ready to come out.

After that night, I had to see her again, and again, and again. Each time we would vow that this was the last time. "Cinco, no mas" we would say to each other. I don't remember where five times came from, but that phrase was our code for "okay not again." I look back, smile, and laugh at myself. The ship had left the dock, and I was on it. I was terrified about coming out to my family. My cognitive dissonance damn near ruined me. I was in love with Emily and in hate with myself. I was crippled by guilt internally and externally every time I lied to my family about where I was or with whom I was spending time. I began to speak in generalized and vague ways: "I am out with a friend" or "a friend and I went to see the Blue Man Group in Chicago." I was disgusted with myself and afraid of others' judgment. I was in a spiritual crisis like I had never faced before. As a child I was taught that homosexuality was a sin and, thus, immoral. While my guilt crushed me, my desire for Emily was too strong to ignore.

To assuage my guilt, I went to confession at my church where I was a lector. *What a hypocrite! I was living a double life. Secretly, I was sleeping with Emily, utterly and hopelessly in love with her.* And yet, on Sundays you could find me in church reading at Sunday mass. I was reading the scriptures to the congregation and asking for God's forgiveness each week. The guilt became too much to bear and I went to confession.

"Bless me Father for I have sinned. It has been many years since my last confession. I have had sexual intercourse outside of marriage with another woman." The priest said to me, "People judge, Jesus doesn't." He gave me absolution along with instruction to say ten *Hail Marys* and ten *Our Fathers* in penance for my "sin." After I dutifully said my prayers, I felt relieved and temporarily committed to not sin anymore.

Part of the sacrament of Catholic reconciliation is to say the Act of Contrition where one vows to not engage in sin again. That was going to be a problem for me. I couldn't stop myself from being with Emily. I was alive in ways I never knew possible because I had repressed my sexuality for so long. I was 31, coming out to myself and truly alive for the first time. I also felt like I was about to die. I had suicidal ideation, but deep down knew I never could commit the act. It would hurt my family too much. My plan was clear though—*I will jump off my third floor balcony.* I quickly changed my mind as I realized that all I would end up doing was maiming myself. *My luck, I wouldn't die and I'd still be gay.*

For a short period of time—perhaps a few months—I told others and myself I was "bisexual." What a joke! There were only three men in my life who I ever felt enough passion for to want sexually. And even sexual attraction did not indicate my sexual orientation. I was a lesbian who was deeply and unequivocally in love with Emily. However, the dogged pursuit of my guilt was unrelenting. Shortly thereafter, my parish pastor asked me to lector at a special Lenten service at another Catholic church. I agreed to do the readings. This service took place over two days. I was required to read on the first night. I completed the reading and sat down to listen to the priest proclaim the Gospel and give his homily. I do not remember his name, but

CHAPTER 7

I do remember that the priest had been ministering to the prison population in Michigan City, Indiana, near where I lived. His homily was on the topic of forgiveness. I was so moved by his stories of the conversations with the prisoners that I knew that I needed to come back to the next night's service.

The following evening, I attended the mass at Our Lady of Grace concelebrated with the priest from the night before and the Bishop of the Diocese. During the service, there was an opportunity to go to confession with one of nine parish priests and the Bishop. The longest lines were for the priest from the Michigan City prison and for the Bishop. I decided that even though the line was long, it was worth the wait to have my confession heard by the priest from the prison. As I waited my turn, my stomach turned with nausea. I was about to reveal my sexuality to a priest and risk ex-communication. Besides being disowned by my family, I could think of no greater travesty of my life.

When my turn finally arrived, I wept as I started my confession saying, "Bless me father for I have sinned. It has been a year since my last confession. I am gay."

There it was—the truth—my confession to God that I was indeed gay. I braced myself for the inevitable chiding by the priest and the order of excommunication from my spiritual home.

He said, "God is the author of your heart, and you give back to God by being who He made you to be." I was stunned by his response. I stood silently in disbelief, and I never felt closer to God than after hearing this priest's words. I felt I was truly in the presence of Jesus Christ. I said, "But what about the church? Should I leave the Catholic Church?" He continued by saying, "Many people do." The sacrament of reconciliation, or confession as it has been known in the past, is guided by the practice that the priest can either give you absolution for your sins or not. This priest refused to give me absolution, which might be interpreted as a form of ex-communication. However, it was not. Instead, he asked God to bless and keep me. He did not give me absolution because he did not see being gay as a sin. I barely made it back to my seat before I wept with joy. Finally, I felt I could set down my guilt. I could embrace what seemed like a paradoxical puzzle of identity—to be both gay and Catholic. I could continue to practice my faith without fear of ex-communication. I could be both even though the public stance from the Catholic Church is that you cannot act upon the feelings. It is fine to be gay, but you must be celibate. His words are forever emblazoned on my heart and brain. "God is the author of your heart and you give back to God by being

66

who He made you to be." The priest did not say, "God is the author of your heart, and you give back to God by being celibate."

I finally felt comfortable with my faith. My family was another matter, as was Emily.

Poor Emily—there was so much pressure on her as my first love, first girlfriend. I had such idealized visions of what true love was and what it meant for our future, and now that I interpreted the priest's words as having a "get out of hell free card" from the Catholic Church, I pursued her enthusiastically. I wanted to woo her and frankly, I wanted to marry her even though marriage equality was a notion yet to be realized. However, she seemed more distant. Could I blame her? No. I was a mess. I was on again/ off-again prior to the confession. I was in love with her, but I would not acknowledge our relationship to my family. I declared "I am gay," then in the next breath "no I am not." Then there was the difference in age. We listened to different music, had different circles of friends, and were in different places in life. She had just finished her undergraduate degree and I was on my way to tenure and promotion. It was a fatal attraction (Femlee, 1998) if there had ever been one, meaning it was doomed from the start. What was undeniably true then and now was that we have an inexplicable attraction. I wanted something from her in terms of commitment that was beyond what she could give. I know she loved me, and still does, but our love was not going to lead to an enduring commitment.

It was clear in my mind what I needed to do. I needed to let her know how I felt, but I wanted to be romantic in my approach. We were leaving in my car for a date, and I had a Marc Cohn CD in the player cued up and ready to play his song "True Companion" (1991).

I said to her, "I want to share something with you." She listened to the song as we drove to dinner. I knew by her body language that it was not going as well as I hoped. In the song, Cohn sings about his "true companion." It is a beautiful love song and I could not think of a better, more eloquent way to capture my feelings for her. Our fingertips touched on the back of the couch moments before our first kiss, and my heart was hers. That kiss was my undoing, my reconciliation with my authentic self, my first foray into the dangerous game of love, and my liberation from my heteronormative life lived thus far. I wanted to spend the rest of my life with her, and I was searching to see if she felt the same about me. She did not. I was too far along in walking her down the aisle, in the fantasy of "us" than what she was comfortable with at the tender age of 23. She may have been 23, but her soul was much older and wiser. She knew it was too much too fast, even with two years of courtship and 15 months of an affair.

We had the passion and some of the intimacy, but not long-term commitment (Sternberg, 2006). I was devastated the day we broke up. My grief was so profound that I found it hard to breathe. My everyday began with thoughts of her, and I could not date again until almost a year and a half after the break up. It was not her fault. It was not my fault. We were at different points in our lives, with different dreams of the future. I would attribute it to timing then, but later realized it was more. As Sternberg writes in *The Psychology of Love* (2006), you have to have passion, intimacy and commitment to have a consummate love. We had no problem with the passion and not much with the intimacy. It was the expectation of commitment that was unfair of me to expect from someone who was only 23, and at the beginning of her journey as an independent adult.

For many years after our breakup, no one could compare to the depth and breadth of passion that Emily and I once shared. Mistakenly, I used that level of passion as a litmus test in future romantic relationships. No one could ever hold a candle to the memory of that first kiss, my first love, and that first realization of who I was. It was an exercise in futility. Even Emily and I would never be able to recreate those moments, because they were less about us, and more about the power of "the first." I now tuck those memories away and cherish them for what they are, which are sweet memories that only Emily and I share. She was a gift to me in that she helped me come to terms with myself. It took me years to realize that and to forgive her for not being able to love me the way I loved her.

***

As we wrapped up our conversation—our co-construction of our past relationship—I walked Emily to the door. She turned to me and said, "If I was not seeing someone, would I be going home tonight?" I said to her, "Darling, that would be entirely up to you." Over the years, we discussed an intention to rekindle if we both happened to be single at the same time. While there were brief periods when this could have been realized, we never have tried to date again. I often think it is because neither of us wants to lose the memory of what we had so many years ago.

However, our passion was alive that night as it always has been. She left and my heart ached, as I knew it would, but it was a pain I could live with knowing now what I did not know then. Although scarred, my broken and wounded heart had healed years ago. Emily and I will always be connected, even though it is unlikely we will ever be together. I often said to her in the past and again that night as she left my house, "You have a permanent residence in my heart. Te amo chica."

One of my favorite poets is Kahlil Gibran. His wisdom on love in the book *The Prophet* (1923) sums up how I feel about Emily:

> When love beckons you, follow him, though his ways are hard and steep. And when his wings enfold you yield to him, though the sword hidden among his pinions may wound you. And when he speaks to you believe in him, though his voice may shatter your dreams as the north wind lays waste the garden. For even as love crowns you, so shall he crucify you. Even as he is for your growth, so is he for your pruning. (p. 11)

What was my growth? My vital lies burned away in the fire of our love; I experienced both the immeasurable joy and excruciating loss of that love; and I finally could accept myself as God had created me.

DISCUSSION QUESTIONS

1. What vital lies have you told yourself about your identity?
2. What role did Cathy's religious beliefs play in her struggle and acceptance of self?
3. Sternberg's consummate love requires passion, intimacy, and commitment. Which one was missing for you in a past relationship? In what ways did your identity change in that relationship?

REFERENCES

Cohn, M. (1991). True companion. *Marc Cohn* [CD]. New York, NY: Atlantic Recording Corporation.

Femlee, D. H. (1998). Fatal attraction. In B. H. Spitzberg & W. R. Cupach (Eds.), *The dark side of close relationships* (pp. 3–31). Mahwah, NJ: Lawrence Erlbaum Associates.

Gibran, K. (1923). *The prophet*. New York, NY: Alfred A. Knopf.

Goleman, D. (1985). *Vital lies, simple truths: The psychology of self-deception*. New York, NY: Simon & Schuster.

Sternberg, R. J. (2006). A duplex theory of love. In R. J. Sternberg & K. Weis (Eds.), *The new psychology of love* (pp. 184–199). New Haven, CT: Yale University Press.

RELATIONAL GIFTS

Keith Berry

I saw the film *Welcome to Marwen* (*Marwen*) in the theatres with my mother on Christmas Day. *Marwen* tells the story of Mark Hogancamp. Based on a true story, Hogancamp ("Hogie") is the survivor of a brutal hate crime in which four assailants beat him to near death after he discloses to them that he loves to wear women's shoes. As part of his recovery process, Hogie creates a model of a town called "Marwen," in which he and five figurines, his heroes, live through battles against unrelenting Nazis. This battle is symbolic of the beating he endured. Each figurine is a woman who has been, and continues to be, instrumental in helping Hogie as he struggles to stay well, and ultimately alive, in recovery. For me, the film is a gripping tale about what it means to navigate difference in a world in which judgment and violence often prevail. It was a painful, but also beautiful gift to receive during the holiday season.

Although my mother and I both saw previews of *Marwen* in advance of watching the film, and knew it dealt with major trauma, neither one of us knew the particularities of its plot. The film's trailers skillfully obscured the most important detail, the difference with which Hogie lives. I figured the storyline would be intense, maybe even gruesome. But I had no idea it would affect me in deeply personal ways. Although I have never been interested in wearing women's shoes, nor have I been the victim of a physical hate crime, I located myself in the relationship shown between Hogie and his figurines. I am "hermeneutically implicated" (Schrag, 2003), or interpretively "in" the lived experience being portrayed in *Marwen*. Put differently, I experienced a significant level of resonance between his story and my own (Bochner & Ellis, 2016). For as long as I can remember, the relationships I have maintained with girls (in my youth) and women have been crucial to my life, and to my survival. Indeed, I have lived my own existential town of "Marwen." I knew girls and women have been important across my life so far (see Berry, 2016). Yet, identifying the meaningfulness and putting their importance into words has been difficult. I left the theater feeling opened up and curious: Which relationships with girls and women have been especially important to me? How did they enrich my life, in terms of my development and overall well-being?

The process of using reflexive writing to explore relational bonds over the course of a lifetime is exciting. It allows us to learn about who we once were, so as to better understand how and who we have become. And yet, this process is often demanding, because the act of using autoethnography to revisit past lived experience may entail *re-living* anxious times and painful episodes (Berry, 2016; Bochner & Ellis, 2016; Holman Jones, Adams, & Ellis, 2013). In turn, this work entails confronting choices made within interaction and relationships, choices that may or may not have demonstrated good care for self and others. Thus, this work can lead to regret, self-critique, and some wicked spells of rumination. In these ways, myriad thoughts and feelings informs this reflexive inquiry. I convey and explore my experiences with these girls and women in this chapter by drawing on a practice of mindfulness. For me, mindfulness entails writing vulnerably, directly, honestly, gently, and sometimes humorously. Similarly, when writing I try to imagine our interactions, the good and bad ones. Sometimes this entails writing as if I am crafting my words *for* or *to* them. Altogether, working in these mindful ways allows me to both acknowledge the important role each person played, and continues to play in my life, and to do so in a spirit of gratitude and love for the care and love they gave, and, with some, continue to give. Small or seismic, the gifts they have given me have been life-altering.

These girls and women are my "sheroes."

***

Rhonda is a close neighborhood friend during my childhood. I hang out with her and our close friend Doug practically every Saturday and Sunday and throughout the week during summer breaks in middle school. The three of us attend school together. Rhonda is a wonderful person who will never say a bad thing about anyone, even when they insult her. Around Rhonda and Doug, I am able to act goofy and be experimental with what I say and who I am. We play school, radio talk show, fake horror films, and more. I don't ruminate when I am with them. In our friendship, I am a freer spirit and have fun. I end the day of playing with them feeling exhausted. We play hard.

Rhonda is quirky and often awkward. She's a bit overweight and suffers with serious acne on her face. I feel bad for her when I see others, including Doug, make fun of her. His attacks can be relentless; he says he's "being playful." He's playing when he calls her "pizza face" because of her acne;

"blubber butt" because of her weight; "bag lady" because she doesn't wear the clothes the "cool kids" wear; and "lonely ugly no one" because "someone with her looks will never find a boyfriend." When I see the hurt look on Rhonda's face during one of his attacks, I often try to intervene. Sometimes I change the subject of our conversation, nudging or abruptly taking us outside to play, or at least to talk about something else. Sometimes if Doug leaves the room to go to the bathroom, or to the kitchen to get a snack, I give her a compliment, to try to make her feel better. "I love that your family has an in-the-ground pool. No one else on the block does." "Your collection of video games is amazing." I am not, however, always affirming.

Sometimes I join Doug when he mocks her by mirroring his insults, or coming up with some of my own. I rarely feel good when I team up with him, and, frankly, I am not at all good at personal attacks. I almost always regret it. Regardless, joining Doug against Rhonda serves me in some meaningful way. Being a rather angelic kid, so I'm told, maybe I insult her because it is fun to be bad. Maybe I feel as though these joint assaults extended toward her will take the attention away from me. If I do not join him, what aspects about me will Doug, and maybe even Rhonda, insult? Whereas the usual playful times with Rhonda gift me with the ability to enjoy myself and be whimsical, participating in the verbal aggression against her gifts me with safety, moments of shade, so to speak, that prevent me from being burned relationally.

***

I meet *Andi* in middle school. She is the first girl I know who is attracted to me and wants to be my girlfriend. She's taller than me, has blonde hair, is thin, and pretty. I don't know her well, but she slips me a note during class one day on which she wrote "I like you, we should hang out sometime." I am thrilled and, I think, interested. Until that point, I am not sure if I will be able to find a girlfriend. Most girls do not seem to be interested in me. During middle school I hear plenty of friends talking about "their first kiss." I am anxious about having *my* first kiss, mainly because I want to be able to tell others I've kissed a girl. I want the kiss, and that disclosure, pretty bad. If other boys can and want to kiss her, why don't I want to do so? I need to make the kiss happen. I don't want the boys at school to bully me. I don't want them to call me "gay." I want to be normal.

One day Andi and I are swimming in the pool at the house of a mutual friend. Andi and I are at the deeper end of the pool, deep enough for the water to come up to my chin on my short body. After a few moments of splashing each other and joking, Andi starts batting her eyelashes at me and smiling flirtatiously.

"I want you to kiss me," she says. I am shocked by her invitation, because until that point, kissing her never came to my mind.

"Umm," I say hesitating, as I look to make sure our friends, located in the shallow end of the pool and on the deck, aren't looking at us. She moves closer to me. I keep moving around, bouncing, and fake dancing while singing gibberish. "La la la la pool dancing, pool dancing."

"I want you to kiss me," she says, again, but this time more insistently. I am torn between wanting her to kiss me, and swimming underwater to the safety of my friends. Finally, she points down to under the water and says "come on ..." We both go under water, and I see her moving closer to me as I begin to close my eyes, to protect them from the harsh chlorine in the pool. Her lips touch mine and Andi grabs my hips. I touch her shoulders and close my eyes even tighter. Our kiss feels weird; when connected our lips feel dry, even though we are both under water. I begin to giggle, which creates bubbles that flow in between our faces, and leads us to stop our kiss and return to the surface.

My encounter with Andi does not progress. We remain casual friends at school, but neither one of us pursues each other romantically, nor do we ever talk about that kiss. It's possible she doesn't want to be my girlfriend—maybe I fell short on the kiss? It's also possible that, because I don't further pursue her, she became uninterested. Then again, it's likely that we don't progress because we are in middle school. What I do know more assuredly is that our kiss feels significant. Even if superficial, that kiss gave me the chance to fulfill my role as a normal boy. It gave me inclusion, albeit temporary, into a life conditioned by compulsory heterosexuality. As a result, I feel proud of my accomplishment. At the same time, I don't tell anyone that we kissed. And in a way, maybe my hidden gay self is thrilled that it took place under water.

***

I first begin my friendship with U.S. Government Agent *Diana* in middle school. Diana Prince is modest and low key in her everyday life, but she has secret identity: she is Wonder Woman, the "princess warrior." I meet her by watching the fictional television show that bears her name. I am quickly hooked on the show and *love* her.

I love the ways Wonder Woman is able to use her superpowers to fight evil villains, restoring order and justice to a dangerous and complicated society, tidily within the short confines of a 60-minute television episode. I love the superhero outfit she changes into when danger calls, including her patriotic tight-fitting U.S. American flag-like shorts, magic bracelets that deflect bullets, magic crown that doubles as a boomerang that often knocks the gun out of villains' hands, and the magic lasso that is attached to her waist and hangs down her right thigh. Also, she has an invisible plane that is fabulous. When duty calls Diana sneaks off to a secret location, much like Superman, holds her arms out by her sides and spins in circles, leading to a large fire blast that envelopes her and allows her to change into a superhero. I love Wonder Woman so much that I dress up like her and spin in circles like she does on the show, in front of a group of girls and my fifth grade teacher Miss Cheek one day during recess (see Berry, 2013, 2016). I think Miss Cheek looks like Diana, and I love that about her. Certainly my spin puts me at risk for ridicule among my peers. A staple in the U.S. entertainment world in the 1980s, I feel a personal and deep kinship with Wonder Woman. I admire, respect, and look up to her. She looks fabulous, does good deeds, and rejects bad ones. She is powerful and resilient. Others admire and respect her. Her being a role model is one of the most important gifts I receive in my youth. Yet, embodying this gift also signals the difference with which I live.

None of my friends, especially the boys, talk about or show signs of loving Wonder Woman. No one tells me they want to *be*, or *be like*, her. Many of my guy friends, much like their fathers, probably admire her more for the ways her fit body and ample breasts appear on the television screen. Unfortunately, Wonder Woman is unable to eliminate objectification, a most insidious patriarchal villain. Instead my school, much like my neighborhood, are filled with boys who enact normative gender performances. They often talk about, love, and emulate male action figures and sports figures. Some boys might orient to Wonder Woman in ways similar to me, but don't pursue similar desires because they are afraid of being labeled "faggot" or a "sissy." While I am afraid of being bullied, those fears don't stop me from wanting her life.

I want Wonder Woman's magical powers, and often visualize situations in which I use them. I want her invisible plane and imagine how cool it would be to travel from place to place without others noticing. In this sense, I want the things that I suspect other kids want. However, I also desire her identity in ways that I don't suspect are common with other boys. I am fortunate to live a safe and happy life in many ways, though I am sometimes an anxious youth. As I suggest in Chapter 1, I suspect my anxiety, at least in part, stems from my difference, especially my not being attracted to girls and likely being attracted to boys. Granted, I am not aware of this attraction at my young age; instead it dwells unnoticed and not discussed. Still, my attraction and desires are likely "there" influencing my life when I feel like "I am different." My mom tells me that many kids feel that way and get anxious, but that doesn't always help. As a result, I love and want to be like Diana, and directly face risk and confront danger when duty calls, without getting hurt, and then return to how I normally live in secret.

I cherish my bond with Wonder Woman throughout middle school, and the gifts she offers me are invaluable. Embodying her allows me times for adventure, excitement, and fun in a generation when there are barely video games to be played, nor is there an Internet to surf. At the same time, the performance of spinning like her, and living with the identification I feel to her, more generally, also lets me mitigate my anxiety. I am freer to experience and experiment with novel selves, new ways of moving through the world that are needed and meaningful. I am able to begin to be the princess warrior that I will need to be for years to come.

***

There are other famous female role models who have been instrumental to my well-being. These women include: Cyndi Lauper, The Pointer Sisters, Cher, Bette Midler, Joan Rivers, "Mrs. Garrett" (from the television show *The Facts of Life*), each of the characters on *The Golden Girls*, all divas from *Dynasty*, Olivia Newton John, Stockard Channing, Madonna, Oprah, Lady Gaga, many singers (including obscure and less-known ones) who sing gay-anthem-like dance songs, and Meryl Streep. The words these women utter and the confidence and sassiness they embody, and the advocacy many of them perform for LGBQ rights, and civil rights, generally, motivates me to love and feel close to them. I make them a constant presence in my life. Even if they are mediated experiences, they are cherished gifts.

***

If I close my eyes, I can picture being at lunch every day during high school. I am sitting by the vending machine in the small eating area outside of the cafeteria. The overhead fluorescent lights are as harsh as the guilt-laden politics of the religious ideology that guides the education I am receiving. I am surrounded by girls, only girls, sitting and chatting while we eat our lunches. Many of the girls are my brother's friends from the marching band.

They think I'm cute, but I never get the impression it is because they feel I'm physically attractive. They never ask me about which girls I am interested in. We mainly talk about classes, school, and other innocuous topics. I survive the daily task of being at school as a result of the safe haven these girls give me. Their presence allows me to avoid sitting in the cafeteria, a treacherous space of bullying (Berry, 2016). I suspect that being with the girls gives them a chance to relate with a guy who is gentle and caring, to be affirmed and not disconfirmed for who they are in that difficult cafeteria.

***

My *mom* is always and already the most significant relational partner, the fiercest hero, who informs my lifeworld (see Berry, 2012, 2016). In large part because of her I am able to grow based on my strengths and talents, and not those that society dictates boys should embody. She's an expert school teacher, so she knows well of the practice of engaging my uniqueness. Although we do not discuss my sexuality until I am an adult, my mom's love, in effect, leaves an opening for the possibility that my being "special" means that I like boys and later men. She never asked me if I was gay until I came out, which has its benefits and disadvantages. Nevertheless, because of mom I am able overcome my toughest battles, and to avoid others that are common to boys like me. I feel the sincerity of her nurturing, her wanting me to be my best self, no matter what happens. My mom will insist that she is imperfect, and, indeed, we all are. Yet, during my childhood and much of my adulthood so far, she loves in tireless ways, sometimes at the expense of her own happiness, or at least doing or having the things she desires for herself. Her sacrifice and endless love are two of the greatest gifts I feel anyone can receive.

Gram, my mom's mother, is much like my mother. I know only the gentlest of care and love from her until the day she died at the age of 95. Gram refers to me as "my boyfriend." She senses how much from an early age I care about her.

Gram and I are especially close in her later years, when she lives next door to my parents. I live at their house for two years when earning my Master's degree, and return to the area for frequent visits during the four years in which I earn my Ph.D., and when I am living and working in my first university faculty position in the Duluth, MN/Superior, WI area. Gram and I often sit in her kitchen during cold months, and on her front porch during the warm ones. I am happy to be by her side, and a loving companion as she gets older and nears death. Regardless of where we are, we drink iced tea together, catch up, and talk about life. We sometimes spend hours chatting with each other, and often go out for "date lunches."

Even after I am out as a gay man, I never disclose my sexuality to Gram. My not telling her falls prey to the popular assumption that suggests that it is "risky," or at least "unnecessary," to tell the elderly about one's LGBQ social location. This wisdom isn't as wise as people think; at least in part, it perpetuates the stigmatizing nature of the closet (Adams, 2011). That being said, neither Gram not knowing, nor her consistent encouragement about me "finding the right gal" to "put a ringer on her finger," diminishes my love for her. Like my mom, Gram offers me the constant gift of a soft landing when I feel uncertain or in times of conflict. Even if we do not talk about these issues, being around her makes me feel better, wanted, and loved. There's never not an abundance of love with her.

My sister *Kathleen* (Kath) and I grow close during my late-teenage years. Like my mom and Gram, she is an expert and tireless mom to her daughters, and loving wife to her husband Kevin. In many essential ways, she is "my person." Kath is the first person in my family who I tell I am gay, a relational gift that draws us even closer. She is a fierce advocate for LGBQ rights who, along with Kevin, convey openness to my nieces, teaching them from the time they are toddlers that whomever they choose to love in life is fine and good. What a gift they give their children. Kath is the sister with whom I attend the Lady Gaga *Joanne* tour. She is also the sister with whom I attend comedienne Amy Schumer's concert, and who jumps to her feet and cheers loudly at the instant Schumer yells to the crowd, "where are my LGBQ people at tonight?" She responds before I even have a chance to do so.

Kath and I manage the busyness and the difficult times in life in some similar ways. For instance, in funny moments of shared styles of shtick, we laugh loudly and from the gut. In sad moments we are there for each other, even if some of those moments are so horrible that silence is all we can manage. I am with my sister when we learn the news of my father's traumatic death at the end of transplant surgery. We sit and cry together in disbelief and sadness. Overall, our time together is familiar, supportive, and fun. Kath lives with her family in Tampa, as does my mom. How lucky we are to live ten minutes away from each other.

Throughout my youth I am fortunate to have a warm relationship with all of my aunts (and uncles), but my bonds with *Aunt Maureen* and *Aunt Ellen* are especially loving and supporting. Like my mother and Gram, Maureen (whom we have always called "Moon") is a middle school teacher. She is also the wacky aunt who thrives on shtick and fun times. Moon takes me, Kath, and our brother Kevin to see the film *Grease* in the theaters together multiple times. Ellen (whom we often call "Ellie Mae") works at CBS/ Channel 2 in downtown Chicago, scheduling television commercials in the traffic department. She brings my brother, sister, and me to work sometimes, and loves to introduce us to famous local television news anchors. As I get ready to graduate with my undergraduate degree, I do an internship and later work at B96, the FM "top forty" music station owned by CBS, which is located one floor above where Ellen works. I love to visit her to chat, and she loves when I stop by to tell her the latest gossip from "upstairs." Together Moon and Ellie Mae are always there and involved in some nurturing way. I think they get their appreciation for shtick and the use of humor, especially in the tougher times, from their mother. *Grandma Berry* is equally loving and wacky, and helps to make my childhood feel special.

***

Throughout my youth I am loved by other women who serve as "bonus moms." These include our neighbors *Lynne* and *Peggy* with whom I spend countless hours over the years visiting and talking with them at their homes (see Berry, 2016). Sometimes we just small talk, usually when I do not feel like hanging out or playing with my guy friends, which happens frequently in my childhood. Sometimes I experiment and tell them things (e.g., my love for Wonder Woman) that I am not yet prepared to tell others, including members of my own family. Another bonus mom is my best friend Kyle's mom (see Chapter 1). Since Kyle and I are together so often, she is like my second mom. Busy with their own families, these women always welcome me into their lives with open arms. As a result, they gift me with a powerful added layer of care and support.

***

A chapter that tells the story of the amazing women in my life is incomplete without speaking to the gifts that women educators play in my development and well-being in my youth. They are teachers who I suspect face ongoing demands from society and their institutions to perform gender in ways that require them to be part of the "boys club," all the while also expecting to take the lead in performing the nurturing that "only women do" or, at least, "women do best." There are too many to list here. Nevertheless, these heroes challenge me, and help me to grow and flourish in good and bad times. I wouldn't be who I am today without the lessons I've learned from the women who have been my teachers.

***

I go on a blind date with *Julia* when I am 19 years old, during summer break after my first year of college. She is Kyle's girlfriend's friend. At this point in my life, I am in denial of my sexuality; thus, I am not out to anyone. I feel same-sex attraction and desire, but feel neither of these for women. Times haven't changed since those earlier years and that underwater kiss with Andi. Regardless of these feelings, there's a way in which I am still confused and unsure. I've never had a relationship with a woman. Informed by the unrelenting rigidity and judgment of our heteronormative and homophobic culture, I tell myself I probably "haven't tried enough" and should "try harder." I decide to go on the date. We have a lovely night out while seeing a movie and eating dinner together. Julia is charming and beautiful, and seems like a person who would make a wonderful girlfriend … for someone else.

At the end of our date, I slowly drive into her family's driveway and prepare myself to say goodnight. This moment is the part I've feared the most, so my rumination is in full gear. *Oh shit, it's "that" time. How do we say goodnight? A normal man makes a move on the woman. He takes the lead. You've seen this in enough movies to know. She's kind and seems like such a great person. We have to kiss. I don't know if I want to but we need to kiss. I need to kiss her. Oh fuck, it's about to happen!* Having parked at end of the driveway by the garage, Julia and I get out of the car. Although I am not quick enough to open her door, I shut it for her, and we then lean on the front of the car. We both look at the ground nervously and begin to engage in small talk.

"This was fun," I say, enthusiastically and probably a bit too loudly. *I hope she cannot hear in my voice how scared I feel right now. I have only kissed Andi, but that really wasn't a kiss, and that was a long time ago and I was a child. Now I'm an adult and I know I'm supposed to kiss her.*

"I had a great time," she says, while looking up at me. "Thank you so much for tonight."

"You're welcome. I … um … had a great time, too." I am being honest, because I really did have a great time—a great platonic time. *The anticipation is killing me. This is awkward.* We both stand upright at the same time, likely also feeling the awkwardness together.

"Well, um, goodnight," I say. I then lean to Julia and begin to kiss her. We kiss for just a couple of seconds and then I abruptly break the kiss and quickly hug her. I hug her tightly and awkwardly for a good seven or eight seconds, and mutter "mmmmmmmmmmm."

"Goodnight." Julia walks into the house and shuts off the outdoor driveway light. I return to my car and drive off quickly and go home. I never hear from Julia again.

I stay in denial and the closet for some time after that date. I don't come out to my sister for another four years, or to my best friend Kyle for another three years. However, I will remember this moment as being significant as one of those times when I "should have known" that I am a gay man. Julia is a person who is kind and nurturing. Those qualities attract me to her, not her physical attractiveness or the prospect of us having a romantic relationship or sex. She's familiar, warm, and safe.

***

At least two bosses perform heroically, or in gift-like fashion, in my lived experience. *Shirley* is the manager at Oakwood Pharmacy, where I first meet Kyle (see Chapter 1). She sees in me at a very early age the potential to be successful. She hires me as a stock boy. She then promotes me to cashier, only to later promote me to the position of pharmacy technician. Those positions help me to gain experience, and confidence, throughout high school and on summer breaks after my first two years of college.

Karen is the News Director and morning show "news chick" (her words) at B-96, the radio station I work at several times after I complete my undergraduate degree. I work as her assistant for a few months, but I don't really enjoy, or do well in the position. When I meet with her, so she can let me know I will no longer work with her, she tells me the news directly but gently, giving me both constructive criticism and compliments. Something caught her attention about the ways that I responded to both, leading her to say, "Keith, have you ever noticed how you take criticism, or negative things about you, easily and really well, but you have trouble taking compliments, or being told good things about you?" I hadn't thought about it at the time, but have never forgotten her relating with and for me in that way.

***

It is no coincidence that my two formal mentors/advisors during graduate school are women who give selflessly. These are relationships that, each in its own way, have allowed me to create a meaningful and lasting professional career.

I first learn about the possibilities for an academic career in the discipline of Communication from *Cathy* (co-author). She serves as my Chair during my Master's program at Purdue Calumet (now Purdue University Northwest). Cathy comes out of the closet during that time and we become close friends as a result.

I learn about hermeneutic phenomenology and ethnomethodology, as well as other philosophical approaches and methods useful to the study of people's lived experience within communication, from my doctoral advisor, *Lenore*. I then begin to explore and rely on ways of looking at communication and culture, and their intrinsic relationship to subjectivity. I begin to truly learn how to write, and think, with Lenore's guidance, which is as skillful as it is tireless.

My relationship with Lenore also provides me with an additional memory, one that I hold dear in my heart. My mom and sister attend my dissertation defense. After I successfully defend my "document," I overhear my mom say to Lenore, "Thank you for bringing out the best in my son." To this day recalling this memory often brings tears to my eyes. I cherish this gift.

Numerous academics who are women support me on a regular basis throughout my graduate school experiences and over many years as a faculty member. They are loving graduate students, department and university colleagues, informal and formal mentors, and administrators. I am surrounded regularly by autoethnographers and ethnographers, many of them women, who give me and others models of vulnerable and candid engagement, assistance, tears, and laughs. The same goes for colleagues who may not use these same methodologies, but still extend themselves to me and others with the gift of close collegiality, friendship, and mentorship.

***

The *drag queens* I have the honor of watching perform, interacting with face-to-face, or watching on television and in films teach me about the importance of the fluidity of gender, and the benefits of "queering" (i.e., disrupting and troubling) static and essentializing gender norms and rules. I learn how to be a better man by the presence of these queens in my life.

***

Women who have participated in my research studies must be included in my story. I'm thinking especially of the six young women who allowed me to use their bullying stories in my research: *Iman, Jessie, Jezebel, Lauren, Ena,* and *Victoria* (see Berry, 2016; Berry & Adams, 2016). Their accounts convey an understanding of the confounding practices and consequences related to being bullied and bullying others; thus, they provide readers with guidance and support for coming to terms with their own relationship to bullying. Yet, I also benefit from my relationship with these storytellers. Working with their stories challenges me to revisit stories of bullying from my youth, and leads me to have a clearer sense of what happened to me so many years ago, and how those experiences shape me today.

***

"Let's get out of here," I say to my mother after *Marwen* ends. I want us to evacuate the theatre as soon as possible. The bold and unapologetic story in *Marwen* makes me think there will be some moviegoers who will not only be surprised by the film, but also confused, and angry. I don't want to hear people spew nasty comments, including violent and bigoted remarks. I don't want the buzz I am feeling to be ruined by others' negativity.

"Okay, let's go," she says, grabbing my hand as I help her make her way to the stairs in the dimly lit theatre. I don't hear comments from anyone; instead people are silent.

"That was some story. It's different—what a *good* movie." My mom gets us started in our ritual of debriefing the movies we see together afterward. Mom and I are walking out of the theater and toward the parking lot. We're off to have lunch together at one of the few restaurants open on Christmas Day.

"I agree. It was a powerful movie. It is important to tell that story, and for people to understand it."

"It is very important. I knew the story was about Hogie being beaten, but I didn't know it was a hate crime, and due to his love for cross-dressing."

"They *conveniently* kept out that part of the story of the trailers. I don't like that, but I also appreciate doing whatever it takes to get butts into seats with a story like that."

"It's also dark and emotional at times."

"Remember my grad school professor and friend Ron Pelias?"

"Yes, he was on your dissertation committee …" I nod to confirm.

"When I was writing my dissertation and rather new to writing personal stories about difficult issues like being gay, visiting the Dachau Concentration Camp and identifying with the 'otherness' of the prisoners who were there, and other tough things, Ron gave me sage wisdom by asking me 'Keith, have you ever seen *doom* done really well? It is difficult to go back, but it can also be a beautiful process.' That advice helped me to write more comfortably. It also helps me to see dark movies like this one."

"Makes sense …"

"I am affected by the relationship Hogie has with his figurines and the women each of them represents. In a way, that's *my* story. I have benefitted from the relationships I have had with many girls and women throughout my youth, and women throughout my adulthood. It is similar to some of the relationships I had with guys growing up, like Cody and Kyle, and several men in my adulthood like Nick, Jay, and Chris. Yet, girls and women have been *instrumental* in my life. Just like *you* have been!"

"Aweee." Mom leans in for a hug. I kiss her on the forehead and hug her deeply, and for about as long as I hugged Julia so many years ago. However, this hug is less awkward.

"My brain is racing after seeing this movie. I think it might be helpful to use *Marwen* and these intimate bonds he has with women as an anchoring point for a story I'm thinking of including in the book Tony, Cathy, and I are writing together. There is something meaningful to these types of relational bonds. Also, I know I'm speaking to a gay male cliché story, but there's more to it than that. So many of these are deeply intimate bonds." We both smile about the cliché line.

"We live in a far more uncertain than certain world. However, I am certain my ability to flourish and survive amid the struggles that I have faced is inseparable from my bonds with girls and women. These strong, loving, and persistent people have been a saving gift. I owe them much."

"I bet they would say that they also owe *you* much, and that they can sense your love for them based on how you relate with them."

"Thank you … probably so. Okay, I've decided I'm going to write the story. Based on what these bonds have meant to me, I know it will be a lovefest. That's fine. But I also want it to demonstrate the invaluable role that girls and women play in my life.

"Go for it, baby doll. Now let's go eat, I'm starving."

"I'm hungry too. Let's do it." I clutch my heart and say, "Here's to the girls and women of *my Marwen*!"

DISCUSSION QUESTIONS

1. What is your *Marwen* like? Who are the people with whom you've built and sustained enriching and highly meaningful relationships? Given the focus of this chapter, who are the women who have gifted you?
2. If you are LGBQ, have you benefited in ways similar to Keith? Different ways? Allies, what examples do you have of LGBQ friends and loved ones who you think would relate to this story?
3. What has been the nature of the platonic relationships you've maintained with girls and women? What do you feel you have learned from girls and women through these bonds? How have they benefited?
4. Do you think relationships across sex/gender are able to be as close and intimate as they are in the relationship between girls and women and gay men, as demonstrated in this chapter?

REFERENCES

Adams, T. E. (2011). *Narrating the closet: An autoethnography of same-sex attraction.* Walnut Creek, CA: Left Coast Press.

Berry, K. (2012). Reconciling the relational echoes of addiction: Holding on. *Qualitative Inquiry, 18,* 134–143. doi:10.1177/1077800411429088

Berry, K. (2013). Spinning autoethnographic reflexivity, cultural critique, and negotiating selves. In S. Holman Jones, T. E. Adams, & C. Ellis (Eds.), *The handbook of autoethnography* (pp. 209–227). New York, NY: Routledge.

Berry, K. (2016). *Bullied: Tales of Torment, identity, and youth.* New York, NY: Routledge.

Berry, K., & Adams, T. E. (2016). Family bullies. *Journal of Family Communication, 16,* 51–63. https://doi.org/10.1080/15267431.2015.1111217

Bochner, A., & Ellis, C. (2016). *Evocative autoethnography: Writing stories and telling lives.* New York, NY: Routledge.

Holman Jones, S., Adams, T. E., & Ellis, C. (2013). *Handbook of autoethnography.* Walnut Grove, CA: Left Coast Press.

Schrag, C. O. (2003). *Communicative practice and the space of subjectivity.* West Lafayette, IN: Purdue University Press.

THE GIRLS

Tony E. Adams and Keith Berry

The scripted U.S. television sitcom *The Golden Girls* (1985–1992) represents the lives of four women—Blanche, Dorothy, Rose, and Sophia, or as they are affectionately known by many gay men, "the girls"—all of whom share a house in Miami, Florida. The women are White; Blanche, Dorothy, and Rose are in their late 50s/early 60s; Sophia is a character in her early 80s. Each episode focuses on comedic, though sometime serious, situations these women encounter. Even though the series ended in 1992, it has been in syndication for more than two decades on several cable channels within the U.S. As of this writing (2019), the series continues to air on *Hallmark*, a channel that foregrounds "family-friendly" programming, and *Logo*, a channel that offers programming for LGBQ audiences. But why might a series that ended in 1992 air on a channel that explicitly caters to LGBQ audiences? One explanation is that the show promotes LGBQ sensibilities, especially those tied to same-sex/gender attraction, sexual desire, reproduction, kinship, and family.[1]

***

"Standby," I say to Tony, interrupting him mid-sentence during one of our nightly telephone conversations. I notice an online news story while Tony and I are talking, and I feel like I must immediately share the news with him. I take a "screen grab" (picture) on my phone and text it to him. "I'm sending you something by text message. It's important."

"Uh oh," he says in a concerned but curious voice.

"Brace yourself …"

"Uh oh … what is it?"

"You'll see … Did you get it yet?"

"Yes, hang on." Tony looks at the text. "Oh no … bless her heart."

The picture is from a blog that shows Betty White, now 96 years old, in one of her rare public appearances.

© KONINKLIJKE BRILL NV, LEIDEN, 2020 | DOI:10.1163/9789004418790_009

"She does not look good!" In the image, White looks considerably frail. Her face is gaunt. She seems confused and scared to be in public. She doesn't look like the vivacious television actor and character we have known and loved for the past thirty years. She looks like death is near.

"She's the last one," I say. The other lead actors on *The Golden Girls*—Bea Arthur (Dorothy), Rue McClanahan (Blanche), and Estelle Getty (Sophia)—are already dead. Each time one of the "girls" dies, we make sure the other knows of the loss. We also often share this news on social media and commiserate with other fans; they are typically friends, partners, and most often other gay men. Each time one of the girls dies, a part of both of us dies with her.

"Awe, poor Rose [Betty White] …" Tony says.

"I know, poor sweet Rose."

"Well maybe she'll finally reunite with Charlie [Rose's deceased husband on the show]."

"True, you know how much she misses him." Rose references Charlie constantly across many episodes.

Neither of us is a stranger to television programs, nor is it uncommon for us to feel a connection or affinity for the actors and characters we watch on television. I (Keith) have loved and emulated the character Wonder Woman from the hit television show by the same name (see Chapter 8; also see Berry, 2013, 2016). I (Tony) love musicians like Cher, The Dixie Chicks, and Dolly Parton. However, there's something special to the ways we relate to/with "the girls" and the series. Neither of us has met these women, nor have we lived their particular lives. But we both feel as though we've "met" and intimately "know" their characters. In addition, we both have benefited personally and culturally, as gay men, because of "our girls." We constantly make references to our girls when we talk, and regularly infuse our conversation about the experiences and challenges comprising our lives in terms of the girls, extracting a phrase from, or a memory of, a particular episode.

In this chapter we work in tandem to explore the ways in which each of us relates to *The Golden Girls*, its characters, and how/we find the series meaningful. We represent our ideas by using a dialogue format in which we each respond to a diverse number of questions concerning the show and its presence and role in our lives.

When did you first "meet" The Golden Girls? *What was that first "meeting" like? What attracted you to them?*

Keith: I first encountered the show in 1985, when I was fourteen years old, during the show's premier television season. I was spending the weekend with Grandma (Mel) and Grandpa (George) Sandor, my mother's parents, who lived about twenty minutes away from our home. After spending the afternoon helping my Grandma sort through memories in her clutter-filled spare bedroom, we had dinner. Then she, my Grandpa, and I watched television in the living room. I sat closely next to Gram, with whom I was always close. My grandpa sat in his recliner. They got to choose what we would watch, and immediately decided upon *The Golden Girls*, a new show they had been watching for several weeks. I knew nothing about the show, and hadn't even heard of it before that evening. Little did I know the program would come to inform my life in such significant and lasting ways.

I have vivid memories of our watching the program together. I remember how shocked I was by the show's storylines and its use of humor. It was the "dirtiest" program I'd ever seen on television, filled with sexual references and innuendoes, and jokes about each character's intelligence (or lack thereof), physical appearance, sexual appetite, and age. In addition, I remember how surprised I was to watch these women, senior citizens, speak to each other in direct, outspoken, and highly candid ways. They were different, and yet I felt connected to them, even if I didn't know or understand the reason for our connection. "They get away with murder," my grandparents would say to each other, and me, after watching some of the more controversial episodes. This many years later, when I think back to that comment, I wonder what they meant. I suspect they were commenting on how the characters really pushed, and sometimes crossed, lines in terms of "appropriate" and "polite" ways of relating. I also wonder if they were "getting away with murder" because they were women who were relating through such unapologetically bold communication? Would it be such a "crime" if the show depicted men in these ways? Regardless, from the first time I watched *The Golden Girls*, I was hooked on the show and these women, and our bond began.

Tony: I too was introduced to *The Golden Girls* by my grandma. Most Saturday nights between 1985–1992, I would watch the show with her. As a young child, I did not understand many of the jokes, but I enjoyed sitting with grandmother on her overstuffed reclining chair, watching the women interact, and taking comfort in my grandmother's laughs. I loved my grandmother tremendously, and I would talk to her about most everything, give her money when she needed it, and spend much of my free time with her. In 2003, my grandmother died suddenly while I was on vacation in Las Vegas. When I watch the program, I feel connected to my grandmother. I regularly fall asleep to episodes of the series, purchase *The Golden Girls* mementos such as greeting cards and drinking glasses, and frequently recite lines and recall favorites scenes with my gay male friends. Even though the series ended nearly three decades ago, it still occupies a prominent part of my daily life.

Keith: My grandparents and your grandma introduced us to the show. In doing so, they introduced us to gay culture.

What is the appeal or attraction to The Golden Girls *by gay men?*

Tony: Several writers have responded to this question (see Halperin, 2012; Musto, 2014). From my perspective, numerous episodes of *The Golden Girls* explicitly address LGBQ issues. Nearly every episode makes at least one reference to same-sex/gender attraction, and some episodes foreground LGBQ issues. The LGBQ references may be subtle, e.g., a quick reference to the "Twinkie defense" (a reference to Dan White's testimony in his murder of Harvey Milk) or when a flamboyant character says, "Well, excuse me for living, Anita Bryant!" The reference may be explicit as well, such as when Rose, Blanche, Sophia, or Dorothy flirt with each other, or when there is the presence of a LGBQ character (e.g., Coco, their gay housekeeper; Laszlo, the gay sculptor). There is one episode when Dorothy's best friend Jean, a lesbian, has a crush on Rose. In another episode, Blanche's brother Clayton tells her that he is gay, and, in a later episode, tells her that he is going to marry his (male) partner. For me, a question about why the show appeals to LGBQ persons is a visibility issue; although they do not always offer favorable representations of LGBQ identities and issues, I imagine that this was one of the first primetime U.S. television shows to hint at or explicitly mention LGBQ topics, and not occasionally, but in nearly every episode.

I also think the show promotes LGBQ sensibilities, especially those tied to same-sex attraction, sexual desire, reproduction, kinship, and family. The content of the series—four unmarried women living together who take care of each other—challenge ideas about what constitutes a family. The women constitute a "chosen family"—a common experience for many LGBQ persons, especially those who feel distanced from, or have been ostracized from their family. In one episode, Rose has a heart attack and the hospital staff will not allow Blanche, Dorothy, and Sophia to visit because they are not Rose's "family." When Rose's daughter, Kirsten, arrives, she also will not allow the women to visit Rose as they are not (biological) family. Kirsten soon realizes the women are indeed Rose's family and arranges for them to visit. There is an episode featuring conflicts over Blanche's (single) daughter pursuing artificial insemination—a topic that disrupts canonical ideas about parenting and reproduction—and in another episode, a city official threatens to fine Blanche for renting her house to too many people (Dorothy, Rose, Sophia). Blanche bypasses the fine by putting all of the women on the title to the house, as it belongs to, and thus should be owned by, all of them. There are numerous remarks about how they plan to take care of each other as they age. For me, the show provides a model for how I would love to live as an aging gay man: I would love to live together with my best friends, and I think it would be great to care for each other.

Other episodes of *The Golden Girls* offer representations of complicated relationships that could be appealing to LGBQ audiences as well—audiences that often must address complicated relationships. One episode features Dorothy's conflict with her White son, Michael, and his desire to marry a Black woman who is nearly twice his age. Another episode shows Rose's struggle with dating a little person.[2]

Further, numerous episodes also unapologetically celebrate aging and foreground the women's sexual desires—desires often framed as peculiar and inappropriate. Throughout the series, there are messages about the sexual attractiveness of these women. All of them are sexually active, and still have numerous discussions about their sexual desires. This is a beautiful, sex-positive aspect of the program that suggests that just because you are a particular age does not mean you are unlovable or should not pursue intimacy and desire. At least for many gay men, there is a common phrase, "you're dead [that is, unattractive] in the gay community at 30 or 40," but *The Golden Girls* offers an alternative storyline.

In addition to these topics within the show, the actors playing the characters are queer icons. Betty White and Rue McClanahan have been staunch supporters of LGBQ rights; upon her death, Bea Arthur donated a significant amount of money to establish a LGBQ youth center in New York; and Estelle Getty participated in early HIV/AIDS activism, and she starred in the classic gay-themed play *Torch Song Trilogy* (Fierstein, 1978). Betty, Rue, and Bea also made regular appearances at LGBQ-themed events such as the GLAAD Awards and gay bookstores.

Keith: For as long as I can remember, *The Golden Girls* have been a fixture in most of the gay bars I know and enjoy. These places normally show clips from the program on the large television screens that hang above the bars. The clips are usually brief, but long enough to show a scene in which the girls are harshly critiquing one another, or performing sexual innuendos (or overtures) with other characters, or critiquing each other's physical appearance or other idiosyncrasies. Clips are a prominent part of the entertainment at Sidetrack, the video bar in "Boystown," Chicago's primary LGBQ district.

I'm sure the campiness and hyper-sexuality of the girls is a major source of attraction between so many queer men and the girls. In this sense, they have always been singing our tune.

I know that attraction to the program also extends beyond campiness. For instance, the show confronted key social issues. In one episode, Rose received a letter from the hospital where she recently received a blood transfusion. The hospital staff are concerned that she received the contaminated blood and want her to get tested for HIV. The episode shows Rose panicking after being tested, as the rest of the girls try to support her while she waits for the results. "Dammit, why is this happening to me?" Rose yells. "I mean, this shouldn't happen to people like me." In response, Blanche confronts her, and says, "AIDS is not a bad person's disease, Rose. It is not God punishing people for their sins" (see Fletcher, 2014). Few programs were engaging with HIV/AIDS at the time, and even fewer addressed the problem in ways that affirmed the community and people who lived with the illness. The girls have always been there for the gay community, and often when many others were not.

What's your favorite episode, and why?

Tony: Bochner (2000) argues that good stories often tell a "tale of two selves" (p. 270), a narrative construct in which a character begins one way but who then, as the story progresses, learns to live differently. My favorite episodes use a tale-of-two-selves construct: the women begin one way but are then transformed into more sympathetic and reflective characters. For instance, in one episode, "Blanche's Little Girl," Blanche begins by disparaging Rebecca, her daughter, who has gained weight. Rebecca also is in an abusive relationship. By the end of the episode, Blanche's acceptance of Rebecca's weight increases and she intervenes, unsuccessfully at first, in the abusive relationship. In another episode, "Dorothy's New Friend," Dorothy's new friend, author Barbara Thorndyke, is dismissive and condescending to Blanche and Rose. Blanche and Rose try to tell Dorothy that Barbara is not a good friend, but Dorothy disagrees and becomes angry with them. Near the end, when the women plan a group dinner, Barbara says that they cannot go to the designated restaurant because Sophia's date is Jewish and not allowed at the restaurant. Dorothy confronts Barbara about supporting an anti-Semitic restaurant, which Barbara disregards. Dorothy ends the relationship.

Keith: The two-part finale to the entire series (1992) is my favorite. These are the episodes when Dorothy and Uncle Lucas (played by Leslie Nielsen) meet and get married. Lucas is Blanche's rich uncle who went out with

Dorothy because Blanche, who was supposed to have dinner with her uncle that evening, wanted instead to go out on a date. When talking over lobster at dinner, Dorothy and Lucas confessed that neither one of them wanted to go out with the other, and that their "date" only happened because Blanche found a better offer. As a result, they decided to seek revenge by telling Blanche, and the other two women, they had fallen in love, and planned to be married. Blanche was beside herself. Several fake dates later, Lucas took Dorothy's hand and, in front of the women, asked her to marry him … "for real." Soon after the two marry and move away to Lucas's estate, effectively leaving the women, breaking up the indelible four-way friendship that they all cherished. What would they do now? How would they go on? What do they do with Ma (Sophia)?

I love the finale because of the twists and turns that comprise the plot line. It's so well written and the idea of having Dorothy and Lucas retaliate with a prank—a big and unexpected one—is clever. Yet, I also love it because awkward Dorothy found love that appears to be true and significant. Watching Blanche, Rose, and Sophia make plans to live together after Dorothy moves out, though sad, was also sweet. That this ending happened at the end of the series tugged at heartstrings even more. It was the end of an era, of a terrific relational story that meant so much to me. I've watched these two episodes hundreds of times; yet, each time I feel as if I learn the story for the first time. I often tear up at the end of the second episode.

The last episode of the program ended with a big finish, when Dorothy said goodbye to Sophia, Blanche, and Rose. It was a beautiful mix of humor and sadness. After initial goodbyes, she left through the front door, sad but knowing she made a good decision to marry Lucas. Yet, once the door shuts, and a few seconds pass, she charges back inside the home to say goodbye and hug the women once again. She exited through the front door again, this time more dramatic than the first, much to the delight of laughing studio audiences. She then re-entered and said goodbye one more time after racing into the living room from the lanai, a move that would likely be impossible in "real life" due to space constraints, but easily accomplished on a studio set. As she said her last goodbye, for real, Dorothy/Bea Arthur broke the "fourth wall" of acting by ever-so-briefly glancing in the camera when she turned around and walked to the door. Blanche and Sophia looked distraught. Rose held the two of them in her arms, as large tears filled her eyes.

It's funny to me that the sad ending of something so special is my "favorite." Maybe one of the reasons I loved it, and still love it today, is because both episodes were so well written and acted. Maybe it is because I do like a "big finish," a dramatic and exciting ending in television programs, and this one hit all of my sweet spots. Yet maybe even more it is because I felt like I could feel real emotions on the part of the actors, and those feelings gave justice to the ending of something so special.

What's your least favorite episode, and why?

Tony: My least favorite episodes are your favorite episodes. Although written superbly, I cannot watch them. The storyline is sad and signals an end to a series—and to feelings—I never want to end. The finale marks a symbolic death of the characters and their cherished on-screen dynamic. The episodes also make me miss my beloved grandma and the series actors who have since passed. I try to avoid the episodes as much as possible. When they are on, I often distract myself or leave the room for the final scene, when Dorothy leaves with Lucas and says multiple goodbyes to her best friends.

Keith: I think just about any episode from the first season counts as one of my least favorite. I can watch any episode across all of the remaining seasons, again and again, but the first season feels "off" when comparing it to later seasons. The characters are less energetic and duller in the first season. To get really specific, even the cinematography seems bland. Although all seasons were groundbreaking, I also don't think the characters' lines were as edgy in the first season as they were in subsequent years. Also, it is in the first season when the very first episode, Coco, the dramatically gay housekeeper, was part of the cast. Coco didn't work for me, and he still doesn't today when I watch reruns. He was too distracting.

At the same time, maybe there are personal reasons for my distaste for him. Back when it first aired, I don't think I would be able to like Coco, at least in open ways. I wasn't aware or able to recognize that I was gay. Talking about that gay man, that "flamboyant" gay man, would've put me at risk for retaliation (questions, teasing, etc.) from others. Maybe that's why my grandparents felt the show "got away with murder." Coco may have been a progressive way for the show to demonstrate inclusion. Today the stereotypical nature of Coco is too heavy handed. I'm glad they quietly removed him from the show. Come to think of it, maybe they got rid of him because complaints from viewers who felt there was no room for a positive gay storyline.

What "critical read" can you give The Golden Girls?

Keith: I am hesitant to read *The Golden Girls* critically. My resistance feels like defensiveness, like I don't want to let anything or anyone get close enough to ask the tough questions about the women and the series. Most storylines demonstrated the girls succeeding in response to adversity, and they demonstrate resourceful ways the women worked through serious problems together. That being said, the program emphasized women who were highly dependent on men for their happiness. Similarly, they typically performed in ways that perpetuated normative conceptualizations of women, and women and men, including the need for all women to be thin and pretty to be liked or loved by men. They also perpetuated the notion that all (heterosexual) men are unsympathetic and sex-craving pigs. Even though most of the episodes ended on a positive and strong note for the characters, and lifted up the resilience and togetherness of women, the normative subtext was always already there.

Tony: As I mentioned, in nearly every episode, there was at least one LGBQ reference or innuendo. I try to imagine what LGBQ representation existed at that time in the United States; compared to sitcoms from the same era, I do not know of another mainstream series that made as many LGBQ references. Although the series excels with LGBQ visibility—and is sometimes referred to as "still the gayest show on TV" (Musto, 2014)— the quality of the representations may now be considered inadequate, at least compared to contemporary standards and expectations. For instance, at times, the strategically-placed laugh track suggests that particular LGBQ topics may be funny and should not be taken seriously (see Manning, 2015). There are moments when characters are ridiculed for engaging in atypical gendered behavior and there are unresolved conflicts about homosexuality, e.g., Blanche never fully celebrates Clayton, her gay brother and, in one episode, Sophie tells Dorothy to not act like Jean, Dorothy's lesbian friend. Yet these representations of LGBQ issues, identities, and experiences may have been welcomed and perceived as progressive when the program first aired.

How have The Golden Girls *been a part of my everyday life?*

Tony: The "girls" are a prominent part of my everyday life. My home and school office have many *The Golden Girls* items, including art and magnets, "Chia Pet" heads, Monopoly (game), and figurines. I have several *The Golden Girls* t-shirts, and friends regularly post Golden-Girl news on my Facebook wall, e.g., as I write this chapter (2019), multiple Facebook friends posted on my timeline about a *The Golden Girls*-themed cruise that will launch in 2020. In the mid-2000s, I purchased DVDs of the series and again when they were released on iTunes. I thus have access to the episodes on my phone, multiple computers, and television (via Apple TV), and I can program episodes to play uninterrupted for hours. I rarely watch specific episodes anymore, but I often turn on the series before I nap or most nights when I prepare to sleep, especially if I am traveling. The reasons why I connect with the show—the abundance of queer content, the progressive, pro-queer actors, and the context in which I first watched the program, that is, with my grandmother in my youth—calm me and allow me to sleep with ease.

Keith: The end of the series (1992) may have stopped us from being able to watch new episodes, but it also increased the ways in which I used the show in my everyday life. In the mid-2000s, I repeatedly signed online petitions calling for the production company of *The Golden Girls* to release all seasons on DVD. I owned all seasons once they finally became available. My family and I would regularly mention the show, and they would gently tease me about being "hooked" on the show. Yet there were never conversations linking the show to my sexuality. I didn't come out to my family until five years after the show ended. Also, members of my family would send me greeting cards for special events or "just because" that had a scene from the show as its theme. You (Tony) for years sent me such cards, probably until you couldn't find any new ones to send.

For years I watched reruns of the show daily, when I woke up in the morning and before I went to sleep at night. The shows made me start the day with laughs, and had a way of relaxing me before bed. I barely broke this routine. The girls were and are predictable. Now I don't watch them as much as I did in the past, mainly because of busyness. I turn them on when I need to relax after a long or stressful day.

The girls are, and always have been, "there" for us.

DISCUSSION QUESTIONS

1. In this chapter, Keith and Tony describe their relationship with *The Golden Girls*. Do you have a similar connection with any media texts (books, films, or television programs)? If so, describe the connection.
2. Why do people establish relationships with media texts and characters, especially texts and characters that are considered to be fiction?
3. How can fictional media texts mirror reality in people's everyday lives? What are risks or dangers of living with mediated texts, especially those representing sexuality?

NOTES

[1]   This paragraph has been revised from Adams (2016, p. 3).
[2]   The last two paragraphs have been revised from Adams (2016, p. 3).

REFERENCES

Adams, T. E. (2016). Queering popular culture. In A. F. Herrmann & A. Herbig (Eds.), *Communication perspectives on popular culture* (pp. 1–11). Lanham, MD: Lexington Books.

Fierstein, H. (1978). *Torch song trilogy*. New York, NY: Random House.

Fletcher, B. (2014). What 'The Golden Girls' taught us about AIDS. *National Public Radio*. Retrieved February 24, 2019, from https://www.npr.org/2014/07/22/333759394/what-the-golden-girls-taught-us-about-aids

Halperin, D. M. (2012). *How to be gay*. Cambridge, MA: Belknap Press.

Manning, J. (2015). The rhetorical function of laugh tracks in situation comedies: Examining queer shame in Will & Grace and Roseanne. *Relevant Rhetoric, 6*, 1–15.

Musto, M. (2014, July 14). Why golden girls is still the gayest show on TV. *Out*. Retrieved February 24, 2019, from https://www.out.com/entertainment/michael-musto/2014/07/14/why-golden-girls-still-gayest-show-tv

CHAPTER 10

LANGUAGE MATTERS

Tony E. Adams

Exercise: Locate two sheets of paper. On one sheet, write the name of the person/thing you fear, dislike, or hate. Examples might include the name of an enemy, snakes, spiders, or a fear of heights or failing. On the other sheet, write the name of the person/thing that you like or love the most. Examples might include a parent or sibling, a favorite friend or relative, or a companion animal. Once you have written each name, take the paper with the name of the thing you dislike and crumple it, tear it apart, pound it with your hand, stomp on it, or roll over it with your wheelchair. Then take the paper with the name of the person/thing that you like or love the most, and repeat the process: crumple it, tear it apart, and pound, stomp, or roll. If you hesitated to complete this activity, explain why.

Exercise: Visit a public space with strangers—maybe a bank, pub or restaurant, coffee shop, grocery store, classroom, bus, train, or airport. When you enter this space, loudly and repeatedly state "Fuck God" or "I hate all [insert racial, gender, religious group]." Document others' reactions. If you would not complete this exercise, explain why.

Exercise: Inform friends, family members, and strangers of your sexuality—state "I am heterosexual," "I am pansexual," "I am queer," "I am a lesbian," "I am asexual," "I am gay," etc. Document others' reactions. If you would not complete this exercise, explain why.

As communication researchers and teachers, we study how language works, how words get others to act (and react), and how/why/when people use words to make sense of society. Words can activate certain meanings and emotions and as ethical communicators we should do our best to consider the ways we use and understand language as well as the ways in which others use and understand language.

***

© KONINKLIJKE BRILL NV, LEIDEN, 2020 | DOI:10.1163/9789004418790_010

I have come to recognize that words can hurt others or make them feel good. I can use words to greet others, ask about their lives, express my appreciation, tell them they are beautiful people. I can use words to hurt others, too: I can tell someone that they have disappointed me, call them bad names, tell them that they are doing an awful job, are a dreadful friend, or aren't deserving of love. I can use language to construct perceptions of society, as well as to elevate others or make them feel inadequate.

For example, when I first heard "they" being used as a gender-neutral, singular pronoun, I reacted terribly.[1] "It violates conventions of grammar," I'd say. I refused to consider the possibility that conventions could change. Then a gender non-conforming friend explained why "he/him" and "she/her" felt inappropriate and inaccurate, hence their preferred use of "they." Initially, I dismissed my friend, refused to use "they" to reference them, and instead used "she/her." I soon felt terrible: Why didn't I respect my friend enough to recognize how "she/her" could inflict harm? Why did I refuse to change my (comfortable, privileged) terms to accommodate and respect them? I strive to be as inclusive as possible and I did not have a preference for the restrictive "he/him" and "she/her" binary; I just didn't think "they" was the best term grammatically. Thankfully, I can change, and so can convention: Thus far, the American Psychological Association, the Associated Press, and the Chicago Manual of Style have approved "they" as a singular pronoun.

If there are terms we use with which we do not have much concern but others find to be inappropriate, what harm exists for us to change our terms? If we could use another term that is more acceptable and accurate, that doesn't hurt someone else, why wouldn't we do so? If someone tells me that "she/her" or "he/him" harms them, then what is my reason for not changing the term and finding a more neutral and respectful term to use? I recognize concerns about becoming too "politically correct" and monitoring language too much, but I know that I want many of the people with whom I interact and care for to feel comfortable, even those with whom I experience conflict. I want to respect their sensitivities.

In this chapter, I discuss various terms related to sexuality and same-sex/gender attraction. I offer this chapter not as a definitive or prescriptive guide to language use—language is always subject to change—but rather to offer insights about some of the everyday language tied to sexuality. I do so in attempt to be more accurate, inclusive, and respectful with the words I use to describe myself and others.

***

"What does it mean to say, 'I am heterosexual?'" I often ask students.

"It means you're attracted to women," they respond.

"If I found men attractive, would I be heterosexual?" I ask.

"No," they say. "You could identify as heterosexual, but people might think you're gay or bisexual."

"Why?" I ask.

"Because you're a man," they respond.

"And …"

"A man who finds men attractive is gay. A man who finds women attractive is heterosexual."

Although I do not want to simplify or dismiss the nuances of sexuality, identity, and attraction, I use the example to demonstrate one way I begin conversations about sex, gender, and sexuality and to show why any discussion of sexuality is simultaneously a discussion about sex and gender.[2]

In these conversations, I tend to ask additional questions: I ask why students think that I am a "man," note that their perception of me as "male" is an assumption about my gender not sex (though they may assume that my sex and gender align, an ascription of "cisgenderism"), and add that sexuality can differ depending on whether it is based on sex or gender. I also introduce additional categories of sexuality such as "queer," "bisexual," "pansexual," and "asexual."

"Sex," "gender," and "sexuality" are complicated, contested, and interrelated terms. "Sex" is the biological classification of persons based on chromosomes, "adequate" genitalia, reproductive possibilities, and hormone levels and responsiveness (Meyerowitz, 2002). Although there is still rampant bias in support of two primary sexes, "male" and "female," there are variations of sex which are sometimes referred to as "intersex" (formerly "hermaphrodite") or captured by the broad and disputed category, "Disorders of Sex Development" (Greenberg, 2012). In everyday interaction, we typically infer the sex of others, especially since we do not have direct access to chromosomes, genitalia, reproductive possibilities, and hormones.

"Gender" is the enactment of language and behaviors often tied to a person's sex; a person "does" (i.e., constitutes or performs) gender by being masculine, feminine, androgynous, genderqueer, etc. (see West & Zimmerman, 1987). Gender connects to sex in at least two primary ways. First, sex assignment often motivates expectations for gender: A child designated "female" at birth may be encouraged to enact gender accordingly, e.g., engaging in stereotypical feminine behaviors such as wearing dresses, liking certain colors (pink), avoiding some activities (football, boxing) while pursuing other activities (cheerleading, cooking). The person who enacts gender differently than expected (based on their designated sex) can encounter resistance and harm (Meadow, 2018).

Second, some people make assumptions about a person's sex based on how they do gender; gender is assumed to be "congruent with genital configuration" (Gagné, Tewksbury, & McGaughey, 1997, p. 479). For example, a person who acts masculine (gender) and who looks and sounds like a man (gender) may be assumed to be "male" (sex). The real or perceived alignment between a person's sex and gender is referred to as "gender conformity" or cisgenderism. In everyday interaction, we tend to infer others' gender, which is often assumed to match their sex, which is typically never known.[3]

Sexuality is an identity rooted in sex and gender, and understanding sexuality often requires understanding sex and gender. As Jackson (2006) writes, the "homosexual/heterosexual distinction depends on socially meaningful gender categories, on being able to 'see' two men or two women as 'the same' and a man and a woman as 'different' (p. 113). Butler (2004) defines sexuality as a "mode of being disposed toward others" and which is contingent upon these others' sex and gender (p. 33). And Ahmed (2006) makes a similar observation: "Desire is, after all, what moves us closer to bodies. To state the obvious: lesbian desire puts women into closer 'contact' with women" (p. 103). With an identity tied to sexuality—e.g., "lesbian"— we also have an identity constituted by sex and/or gender—e.g., "women."

Sexuality is complicated when we try to determine if it is based on sex or gender, especially in instances when sex and gender do not align. Is *hetero*sexuality determined by one person's sex and this person's attraction to a different sex? Or is *hetero*sexuality determined by one person's gender and this person's attraction to a different gender? Is a lesbian identity—one which "puts women into closer 'contact' with women" (Ahmed, 2006, p. 103)—determined by the sex or gender of these women?

As an example, consider Greenberg's (2000) analysis of the tumultuous experiences of Christie Littleton, a person who, at birth, was named Lee Cavazos and classified as male. In 1977, Christie legally changed her name from Lee to Christie Lee. In 1979 and 1980, Christie underwent sex reassignment surgery—surgery that allowed her to (legally) change her birth certificate from "male" to "female." In 1989, Christie married Jonathon Littleton in Kentucky, a (legal) heterosexual union that further classified Christie as female (that is, since same-*sex* marriage was still illegal in Kentucky). In 1996, Jonathon died from medical error, and, in 1999, Christie, as Jonathon's spouse, filed a malpractice suit against Mark Prange,

Jonathon's doctor. Yet, Prange argued that Christie was and would always be male because of her original sex-at-birth classification. Prange won the case: judges ruled that Christie had no right to marry a man, a person of the "same sex," therefore invalidating the once-legal, decade-long marriage between Christie and Jonathan and thus providing no way for Christie to sue for malpractice.

As Greenberg (2000) demonstrates, Christie was, at times and for specific audiences, "male." At other times Christie was "female." Such assessments influenced how she, her husband, and their relationship were evaluated, particularly whether each was worthy recipients of particular rights (that is, either by way of marriage, or the rights that might result from the malpractice suit). I assume Christie did her best to prepare for such assessments, but who Christie was, in legal contexts, changed depending on the clerk, lawyers, and judges. In other words, sometimes Christie effectively used her female identity to accomplish particular tasks (e.g., changing her name, having sex-reassignment surgery, getting married), but others, such as Mark Prange and the judges, effectively used her sex-at-birth "male" identity to accomplish tasks such as framing Christie's and Jonathan's marriage as a "same-sex" marriage, thus, making it illegal, and thereby allowing the court to rule in Prange's favor. In this situation, sexuality was tangled by sex and gender, and, more specifically, sex-at-birth and sex-after-treatment/surgery.[4]

Although Littleton's situation happened two decades ago, cisgender bias, transphobia, and the sex/gender distinction still materialize in multiple contexts. In the U.S., there are legal debates about sex/gender bathroom usage—often referred to as "bathroom bills"—dictating who can (not) use "male" and "female" bathrooms (Drew, 2018). The Michigan Womyn's Music Festival ended in 2015 because of adhering to a "womyn born womyn" policy, one that prohibited attendance by women not designated "women" at birth (Ring, 2015). And some sex/gender-specific contexts such as colleges (Moyer, 2015), the U.S. military (de Vogue & Cohen, 2019), and sports (Navratilova, 2019) debate removing or enforcing transphobic, essentialist, and cisgender-only policies. Problems arise with incompatible assumptions about sex and gender and when people adhere to assumed and rigid definitions of taken-for-granted words such as "male" and "female."

Sexuality can also be influenced by the sexual acts that occur between people. The terms "gay" and "lesbian" have been used to describe persons who are attracted to persons of the same-sex or gender, yet even these terms are complicated. Some people believe that men are only "gay" if they assume a passive, penetrated role in sex. In this usage, a gay label does not apply to active, masculine penetrators. A man who "has sex with another man has little to do with 'gayness,'" Nadya Labi (2007, p. 74) writes. "The act may fulfill a desire or a need, but it doesn't constitute an identity" (p. 74). It is "being a bottom" that is "shameful" as bottoming "means playing a woman's role" (p. 78). This criterion not only illustrates a Eurocentric understanding of sexuality, but also the masculine and misogynistic biases of gay identity, specifically how "playing a woman's role" is framed as being shameful (Rao & Sarma, 2009). "Gay" may not apply to men who masturbate together or who engage in oral sex (see Balay, 2018; Ward, 2015), and there are even "apps" and sites that promote non-gay, male-on-male sexual contact, such as "Bro" and "Bateworld" (Mustain, 2018).[5]

Conversely, "lesbians" have been excluded from definitions of sex acts, particularly when/if sex is conceived of as something that occurs only when a penis penetrates a vagina or when a penis ejaculates; these criteria exclude any possibility of female-female sexual relations (Frye, 1983; Hans, Gillen, & Akande, 2009). "I was never in danger of being thrown in jail for practicing sodomy," Julia Creet (1991) writes. "Not surprisingly, what constitutes homosexual sex in the public eye has always hung on the penis" (p. 29).

There are terms that introduce more fluidity with sex, gender, and sexuality. A person attracted to two sexes or genders might identify as "bisexual"; someone who celebrates non-normative desires (e.g., fetishes), relationships (e.g., swinging, open relationships, polyamory), or who does not feel as though existing identity categories such as "homosexual," "gay," or "lesbian," are helpful or accurate might identify as "queer"; or a person might identify as "pansexual," a more inclusive term for people who are attracted to others of any sex/gender or for whom sex/gender are irrelevant.

Sex, gender, and sexuality relate in other ways as well. Although "transgender" is a category rooted in gender, not sexuality—e.g., a person can be "transgender" and "heterosexual," "transgender" and "gay"— gender (identity) and sexuality are sometimes grouped together because of overlapping concerns and histories, e.g., LGBQ. Gender nonconformity (sometimes referred to as "gender inversion") exists when a person's perceived sex and gender conflict, when their enactment of gender differs from the gender associated with their assumed/assigned sex. Gender nonconformity can mark a person, for others, as possessing a particular sexuality, e.g., a masculine woman may be perceived to be a lesbian; a feminine/effeminate man may be perceived as gay. We can observe this assumption at play when others assume a person's sexuality based on how they sound and appear and based on their assumptions about the person's gender (or sex, which we often do not know). Transpersons navigate gender nonconformity as well given that their gender typically differs from their (assigned-at-birth) sex.

Yet, there are key differences between sexuality and gender (identity). As Booth (2011) writes, transpersons often engage in rhetorical battles to affirm their male or female identity, a perpetual telling and justifying to others why they (do not) fit these categories; conversely, LGBQ persons often do not need to engage such battles. Transpersons may have "ghosts" of female- and male-ness with which to contend, histories of being differently sexed and gendered for which they can be held accountable, histories with which LGBQ persons do not typically contend. And coming out for LGBQ persons "may require courage and might entail certain risks," but does not "require multiple psychiatric appointments or thousands of dollars in out-of-pocket medical expenses"—common characteristics of the experience of transpersons (p. 188).

***

In recognizing that language matters in complex, complicated, and sometimes confounding ways, I conclude by cataloging my least favorite terms tied to sex, gender, and sexuality—terms that I witness people continue to use in a variety of contexts.

"Homosexual" makes same-sex/gender attraction seem like a "disease." "Homosexuality" was removed from the Diagnostic and Statistical Manual of Mental Disorders (DSM) in 1974; no longer did the American Psychiatric Association consider it a mental disorder. Yet, as long as the term "heterosexual" exists, "homosexual" will comprise part of the "hetero-homo" binary that shapes and, at times, controls social order.

"Fag" is a term used to disparage others. Sometimes "fag" is used in reference to a person's same-sex/gender attraction, and sometimes it is used in reference to a person's (often a cisgender man's) inability to do gender appropriately. For example, a "weak" cisgender man might be called "fag" not because he is gay or queer, but because he is perceived to not be masculine enough (Pascoe, 2012). Fag seems to be male-specific; I have never heard of a cisgender woman being referred to as a "fag."

I imagine the female equivalent to fag would be "dyke," a gendered term often used toward cisgender women who may be more normatively masculine ("butch") than feminine ("femme"). Lesbians who align with assumed

105

expectations of how cisgender women should act and appear need a special term—e.g., "lipstick" lesbians—to distinguish them from more masculine, gender nonconforming lesbians. I have never heard of a cisgender man being referred to as a "dyke."

There are derogatory phrases rooted in, and which suggest erroneous ideas about, sex, gender, and sexuality. For example, "mother fucker" is used in reference to something bad or an agitated state, but why must a gendered identity ("mother") and a sexual act ("fucking") be used as an insult? What might "father fucking" mean?

Or consider "cocksucker": Why must a kind of oral sex—cock-sucking—be used to disparage someone (see Adams, 2006)? Is the use of this term gendered—are cisgender women disparaged by the term "cock-suckers," or is the term primarily used toward cisgender men? There are additional sex/gender-based and homophobic terms and phrases as well, including "take it in the ass" and its derivatives "bend over backwards," "cover your ass," and "butthurt"—all of which imply that asses are not to be touched and that ass-play (sex) is abject and not ideal.

And then there are the multiple disparaging terms tied to gender. These include terms such as "douche," "cunt," and "pussy" and other phrases based on body parts associated with females/women. There are phrases such as "grow some balls" to encourage someone to be masculine and strong (and similar attempts to embrace the phrase to "grow some ovaries"), and there are phrases used against cisgender, heterosexual men such as "don't be a pussy" and "girly man" (Pelias, 2007).

***

Meanings and uses of words change with time and place, and words have histories. A term that may have once been appropriate ("homosexual") is no longer so; a term that may have once been inappropriate ("queer") is increasingly accepted and celebrated by some communities, e.g., the addition of "Q" to "LGB." We can do things with words, and improve and harm relationships based on what we say and don't say. Might we receive accusations of being too "politically correct" for monitoring language? Possibly, but I welcome this accusation. I want the people with whom I interact and care for to feel comfortable. I want to respect others' sensitivities and hope that they too will respect mine.

DISCUSSION QUESTIONS

1. In this chapter, I included a list of terms that I find to be offensive. What might be some alternative, more respectful words and phrases to use instead of these terms?

2. How should we respond to someone who uses an offensive word but who disagrees about the word's offensiveness? If a word hurts another person, especially a person you care about, would you change the word you use? Explain.

3. Consider facilities and organizations that make use of sex/gender terms such as "male," "female," "women," "men," "girls," and "boys" (e.g., bathrooms; Girl Scouts; Catholic priests can only be "male"). Are these terms indicative of sex, gender, sex-at-birth, or sex-after-treatment/ surgery? What if one person determines that a term designates sex and another person believes the term designates gender? Explain.

NOTES

[1] Merriam-Webster included the term "thon" in its dictionaries between 1934–1961. Thon was a "proposed genderless pronoun of the third person" and short for "that one." It was removed from dictionaries due to infrequent use (Merriam-Webster, n.d.).

[2] For comprehensive overviews about the language of sex, gender, and sexuality, see Pascoe (2012), Killermann (2017) and Stryker (2017).

[3] Parts of this section have been revised from Adams (2011, pp. 29–31).

[4] The last two paragraphs have been revised from Adams (2010, p. 744).

[5] The last two paragraphs have been revised from Adams (2011, p. 169).

REFERENCES

Adams, T. E. (2006). Seeking father: Relationally reframing a troubled love story. *Qualitative Inquiry, 12*, 704–723. https://doi.org/10.1177/1077800406288607

Adams, T. E. (2010). Social constructivist approach to personal identity. In R. L. Jackson, R. C. Arnett, J. Bryant, J. H. Rolling, C. D. B. Walker, & M. Western (Eds.), *Encyclopedia of identity* (pp. 742–745). Thousand Oaks, CA: Sage.

Adams, T. E. (2011). *Narrating the closet: An autoethnography of same-sex attraction.* Walnut Creek, CA: Left Coast Press.

Ahmed, S. (2006). *Queer phenomenology: Orientations, objects, others.* Durham, NC: Duke University Press.

Balay, A. (2018). *Semi queer: Inside the world of gay, trans, and Black truck drivers.* Chapel Hill, NC: University of North Carolina Press.

Booth, E. T. (2011). Queering Queer Eye: The stability of gay identity confronts the liminality of trans embodiment. *Western Journal of Communication, 75*, 185–204. https://doi.org/10.1080/10570314.2011.553876

Butler, J. (2004). *Undoing gender*. New York, NY: Routledge.

Creet, J. (1991). Lesbian sex/gay sex: What's the difference? *Out/Look, 11*, 29–34.

de Vogue, A., & Cohen, Z. (2019, January 22). Supreme Court allows transgender military ban to go into effect. *CNN*. Retrieved February 23, 2019, from https://www.cnn.com/2019/01/22/politics/scotus-transgender-ban/index.html

Drew, J. (2018, June 25). North Carolina's transgender rights battle isn't over. *USA Today*. Retrieved February 23, 2019, from https://www.usatoday.com/story/news/nation/2018/06/25/north-carolina-bathroom-bill-transgender/729791002/

Frye, M. (1983). *The politics of reality: Essays in feminist theory*. Trumansburg, NY: Crossing Press.

Gagné, P., Tewksbury, R., & McGaughey, D. (1997). Coming out and crossing over: Identity formation and proclamation in a transgender community. *Gender & Society, 11*, 478–508.

Greenberg, J. A. (2000). When is a man a man, and when is a woman a woman? *Florida Law Review, 52*, 745–768.

Greenberg, J. A. (2012). *Intersexuality and the law: Why sex matters*. New York, NY: New York University Press.

Hans, J. D., Gillen, M., & Akande, K. (2009). Sex redefined: The reclassification of oral-genital contact. *Perspectives on Sexual and Reproductive Health, 42*, 74–78. https://doi.org/10.1363/4207410

Jackson, S. (2006). Gender, sexuality and heterosexuality: The complexity (and limits) of heteronormativity. *Feminist Theory, 7*, 105–121. https://doi.org/10.1177/1464700106061462

Killermann, S. (2017). *A guide to gender: The social justice advocate's handbook* (2nd ed.). Austin, TX: Impetus Books.

Labi, N. (2007). The kingdom of the closet. *Atlantic Monthly, 299*, 70–82.

Meadow, T. (2018). *Trans kids: Being gendered in the twenty-first century*. Berkeley, CA: University of California Press.

Merriam-Webster (n.d.). We added a gender-neutral pronoun in 1934. Why have so few people heard of it? *Merriam-Webster.com*. Retrieved December 21, 2018, https://www.merriam-webster.com/words-at-play/third-person-gender-neutral-pronoun-thon

Meyerowitz, J. (2002). *How sex changed: A history of transsexuality in the United States*. Cambridge, MA: Harvard University Press.

Moyer, J. W. (2015). Smith College to admit transgender women in historic policy change. *The Washington Post*. Retrieved February 23, 2019, from https://www.washingtonpost.com/news/morning-mix/wp/2015/05/04/smith-college-to-admit-transgender-women-in-historic-policy-change/?utm_term=.658e62c44236

Mustain, K. (2018, December 13). Helping a brother out. BateWorld hosts a vibrant community of straight men who enjoy masturbating together. How they make sense of that says a lot about the nature of male sexuality. *Slate.com*. Retrieved January 21, 2019, https://slate.com/human-interest/2018/12/bateworld-straight-gay-masturbation-meaning.html

Navratilova, N. (2019). The rules on trans athletes reward cheats and punish the innocent. *The Sunday Times*. Retrieved February 23, 2019, from https://www.thetimes.co.uk/article/the-rules-on-trans-athletes-reward-cheats-and-punish-the-innocent-klsrq6h3x

Pascoe, C. J. (2012). *Dude, you're a fag: Masculinity and sexuality in high school* (2nd ed.). Berkeley, CA: University of California Press.

Pelias, R. J. (2007). Jarheads, girly men, and the pleasures of violence. *Qualitative Inquiry, 13*, 945–959. https://doi.org/10.1177/1077800407304413

Rao, R. R., & Sarma, D. (2009). *Whistling in the dark: Twenty-one queer interviews.* Thousand Oaks, CA: Sage.

Ring, T. (2015, April 21). This year's Michigan Womyn's Music Festival will be the last. *The Advocate.* Retrieved February 23, 2019, from https://www.advocate.com/michfest/2015/04/21/years-michigan-womyns-music-festival-will-be-last

Stryker, S. (2017). *Transgender history: The roots of today's revolution* (2nd ed.). New York, NY: Seal Press.

Ward, J. (2015). *Not gay: Sex between straight White men.* New York, NY: New York Press.

West, C., & Zimmerman, D. H. (1987). Doing gender. *Gender & Society, 1*, 125–151. https://doi.org/10.1177/0891243287001002002

RUMINATION

Catherine M. Gillotti

Ruminate: to meditate, ponder, chew the cud.
—*Oxford English Dictionary & Thesaurus* (1997, p. 699)

Why did she break up with me? What could I have done differently? I am almost 8 years older than she is. Am I too old for her? She likes to go out and dance in the city, and I am too busy with work. She didn't introduce me to her friends. Did I embarrass her? No—I cherished her. I loved her with all my heart. I came out for her. Why did she break up with me?

***

In this story, I take you on the journey of the aftermath of my breakup with Emily. At the end of "True Companion" (Chapter 7), I speak to the ways in which I grew from that relationship. What I did not include in that chapter was that I believe there is no growth without pain. This current chapter conveys both my thoughts and actions after the breakup as I worked to understand what happened, what I could do differently, and heal from the pain of love lost. Intermittently, my thoughts appear in italics, to show the rumination I endured. I also include memories of past events during the course of the relationship that I pondered on my daily runs. I never enjoyed running, but the monotonous punishment of the pavement gave me the mental space to work through my grief.

***

Each step feels like I am running in concrete shoes. My feet are as heavy as the black hole left in my chest where my heart used to reside. I run every day in between sessions of writing the chapter for the *Handbook of Health Communication* (Gillotti, 2003a) and teaching summer classes, trying to eradicate my feelings of love for her. Sister Magdalene Marie, my fourth grade teacher, always said, "Where there is a will, there is a way." I can will my love away for Emily.

© KONINKLIJKE BRILL NV, LEIDEN, 2020 | DOI:10.1163/9789004418790_011

I will stop loving you, Emily. I will. There will be a day and I will wake up and I will not be in love with you anymore. Each day I will literally run you out of my system.

Boom, boom, boom, boom—the pounding of my heart syncs with the beat of the song as I run through the neighborhood playing over and over in my head the lyrics to Journey's "Separate Ways." I am searching for my heart that has been shattered and scattered to the wind—my untainted heart, my unbroken heart that she tossed out like garbage.

I saw her yesterday driving. Her windows were down and she was singing to the song on the radio. How could she? How could she be so happy when I can barely put one foot in front of the other?

These thoughts rush through me like an unrelenting tide. The waves come crashing in on me and I wonder if I will ever be able to take another breath. I am wrecked, and it is the almost unbearable pain that keeps me running. I pound my feet with every step, hoping that I can stomp out the pain, stomp her out of what is left of my heart. I feel like I have lost everything important to me, and while I know it is impossible, I have to try.

***

Where did I go wrong in our relationship? I was honest about my uncertainty about my sexual identity. I told her I was unsure I was a lesbian and she seemed so understanding. God Emily, I told you after our first night together that I was not gay. We laughed. Seriously, who makes out with someone for 8 hours and then says, "no offense, but I am not gay." I know it was ridiculous, but I was not ready to accept who I am.

Did she break up with me because I went on that date with John? I told her I had to go out with him. Granted, I felt bad because we were dating for many months at this point. But I had to find out what it would be like to go out on a date with a guy again—this particular guy. She seemed so understanding. She told me to go find out. Was she being honest with me or was this just some test to see how committed I was to her? I was being transparent—too honest. It made me all the more vulnerable.

***

The pounding of my feet on the concrete sidewalk brings me back to the present moment.

Emily is rekindling with her ex-girlfriend right now. I feel it in my bones. Pound it out, Cathy. Pound out the pain and the tears and the hate, and the love.

***

The song lyrics interrupt my thoughts as Steve Perry sings about the possibility of the new lover hurting the woman who leaves him.

You sure as hell hurt me, Emily. You pursued me for two years before anything physical ever happened between us. Was this all a game to you? Did you ever love me? You went out with your ex while you were seeing me. I found out you were doing this only because Keith saw you out with her the same night you had gone out with me. No, it has to be something I did. Maybe it was because I went out with John.

***

John and I met at a pub-crawl in Chicago I attended with other friends from my university. There was an instant, primal attraction between us. Each pub and each glass of beer lowered our inhibitions. By the end of the night, he was offering to share a cab ride. I agreed and then made out with him the entire ride. I am not proud of making out, in the back of a cab, with a man I just met.

Anyone watching us that night would have thought we were long-time lovers, not strangers who had just met. The cab dropped me off at my car where John and I shared one more kiss. I got in my car, pulled myself together and sat there contemplating what I had just done. I don't normally throw myself at complete strangers. I could not explain it, but I was wildly attracted to him. Maybe it was the alcohol? I don't know, but the attraction was undeniable. I had the same feeling once before for a guy I worked with during college.

Months later, when Emily and I were dating and I was struggling to accept myself as a lesbian, John called me. I answered, and after some polite chit-chat, he asked me out and I accepted. I felt guilty for accepting the date without first talking to Emily since she and I were seeing each other, but I knew as soon as I hung up with John I would call and tell her. I told Emily before the date, and we talked about my needing to find out who I was. I also told Emily that I did not know why I was so attracted to this guy and her at the same time.

I said to her, "Maybe I am bi, Emily?"

"You need to go figure it out."

It was only later that I stepped back and saw how hurtful that conversation had to have been for Emily.

On the night of our date, John picked me up at my apartment for dinner and a movie. I heard him knock at my door while I was talking with Emily on the phone. She was sweet and understanding, and I only felt more guilty about doing this to her. My mind chewed on thoughts of self-doubt.

What kind of girlfriend goes out with a guy and calls the woman you love minutes before your heterosexual date arrives? What kind of person accepts a date from a guy when you have a girlfriend?

***

I opened the door and saw John looking at me with his dark brown, penetrating eyes. He smiled and I smiled back. We briefly embraced. He entered my apartment and we sat on the couch and made small talk for a few minutes. There was not much time to chat before we left for the theatre. Staying in the privacy of my apartment was too precarious given our attraction. I had second thoughts about even going out with him as we drove to the theatre. My attraction for him was as powerful as what I felt for Emily before we started dating.

***

Maybe I am addicted to the relational chase? Maybe it is about the getting to know you phase coupled with the physical attraction that makes John and Emily both so appealing? But I know Emily. I have known her for three and a half years, and I don't know John.

***

We arrived at the theatre. Once we took our seats, the lights dimmed and we settled in to watch *The Talented Mr. Ripley* (Minghella, 1999). It is only later that I really began to contemplate the fitting symbolism of this particular movie for this particular date. *The Talented Mr. Ripley* is a movie about a young con artist, played by Matt Damon, who falls in love with a wealthy aristocrat, Jude Law. Damon's character, Tom Ripley, is masterfully duplicitous as he makes himself over and over again for personal gain. As Damon's character appears on a European beach, pretending to be a wealthy U.S. American on holiday, the audience can see how out of place he is. His complexion is pale, a stark contrast to the tanned, toned, and vibrant people who have been there for some time. Amazingly, he smiles and pretends that he fits in with this crowd. I feel implicated by this story. *Is that what I am doing? Pretending to be attracted to John so that I do not have the face the reality of being gay?* My thoughts distract me from being able to focus on and enjoy the film.

***

Who are you Cathy? Are you a con artist? You are in a relationship with Emily. He smells good. I wonder if he is going to put his arm around me or hold my hand? What I am thinking? You have a girlfriend! You have been sleeping with a woman for the last 6 months. Are you going to just leave that part of your dating history out? What if John wants another date? What if you do?

***

Two and a half hours later, the movie ended leaving the audience with much to contemplate and much to admire about the actors' performances. John and I went to a Bennigan's restaurant about five minutes from the theatre. We started to talk about the movie in the car. It seemed like a safe topic to start conversation. We parked, and headed into the crowded restaurant. It is Friday night and the place was packed. We grabbed a table in the bar area. We were both starving. After placing our orders, we resumed our conversation about the movie as we shared appetizers and drinks. He began by asking me a general question about what I thought of the film. I responded by telling him that I like "dark films," but this one was much more complicated and darker than I thought it would be.

"Damon's character obviously had this dark side," I say. "But it seemed like he did not want to be the person he was. He reminded me of a child who just kept digging the hole of lies deeper in order to not be caught. Once he was caught, he had to eradicate any evidence of his lies. The really pathological piece though occurred when he assumed the identity of the person he killed."

John said that he did not expect there to be an attraction between Matt Damon's and Jude Law's characters.

I asked him, "Do you think Damon was in love with Law?"

"I do, and if he could not have him then no one else could."

"One of the research projects I am working on with my colleague, Theresa, is about the representation of lesbians in film. We are studying three films: *Basic Instinct, When Night is Falling*, and *High Art*. Have you seen any of these films?"

"I have seen *Basic Instinct*, but not the others. What have you found in your study?"

"We are looking at a concept Theresa calls 'intimate danger' (Gillotti, 2003b). Intimate danger is the idea that media representations of lesbians are simultaneously threatening to both lesbians and to the straight community."

"How so?"

"For the straight community, the audience sees two women in an intimate relationship that mirrors their own with the opposite sex, which only challenges heteronormative ideals. For the lesbians, mainstream films, like *Basic Instinct*, exploit same-sex, female attraction as a way to arouse men, which implicitly undermines the legitimacy of the attraction."

We continued our conversation throughout dinner about the movie, the research, and his work. I was delighted to be sharing with John the details of this research. The conversation was intellectually stimulating.

John generously paid our bill and we exited the restaurant making our way to his car. Our conversation about *The Talented Mr. Ripley* and society's view of homosexuality continued on the drive back to my place. My mind began to race again as I thought about what to do once we got there. I wondered what he was expecting next.

***

What the hell am I going to do? I guess I will offer him a drink. I feel so guilty. I am having such a good time, but I am betraying Emily. This date feels so different than when I am with Emily, because it is so normal for men and women to go to dinner and a movie. Every time she and I go out, our time together is amazing, but I am also terrified that people will recognize us as lesbians.

***

When we arrived at my apartment, I invited him in for a drink. We sat on my loveseat, and picked up our conversation about Ripley where we left off with it in the car. Our conversation was turning from an academic discussion of homosexuality to our personal experiences, and even though it was logical to anticipate that John would ask me about my history, I was still a bit surprised when he broached the subject.

"Have you ever done anything sexual with a woman?" There was a hopeful glint in his eyes.

"I am dating a woman. Her name is Emily."

"Does she know we are out tonight?"

"Yes. I spoke to her on the phone right before you came to pick me up. Have you ever been attracted to a man?"

"I have, but I have never done anything sexual with a man."

His disclosure gave me another reason to like him. He was also comfortable with his sexual identity and willing to share openly with me without being homophobic. My attention turned inward.

***

He is so secure and sure of himself, which is attractive to me. I love it when people are comfortable in their own skin. I wish Emily were here and a part of this conversation. I would like to know what she thinks about the fluidity of sexual orientation, and her opinion of John's self-assuredness.

***

"What is Emily like?"

"She is really special, and sweet, and wise beyond her years." I proceed to tell him how we met, and what I love about her.

***

Emerging from my memories, I pick up the pace of my run as the fatigue sets in and the despair of facing my empty apartment with hours to go before I can close my eyes and say that I made it through another day without Emily. My grief is crushing me, but I only pound the pavement harder to literally run my sadness out of my body. I think back to the end of that date with John.

***

After I went on about how much I love Emily, John and I looked at each other for a prolonged moment. We both knew nothing else was going to happen between us. It was as if there was nothing left for us to say, so he politely made his way to the door. We embraced as friends knowing we would never see or talk to each other again.

The next day, I went to Emily's apartment to pick her up for a shopping date to IKEA. We never made it there. Emily and I talked about my date with John, and then spent all day in bed. Perhaps Emily was not as immune to jealousy as I thought she was, since she practically jumped me when I got to her apartment. I was glad. It felt good to be wanted. At that point in our relationship, I always felt that Emily had the upper hand when it came to if, and when, we saw each other. While I knew we had strong feelings for each other, I also felt like I needed her more than she needed me. What happened in that cab with John, although passionate, did not match what I felt for Emily. What I felt for John was sexual attraction, but what I felt for Emily was love.

***

The music grows louder in my ears, and brings me back to my daily self-punishment. The tears roll down my face as I work to pound that love out of my heart with each and every aching mile. In between verses of Journey, I let the rumination wash over me and repeatedly think: *I fell in love with you and I will fall out of love with you.* Every run I look for the pieces of my shattered heart. I imagine picking up broken pieces of glass on every run, collecting what is left of me. It takes 15 months to find them. With Emily I was authentic, alive, in love, and worthy of being loved. Without her, I was not—at least until I learned to love myself.

DISCUSSION QUESTIONS

1. What does our first love teach us about ourselves?
2. Why do people base their self-worth on their relational status?
3. How did Cathy's rumination both hurt her and simultaneously help her to heal?
4. Was Cathy's date with John a betrayal to Emily? Why? Why not? By going out with John, did Cathy betray herself?

REFERENCES

Gillotti, C. M. (2003a). Medical disclosure and decision-making: Excavating the complexities of physician-patient information exchange. In T. Thompson, A. Dorsey, K. Miller, & R. Parrott (Eds.), *Handbook of health communication* (pp. 163–181). Mahwah, NJ: Lawrence Erlbaum Associates.
Gillotti, C. M. (2003b). Verbal and nonverbal displays of intimacy in lesbian relationships in film. In T. Carilli & J. Campbell (Eds.), *Women and the media: Diverse perspectives* (pp. 35–43). Lanham, MD: University Press of America.
Minghella, A. (Director). (1999). *The talented Mr. Ripley* [Motion Picture]. Hollywood, CA: Paramount Pictures.
Oxford Pocket Dictionary & Thesaurus (American ed.). (1997). Oxford: Oxford University Press.
Separate Ways (Worlds Apart). On *Journey's Greatest Hits* [CD]. New York, NY: CBS Records Inc.

THE SEXUAL RELATIONSHIP

Billy Huff

"There's no such thing as a sexual relationship" (Lacan, 1975, p. 12). This is one of the most notable quotations from the later work of psychoanalyst Jacques Lacan. As an aspiring Lacanian scholar interested in gender and sexuality, I struggled to understand this notion for years. It seemed integral to my thinking about queer sexuality and my strong belief that sex and identity are ultimately unassimilable. As is the case with most of Lacan's writings and seminars, I grasp the ideas, but my understanding flees the second I attempt to articulate them in my own arguments. I always feel like I am simultaneously so close and so far away. "There's no such thing as a sexual relationship" was especially troubling. That is until I experienced the truth of this statement directly and personally.

I remember the first time I saw him. It was the first faculty meeting of the fall semester, and he was sitting uncomfortably in the first row. I was behind him. The department chair began the meeting by introducing the new faculty. My new colleague stood up, turned around, and wryly waved, a blush forming on his brown cheeks. I elbowed the colleague sitting beside me. "The new guy is hot!" He was tall with black hair and eyes and dark skin. He had a well-manicured black beard and moustache. I was distracted throughout the entire meeting. I couldn't stop staring at his black, leather belt peeking out of the back of his chair. I imagined him taking it off and beckoning me to bend over.

You can imagine my jubilation when I learned that his office wasn't yet ready and he would have to share mine for the first two weeks of the semester. At the time I had long hair. I had recently lost over one hundred pounds, and I was obsessed with wearing the petite dresses my larger body was always denied. I wore makeup that always matched my nail polish. I had one small tattoo, the BDSM pride symbol, on the inside of my left wrist. He was married, and I was at the end of a ten-year relationship. I decided to be the only member of his welcoming committee, and we quickly became close friends.

© KONINKLIJKE BRILL NV, LEIDEN, 2020 | DOI:10.1163/9789004418790_012

We talked about almost everything. I told him about some of my most intimate fantasies. He admitted that he was aggressive in bed. He had never tried BDSM, but he assured me that as a guitar player, "I know just how hard to hit the strings without breaking them." I wanted to watch him play guitar all the time after that. Over the course of the year both of our long-term relationships ended, and our friendship strengthened. I sent him a text message: "I got a hotel room. Interested?" He was interested, and the sex was phenomenal from the start. When Lacan says that "there's no such thing as a sexual relationship," he surely hadn't met us. We started calling each other "best friends," and the sex only improved. He was the right kind of dominant, and was not afraid to hit me hard. Before him so many men were hesitant with me. They seemed unable to get past the prohibitions they learned as boys against hitting girls and women. He allowed me to do things to him that no girl had done before. The first time I reached for his ass he stopped me. "I'm not gay," he said. I convinced him that it was okay—I was a girl after all. He was addicted.

Time passed, and I moved in. We watched football together, played video games, and had a lot of sex. Neither one of us remembers the first time he called me "Billy," but he recalls that "you think like a man, but you have the sexual curiosity of a little boy." I have no interest in romantic or monogamous relationships, I enjoy the most perverse sex, and I want to do it a lot. He seems to enjoy the things about me that resist stereotypically feminine behavior. He nurtures the questions I have about what it feels like to be a man. "Do penises sweat?" I remember asking one day. He didn't know the answer. I have never told him that for almost twenty years I've been thinking about transitioning, and I don't tell him about the immense joy I feel every time he unknowingly validates my boyish masculinity. It's a recognition I've rarely experienced before.

When I told him I decided to transition, I expected him to be surprised, or at least to try to talk me out of it. He didn't. He couldn't have been more supportive. I started injecting testosterone and legally changed my name to Billy. He transitioned easily with me. He had already been calling me Billy in private for two years. Every day that passed and every time I plunged that long, thin, testosterone filled needle into my thigh, I knew I would soon cross a line and he would be unwilling to follow. I knew how invested he was in being a "straight" man. Every time we had sex could be the last. Would it be the thick, black hair sprouting on my legs and armpits? Would it be my deepened voice that changed my exclamations during sex from high-pitched screams to low grunts? Would it be too much when my boxer briefs mixed with his in the laundry? I remember returning to our hotel room one night after a wedding to change our clothes. We laughed hysterically when we looked in the mirror, standing side by side, and realized that we were wearing matching underwear, white undershirts, and black socks. "Look, we're brothers," he laughed. I thought we looked like gay lovers.

"There's no such thing as a sexual relationship." I've been on testosterone for two years now, and we're still having amazing sex. I have a shaved head and hair growing all over my body. I call my enlarged clitoris my "tiny cock." He doesn't mention it. When we have sex, I imagine us as daddy and boy. It's the hot gay sex I've always wanted. When I touch his cock, I sometimes pretend that it's attached to me. I don't know what he's imagining that allows him to experience pleasure with me. I do know that it's not the same fantasy that animates me. What is he thinking that allows him to look down at my shaved head as I suck his cock with anything other than disgust? I'm not sure I need to know the answer. His identity as a straight man seems to be invalidated by the sex we're having, but it somehow isn't.

"There's no such thing as a sexual relationship." When we have sex, we cannot experience each other directly. We touch each other's bodies through the screens of two very different fantasmatic frames. We are not the only people in the room. I realize that this has always been the case. The image of sexual union I thought we once had was just that—imaginary. The pleasure I thought we experienced together was always individual and wholly resistant to communication. This is, however, the closest to love I've ever been.

"There's no such thing as a sexual relationship." We meet time and time again through the necessary missed encounters that characterize the gaping abyss of desire. The assurances that stabilize our identities destruct. "Man" and "woman," "gay" and "straight," and even "trans*" exist only as supports of our fantasies. The ground we stand on is ungrounded. Were we to appear together in pubic, strangers would insist we were gay lovers. Only two years ago, we would have appeared straight. No matter how many questions I ask him, he is unable to explain what it is to be a man. No matter how many times I inject testosterone into my thighs, I am unable to articulate how this foreign substance feels in my body. Is the pleasure we feel in orgasm the same? How can we ever know?

When Lacan tells us "There's no such thing as a sexual relationship," he means that sex cannot assimilate itself to reality. It resists sense and communication. We have developed so many different identities and fantasies to come to terms with that for which there are no terms. Our gender and sexual identities give us anchors. They tell us who we are on the most fundamental level, and they tell us how we are related to others. They allow us to believe that we can encounter each other directly, that two can become one, and that union between self and other is possible. My experience tells me differently. The only constant is our desire as an abyss that can never be filled. We come together to experience our singularity. My sex knows nothing about women and men or about gay and straight. My sex only knows pleasure.

DISCUSSION QUESTIONS

1. How does Billy's gender transition complicate fixed sexual identity categories like gay, straight, lesbian, and bisexual?
2. In this chapter, Billy argues that sex and identity are unassimilable. Do you agree? Why or why not?
3. Billy discusses the difficulty in communicating to another what "man" feels like? Do you agree? How would you describe to another how your gender *feels* to you?
4. After reading this chapter, how would you explain Lacan's statement that "there's no such thing as a sexual relationship?"

REFERENCE

Lacan, J. (1975). *Encore, the seminar of Jacques Lacan, Book XX: On feminine sexuality, the limits of love and knowledge, 1972–1973* (B. Fink, Trans.). New York, NY: W.W. Norton.

MONOGAMY

Tony E. Adams

We may believe in sharing as a virtue—we may teach it to our children—but we don't seem to believe in sharing what we value most, our sexual partners. But if you really loved someone, wouldn't you want to give them the best thing you've got, your partner?
—Adam Phillips (1996, p. 15)

One way of loving people is to acknowledge that they have desires which exclude us; that it is possible to love and desire more than one person at the same time. Everyone knows that this is true, and yet we don't want the people we love to start believing it about themselves.
—Ibid. (p. 115)

He enters your life unexpectedly and at an inopportune time. You're trying to date Someone-Else, but your nerves flutter when he's around. He's beautiful, caring, intelligent, and entertaining. You want to spend time with him, as much as possible, but fear that he will reject and judge you. You engage in subtle flirting, which he reciprocates, but soon learn that he doesn't flirt as much because he doesn't want to interfere with your budding relationship. Your relationship with Someone-Else soon dissipates and, immediately, he asks you on a date, and then another. You begin to spend most days together and, a year later, share an apartment.

He is easy to get along with and seems to only have one core belief about himself/us: he does not believe in monogamy. Never has, never will. Yet, he says, he will tell you immediately if he ever has sex with another man. He often reminds you of this belief: on the first date; after a month of dating; two, three, and six months later; when you search for the apartment together; when you move in together; and again, a few months later. At the time, you believe in monogamy but can't articulate why—it's what you've been taught, something to which you've been oriented and expected to believe.

© KONINKLIJKE BRILL NV, LEIDEN, 2020 | DOI:10.1163/9789004418790_013

Naïve-Self thinks you can convince him otherwise, especially since after more than a year together, he has not had sex with anyone else.

But he soon does. As promised, he tells you the first time he sees you post-sex. He says it happened when you weren't home, and that it was just sex—no emotion or love, only pleasure. He loves you and wants to be with you. He tries to convince you that who he has sex with shouldn't indicate his care for you. Naïve-Self thinks otherwise: Although you appreciate his honesty, the relationship must end—he has violated your expectation, had an affair, cheated. Saddened by your hurt, he is also not sure how to apologize. After all, he has been honest about his beliefs about monogamy.

***

According to the *Oxford English Dictionary* (n.d.), monogamy includes "the practice or principle of remaining faithful to one person during the course of a sexual relationship other than marriage." Yet, what constitutes a "sexual relationship"? Any intimate physical contact, e.g., kissing, hand-holding, oral sex, or only sex-acts such as penis-vagina penetration, ejaculation, and anal sex? What constitutes "faithfulness"? Does an emotional connection with Someone-Else disrupt monogamy? Can we still maintain monogamy yet watch pornography (others engaging in sexual acts), or fantasize about (absent) others while having sex with one person, fantasies about which the person with whom we're sexual may never know? As Phillips (1996) writes, "For some people it is a betrayal to dance with someone else; for other people only intercourse counts, so you can do everything else with impunity" (p. 33).[1]

***

During a visit to a local pub you sit at the bar, order a beer, and watch the crowd. The bartender serves you another beer, saying a man across the bar purchased it for you. You thank the bartender and wave at the man, who then comes to greet you. He is attractive and witty and, based on the initial conversation, has a good personality. The two of you have a few more drinks and then go to his apartment to have sex. The next morning, before you leave, you exchange telephone numbers.

He texts you throughout the day, telling you about the great time he had and how he'd like to see you again. You too had a great time and arrange to meet in a few days. He comes to your apartment, you have more sex, go to dinner and to another bar, and invite him to stay the night. Like you, he enjoys cuddling and kissing; his lips are sweet, his body smooth. The next morning, you have more sex, then breakfast, and he leaves for work. He texts, thanking you for a great time; you reply, thanking him too.

The following week he asks you to dinner and invites you to stay the night. At dinner, he says he is bisexual, not gay, and has a girlfriend of more than two years. He loves her, is committed to her, but enjoys having sex with men. According to him, she knows he has sex with men. None of this information bothers you because you enjoy spending time with him, having good sex, and are not looking for (monogamous) commitment.

The next two months continue in a similar pattern—seeing each other every few days, spending nights together, having sex and drinks and dinners and breakfasts. Soon two things occur: First, he tells you that he is attending an out-of-town wedding with his girlfriend and asks if you want to travel separately and stay nearby, so that when he is not with his girlfriend, he can have sex with you. You decline the invitation and wonder if/how much she knows. Second, you begin to develop stronger feelings for him and want more commitment. You ask him to take a weekend away, just the two of you. He declines and says he is not sure he can be away from his girlfriend for so long. Out of care for yourself, you tell him that you can't continue seeing him. He says he is sad, understands, and does not know how to proceed otherwise; he loves his girlfriend.

You stop contact for a week, but he soon asks if you still want to go on a weekend away together. He thinks he can do it. You are excited by the idea but assume your desire for a more established relationship will escalate and worry about being disappointed. You can't blame him too much—with you, he was honest about his sexuality and relationship. You decline the trip but hope to see him again.

You don't see him again and, during the next few months, return to the bar where you met. You talk with the same bartender, drink the same beer, and hope he appears. You miss him, wish the relationship hadn't been so complicated, and regret having these feelings. Six months later, your phone breaks and you lose his number. You have no trace of him and do not know his last name.

***

You have learned to disavow monogamy for two reasons. First, you recognize that across a lifetime a person may find more than one person sexually attractive. Second, in an intimate relationship, you value honesty more than secrecy and lying, even when this honesty may hurt.

There are billions of people in this world. To assume that each person is only attracted to, or destined for, one person is ridiculous. Instead, you believe in several intimate and relational possibilities for people, people for whom we develop crushes and attractions. To ask ourselves and others to deny or "turn off" these crushes and attractions once we enter a monogamous commitment seems suffocating and cruel. You think monogamous relationships can probably exist, as long as both people recognize that they might still view others as attractive.

You also imagine many monogamous couples are not willing to accommodate—and be honest about—these crushes and attractions, thus, introducing the second reason you disavow monogamy: in your intimate relationships, you value honesty more than secrecy and lying, especially when such secrecy and lying involves an attraction to others. You would rather know if a person might have sex with another person. With this knowledge, you can determine if you want to stay in the relationship, as well as if your health and safety is at risk. If your partner says they might, or did, "cheat" on you, or if they have a serious crush or attraction to someone else, you have the knowledge to take care of yourself and make an informed decision based on what you want in a relationship. Further, by loving the other and recognizing the other may be attracted to others, you may even learn what/who they like.

***

Although pornography has existed for centuries, it did not exist in the same ways as it does now. Pornography consisted of erotic stories and drawings, which only became widely available with the invention of the printing press; images and videos only came into existence with photography and other recording technologies. In these pre-online forms, pornography was difficult to acquire. In the United States, from 1873 until the late 1960s, the Comstock Laws prohibited the mailing of obscene and immoral—often erotic—materials. In order to acquire pornographic material, you might have to physically locate an underground community or an "adult" bookstore. With pre-online forms of pornography, there were space/time constraints: a person was limited to the stories and images contained in the physical object/text. In such an era, would objectifying others for personal pleasure be a violation of monogamy? More specifically, would having a subscription to *Playgirl, Hustler, Sports Illustrated Swimsuit Edition*, Cinemax (or "Skin-emax" as it was once called because of its sexual content), or reading an erotic romance novel (Radway, 1984) constitute "cheating"?

Currently, online technologies make it easy and free to find new scenes and objects of attraction, and many people can't imagine, or ever know, a world without such access. There is Craigslist, Tinder and Scruff, Bumble and Match, Instagram and Tumblr, Pornhub and Xtube, and you can use your computer or cell phone ("hand-held device") to watch couples have live sex on sites such as Chatterbate, Tinychat, and Cam4. The abundance of porn—only possible with online technologies—creates new relational challenges: You can find a new person to watch every minute of every day without ever having to leave your residence, "log-in" or "pay-per-view," or subscribe to a magazine or cable channel.

***

On Grindr, a sex/dating application for mostly cisgender gay men, a man with a blank profile messages you, inquiring about the possibility of sex. He says you know him. You ask for a photo. He sends an image of himself and his partner. You used to work with them. He says "Partner knows" he is on Grindr. You wonder what "Partner knows" means.

***

You think about the (assumed) heterosexual, cisgender, married men at professional conferences who invite (assumed) heterosexual, cisgender women, graduate students and early-career scholars, to sit on their knee, sometimes their lap, on display for attendees. You notice these senior scholars, often (always) men, caress the women's arms, legs, and butts, in lobbies, hallways, and hotel bars. You feel that their intimate activities are not necessarily your business, unless the touching was non-consensual, or if these (assumed) monogamous folks were staunch advocates of/for monogamy.[2] As someone who has attended conferences for many years, you have witnessed a significant amount of flirting and touching by self-identified monogamists, but wonder if such acts constitute cheating?

And then there are couples who proudly identify as monogamous, but, in practice, you would not refer to as such. These are the couples who reveal the cracks in their monogamous practices when asked particular questions:

- Have you ever cheated, had sex, or flirted while in a (monogamous) relationship?
- What do you do, sexually, when traveling or living apart?

- Do you ever engage with erotic materials, watch porn, or fantasize about others?

Some will quickly deny the possibility that they've ever done any of these acts. But then they'll respond with statements such as, "We don't talk about what happens when we're away from each other," "Watching porn isn't 'cheating' although we have never discussed it," and "I had an affair once (or twice) but will not do so again." Some say being in a different city/ nation makes it acceptable to have sex with others. The hypocrites frustrate you—they praise monogamy and judge others who are not monogamous. Yet, in practice, they do not align with how you understand monogamy, that is, as "the practice or principle of remaining faithful to one person" (*Oxford English Dictionary*). You are not frustrated by their sex acts and violations, but rather their denial that monogamy has been violated. You realize people may be monogamous until they are not; they may claim commitment to only one person, but then mess up, have an affair, apologize, and return to monogamy—until they mess up again.

***

At a pool party with friends. Persistent approaches you in the water, smiles and winks, touches your back, out of sight of his Partner. You reciprocate— you find Persistent fun and cute. Partner notices Persistent's smiles, winks, and touches with you and begins to follow Persistent around the pool. You sense Partner assumes they are monogamous, yet Persistent must not. Partner leaves the pool area, and, once out of sight, Persistent grabs your hand and thrusts it in his pants. You ask, "are you two 'open?'" "No," he replies. "I want to be, but Partner wants monogamy." You remove your hand from his pants and swim away. Regardless of desire, you do not intervene on the couple, both of whom are friends.

***

You cannot control others or their relationships. You do not ask strangers you watch online or with whom you may have sex if they are in a monogamous relationship; having sex with someone else is a decision they make. If you do learn the other is in a supposedly monogamous relationship, you might hesitate to act, but not always. There might be reasons why a person may not be sexually content in a relationship. Granted, with monogamous couples with whom you are friends, you would typically refuse sex with only one of them, especially if the sex is a secret. You do not want to damage the friendship, especially if you sense that at least one friend understands their relationship as being monogamous.

***

For you, monogamy only exists in two-person relationships in which neither person "cheats" physically or emotionally, flirts with others, or finds others attractive. For you, monogamy cannot exist if at least one part of a couple desires pornography, flirts with or fantasizes about others, or uses social apps (e.g., Tinder, Grindr, Bumble). Couples are monogamous until they are not, yet may return discursively to monogamy, e.g., framing a sexual violation as a "mistake." The monogamy pact may be violated again (another affair; more pornography; additional flirting/fantasizing). Given these assumptions, for you, the concept of monogamy feels sad, silly, arbitrary, and elitist.

Yet, non-monogamy does not mean any sex can happen within a relationship. In your relationship, there are rules: unless you both are involved, the other(s) with whom you have sex must occur in the guest bedroom; staying the night with someone else, when your partner is present, is not acceptable; sleeping with friends is delicate and sometimes discouraged; and you must disclose your relationship to all sexual prospects, as you do not want to foster a false impression of singleness. Together, you recognize the possibility that "mistakes" may happen and neither can predict what these mistakes might be, only that you will discuss how/why sexual acts with another person may have motivated discomfort within the relationship.

***

With time and experience, relationships and desires will change. Partners might feel lust at first, but lust may decrease with time. What might be attractive at 23 might be unattractive at 48 or 72. We age and change physically—you (and your partner/s) will look differently in 10, 20, 30 years. With time and experience, you also learn what hurts—the pain of secrecy, the injuries of lies, the aches of growing distrust—as well as what feels good— talking about fantasies, curbing dishonesty and guilt, celebrating freedom, and supporting desires.

You are not necessarily against the idea of monogamy and recognize that some partners may do monogamy well. Instead, you are disheartened by the unquestioned allegiance to the principle and how such allegiance makes secret sexual affairs possible and difficult to discuss. You also assume many monogamous couples do not believe that flirting, sexting, pornography, and the use of social apps such as Tinder, Bumble, and Grindr violate monogamous pacts. Yet, you wonder about the crushes they've had, their flirts and affairs, the times when they've fantasized about others while being intimate with their current partner, and the lies they tell themselves (and their partners) about their desires.

You realize monogamy isn't for you. It is limited, limiting, and suffocating, an unnecessary ruse. You enjoy the beauty of others, of activating desires in mundane interactions, of celebrating the sexual life of everyday affairs.

DISCUSSION QUESTIONS

1. When should two people in an intimate relationship discuss their beliefs about monogamy? On the first date? After two months of dating? If/when they get married? Never?
2. What does it mean to "cheat" in a (monogamous) relationship? Cheating is often assumed to happen when one person in a relationship does not tell their partner about a sexual affair. Yet, what if the person has an emotional affair? What if one person develops a crush on another person, thinks about another person often, and maybe even while having sex with their partner—is this person cheating? Does cheating happen if a person finds someone else attractive—the teacher, the bartender, the stranger on the street—and says nothing to their partner? If one person is aroused by pornography, and the other person does not know about the porn, would this be considered cheating? Why (not)?
3. How important is sex in a committed relationship? What happens if sex disappears, or does not exist, in a relationship? What happens when a couple no longer wants to have sex with each other? What if sex disappears from a relationship, after two years, or ten years, or forty years? What happens if one person is less able to have sex—maybe because of a health condition, or a physical accident—or becomes less attracted to the other because of a physical change (e.g., gaining or losing 100lbs), or simply because their desire has changed? Does one person have the ability to regulate the sexual activities and desires of another person?

NOTES

[1] What counts as "sex" for one person may not count as "sex" for another person. If being monogamous means not having "sex" with another person, then both people in the monogamous relationship need to establish what acts count as "sex." See Frye (1983), Hans, Gillen, and Akande (2010), and Peck, Manning, Tri, Skrzypczynski, Summers and Grubb (2016) for various definitions of "sex."

[2] This paragraph has been revised from Faulkner and Adams (in press).

REFERENCES

Faulkner, S., & Adams, T. E. (in press). #YouToo: Notes on sexual harassment and assault in the academy. *International Review of Qualitative Research*.

Frye, M. (1983). To be and be seen: The politics of reality. In. M. Frye (Ed.), *The politics of reality: Essays in feminist theory* (pp. 152–74). New York, NY: The Crossing Press.

Hans, J. D., Gillen, M., & Akande, K. (2010). Sex redefined: The reclassification of oral-genital contact. *Perspectives on Sexual and Reproductive Health, 42*, 74–78.

Oxford English Dictionary. (n.d.). *Monogamy.* Retrieved July 20, 2014, from http://www.oed.com

Peck, B., Manning, J., Tri, A., Skrzypczynski, D., Summers, M., & Grubb, K. (2016). What do people mean when they say they "had sex"? Connecting communication and behavior. In J. Manning & C. M. Noland (Eds.), *Contemporary studies of sexuality & communication: Theoretical and applied perspectives* (pp. 3–13). Dubuque, IA: Kendall Hunt.

Phillips, A. (1996). *Monogamy.* New York, NY: Pantheon Books.

Radway, J. (1984). *Reading the romance: Women, patriarchy, and popular culture.* Chapel Hill, NC: University of North Carolina Press.

THE JOY

Catherine M. Gillotti

A friend once told you that when it comes to romantic relationships, eventually you get to play all of the roles. Sometimes you are the one who leaves. Sometimes you are the one who is left. Sometimes you are the one who is certain about your feelings for the other person. Sometimes you are the one who is ambivalent. As you do the post-mortem examination of each relationship, you might not even recognize yourself depending upon what role you played, and if you do, you might not want to even acknowledge who you were. While there are many roles to play, the roles you know and have played best are those of "the codependent" and "the narcissist."

You learn through your reading of codependence literature that all humans are codependent. People rely on one another for survival, stimulation, and companionship. As Charles Whitfield (1991) argues, it just depends upon whether it is a healthy codependence or an unhealthy one. Healthy codependence entails interdependence; unhealthy codependence is "the disease of lost self-hood" (p. 3). Looking back on relationships that ended, you certainly lost yourself more times than you care to remember, but the remembering is essential to who you have become and the kind of partner you hope to be.

"THE JOY—THE JOY—THE JOY"

He just kept repeating these words as he laid his hands on top of your chest. You were lying on a bearskin rug in the middle of a filthy floor surrounded by two large but gentle Huskies. You agreed to a "reading" by a Native American shaman, out in the desert outside of Sedona, Arizona. Supposedly he is going to read your energy, your memories, past lives or something. While you are open to different ways of knowing and healing, you just don't have a good feeling about this situation given the remote location and condition of his home. As this stranger lays his hands on top of your chest babbling about joy and laughing uncontrollably like a little kid, you cannot believe you

© KONINKLIJKE BRILL NV, LEIDEN, 2020 | DOI:10.1163/9789004418790_014

signed up for this experience with your girlfriend. You had already paid more than $200 for a chakra treatment that ended up being nothing more than a mediocre massage. But hey, you are just happy to be on a trip with her. Most importantly, you want her to be happy and to be happy with you.

Oh the things you will do for love. So far in this relationship, you have spent six months underestimating your value by bowing to her every whim, and here you are lying on this stranger's family room floor because your girlfriend really wanted to do this.

You lie there wondering how long this is going to last. Your girlfriend is lying next to you with her eyes closed listening to his laughing and then the uncontrollable crying. It was difficult not to laugh. When he finishes your reading you stay still as he moves to her. You quietly lay there listening to his reading of her. You think he is making it all up. There is some talk of "staircases" and "doorways" and "transitions." She did not like her reading either. Hundreds of dollars for you both, but you still hold onto a measure of hope that something might come out of it that is insightful.

After he finishes her reading, the three of you sit on the floor, petting the giant dogs and interpret the reading. You start with how he began your reading by repeating the words "The Joy" and wonder what that could mean in the grand scheme of your life. As you repeat the phrase, you reflect on October 1967 when you were born on the heels of your grandmother's death. Your mom's mom had ovarian cancer and died that year. Perhaps, there was an unconscious expectation that your arrival would ease your mother's grief, and bring her joy in the wake of her grief. You also reflect on the ways you spent your life trying to live up to the expectations of others—pleasing everyone around you, not because you were told you had to, but because you wanted to. You believed that if you could please others that would be enough for you to be pleased with yourself. You did everything you could to make your parents proud of you. You tried to be the "good" Catholic girl they raised you to be. You did not do drugs or stay out after curfew, not that you really had one because you were always home at a reasonable hour. You did not even begin to date until you went to college. It is only years later when you came out as a lesbian that you realized why you weren't interested in dating at that time.

And here you were again, trying to please the woman you loved. Who were you in this relationship? Whoever it was, you did not like her very much, and you had been different versions of this codependent self before. No wonder your girlfriend always seemed irritated with you. People-pleasing is not a sexy quality, and she told you from the beginning that she wanted to be with someone who was assertive. Initially you were, but somehow you fell back into your comfortable, familiar, over-accommodating, codependent self. This relationship was not the first time you played this role. No, this was simply the most recent incarnation of it.

***

While this people-pleasing proclivity was cultivated throughout your life, it fully showed itself thirteen years ago during your first serious relationship. There might as well have been the word "welcome" tattooed on your chest because you allowed yourself to be walked on frequently. You remember the time your first girlfriend was going to make you dinner. This was a very rare occurrence. You didn't want her to go to too much trouble, so you offered to make the side dishes. You also did not trust that she would plan the meal well enough, so your offer to share in the cooking was actually a veiled attempt at control. This inconsistent nurturing/controlling dynamic is characteristic of codependent relationships (LePoire, Hallet, & Giles, 1998). When she arrived with a frozen chicken at 9 p.m.—a few hours late—with all of the sides overcooked, you were just happy to see her. Oh yes, part of you was angry that she was profoundly late and unprepared to deliver on what you had hoped would have been an enjoyable evening together. Instead, you stomped those feelings down to keep the peace and the illusion of a happy, fulfilling relationship.

The relationship exploded when your girlfriend insisted on going to Chicago on her own to be with her friends, something she did often. That was fine and healthy in a way, but also hurtful because you felt like she was keeping your relationship a secret. You were not sure how many of her friends knew about you. You had met some high school friends once or twice, but no one from Chicago. Instead of asking to join her, you kept quiet about your feelings. You did not want to jeopardize the perceived stability of the relationship; she was your first love and you saw yourself spending the rest of your life with her. She was the fairytale come true. You thought you had it all. That relationship made every other part of your past make sense. It explained why you had never fallen in love with any of the men you dated. You hung all of your ideal relationship fantasies on her, which was not fair to her.

Anytime the two of you got close to a fight, you smoothed over the rough edges, and apologized when there was nothing for which to apologize. No fighting meant bliss and bliss meant a relationship, and a relationship meant you were worthy of love. Someone loves you. You forgot—and maybe at that point you never really knew—that YOU were someone too and perhaps the love you most deserved was self-love. No one else could fill this void.

Sternberg (2006) argues that a consummate love requires three elements: passion, intimacy, and commitment. It was not until years later that you realized that all you had with your first love was passion with a sprinkling of intimacy. The house of cards folded when Keith, your dear friend and co-author of this book, had the courage, integrity, and love to let you know he saw her on a date with someone else while she was dating you.

Then there was the first girlfriend who you referred to as your "partner." This was, for you, a big deal. She was the one for whom you fully "came out" to yourself, and the one you were with when you came out to your family. You even bought commitment rings for each other that were engraved with the words "stay forever." She lived 90 miles away. You were going to buy a house together, and for over half of the relationship, you equally shared in the driving to see one another. To this day you can name almost every highway exit between your house and hers, because you made that drive so often near the end of the relationship. Her work, the renovation of her house, her animals all took precedence over your life, work, and household responsibilities.

One of the most profound examples of your codependence came when you agreed to a trip to Venice Beach, Florida. You love the Gulf coast of Florida, but you had been to Venice Beach and knew that it did not compare to the beauty of Siesta Key where you had vacationed with your family for many years as a child. She wanted to go to Venice Beach, which coincidentally was where she and her ex had vacationed. You acquiesced, and spent the trip resenting each and every reference she made to what she and her ex did there. You look back and wish that you had insisted on vacationing somewhere else, where she had not spent time with her ex. Instead you silenced yourself, and the sad fact is that your partner would have been amenable to a different vacation suggestion if you just had asserted yourself. Unfortunately, you were deeply rooted in the codependent role. Your family could see how passive you were given that your father called her "management" and you "labor." Your mother even insisted that the only reason you painted your bedroom the color of yellow was because of her. You chose the color and your partner surprised you by staying an extra day to paint the room while you were at work. She did many kind things for you like slipping 10 romantic cards in your suitcase (one for each day) when you were going on a trip. Only in retrospect did you realize that perhaps if you had not been so codependent, your partnership might have stood a better chance of surviving.

There is a saying that suggests there are always at least three sides to every story—yours, the other's, and the truth. The truth is you also played the starring role of "the narcissist" in several relationships.

Let's start with your girlfriend from Wisconsin. She was incredibly thoughtful, sweet, accommodating, intellectually stimulating, and wonderfully kind. Why the hell did you let her go? Sternberg (2006) provides a possible answer. Although you had the intimacy and the commitment, you did not feel the passion. You wanted to feel it, but passion cannot be manufactured. You discussed your ambivalence in candid terms. She tried so hard to make physical adjustments to be more desirable for you. You remember the many accommodations over the course of that on-again, off-again 15-month relationship and wonder how much damage you did to her. You wanted to want her. How could you not? She was so thoughtful, and once had Kentucky silk pies shipped in dry ice from Lexington to your house to bring back a fond memory of your years of living there when you earned your doctorate from the University of Kentucky. What made your behavior so narcissistic was the self-congratulatory internal monologue of your superiority to her. You were younger, more educated, and financially more stable. In your mind, you were quite the catch. You are embarrassed to admit your arrogance.

Years later, you were cast again as the narcissist with the one and only significant other with whom you have lived. Like your girlfriend from Wisconsin, the passion passed quickly, and you probably should have been just friends from the start. You were aging and anxious to settle down with someone—the embodiment of the pragma lover (Lee, 1988). There were significant differences between you in terms of age, hobbies, education, finances, and household habits. You pushed all of these away to once again be in a relationship—a little bit of your codependent self showing up. You so badly wanted to be in a relationship that you convinced yourself that you were compatible when deep down you knew you were not. The underlying truth spiked your anxiety, which caused you to want to control everything around you, and one way to do that was to control yourself. So you went on a diet, and obsessively lost 25 pounds. The smaller you got, the larger she got; the differences were cemented, and your narcissist claimed her starring role. Your girlfriend had started a business, was pursuing her master's degree, and trying to be sweet to you. Yet, nothing was good enough. You once even cut the grass the same day that she had cut it because it wasn't short enough. You felt superiority in all things—wisdom because of your age, intellect because of your education, finances because you had a full-time job, and physical attractiveness because of your recently acquired status as a lifetime member in Weight Watchers. No matter what she did, you were irritated with her. Of course, there were many other contributing factors that went into the demise of the relationship besides your narcissistic tendencies, but in voicing your own contributions to its dissolution, you fully own your actions.

Now you found yourself in the desert in Sedona with a girlfriend who was irritated with you. There was nothing you could do that was good enough. How ironic? Or maybe it was not at all ironic. Remember, over time, you get to play all the roles. After touring the Sedona vortexes, hiking, and building a tower of stones as a prayer offering on the bank of the river that cuts below Cathedral Rock, your self-deceit took its roots. You told yourself how great this relationship was and how much fun you were having. You decided to self-medicate with tacos and margaritas—they would help to keep your mouth occupied so that you did not tell yourself or her the truth. Ironically, the stark and arid Arizonan background was a fitting metaphor for your relationship. You continually blanked out the memory of sitting in her apartment in the early weeks of the relationship where you said, "I don't think you are nice enough for me."

That is right, you said that to her. "I don't think you are nice enough for me." Listen to yourself. You sensed this was not the right person, and while your codependent self was in the lead role, your narcissistic understudy was there too. Why didn't you listen to yourself? Why didn't you love yourself enough to trust your own instinct? It was all there. But you knew why then and you know why now. You needed to be in a relationship to feel worthy of love.

Near the end of the Sedona trip, you sat with her in a coffee shop, pathetically falling all over yourself to please her. She was upset about something. It might have even been the first time she said, "I don't feel deeply connected to you." Those words struck pain every time she said them because what *you* heard was "I am not in love with you."

Many things happened in the months and years that followed the Sedona trip, but the more codependent you became, the more narcissistic she became. You both lost a lot in this relationship. It was the dynamic between you—between the codependent and narcissist—that took two relatively decent people and transformed them into their shadow selves (Ford, 1998). You do recognize that all of us have a shadow side; those qualities that are not the most functional or becoming.

Many people think that the codependent is passive as you were much of the time with your first girlfriend. Yet, experience has taught you differently. It is not that simple or linear. Your codependent self had matured into a version of simultaneous nurturer and controller (LePoire, Hallet, & Giles, 1998). For example, sometimes you would unconsciously say "I love you" to her to invoke reciprocity in self-disclosure. Naturally, she would feel compelled to say it back to you. However, she did not always feel compelled to do so, because she knew you were saying it for a response and not as an authentic expression of feeling. The narcissist could see through the co-dependent's attempt to control her behavior. The two of you even discussed this dynamic and struggled with how to manage each of your tendencies to fulfill what felt like prescribed roles.

After four and a half years of being together, neither of you could do it anymore. So when she said for the third time, "I don't feel deeply connected to you," you found the strength to be honest with yourself and with her. You didn't feel deeply connected to her either, and had not for a very long time.

The relationship was a necessary mistake. Sure, you lost time; you also lost a lot of money trying to live a lifestyle that was outside of your means; you lost opportunities; and you even lost some friendships. But in the end, you came home, so to speak, to a healthier version of you. You were no longer *Echo* in the story of Narcissus. *Echo* repeats everything back to Narcissus in the hope that Narcissus will see and love her (Whitfield, 1991). It was not her responsibility to love you. It was your responsibility to love yourself first, so that you could build a consummate love with her. As painful as it was to end the relationship, you handed her the keys to her apartment, reclaimed the self-worth you ransomed for the illusion of happiness, and embraced the uncertainty of what the future would hold.

In *Fierce Conversations*, Susan Scott (2002) argues that a couple's conversation indicates the health of the relationship. What you talk about reflects the passion, intimacy, and commitment in the relationship. Altman and Taylor (1973) describe how intimacy decreases when couples do not mutually self-disclose. You both had backed off from sharing anything of import. Many hurts from you both led to the inevitable end, but you came out on the other side grateful for being shown, once again, that relationships need a balance of give and take by both partners.

You now more readily accept that people are imperfect. Maybe author and social worker, Brené Brown (2015), is right when she argues that people are just doing their best. The upside to the codependent self is that she is a nurturer—the giver. The upside to the narcissistic self is that she is willing to put herself first and to "take." As you recounted above, you have played both roles, sometimes in the same relationship.

In an episode of the television program *Inside the Actors' Studio* where host James Lipton (2003) interviewed the creator and cast of the show *Will and Grace,* you recall a question relevant to your relationships and the current story. Lipton asked, "How did you come up with the names of the characters—Will and Grace?" The creator responded by saying he was reading Martin Buber's *I and Thou* (1970). In the book, Buber argues that you must have the *Will* to love and the *Grace* to receive it.

You think back to that dirty floor with the bearskin rug and the giant Huskies. You hear the drum beat and chanting from the shaman. You hear the echo of the words "the Joy, the Joy, the Joy."

Lying on the floor of that shaman's house, you, indeed, found your Joy.

It took 49 years to realize that you, indeed, have played both roles.

You, indeed, are mutually accountable.

You, indeed, must give and take in a healthy relationship.

You, indeed, finally were able to love yourself more than loving the idea of someone else, so as to not cheat either of you from a consummate love.

And you, indeed, are worthy of love, not because of what you do for other people that may bring them *joy*, but simply because you are.

DISCUSSION QUESTIONS

1. After reading Cathy's story, describe aspects of Cathy's behaviors that indicated codependency in her relationships.
2. When and how have you engaged in unhealthy codependent behaviors in a relationship? When and how have you engaged in narcissistic behaviors? How have these behaviors been communicated?
3. What does this story teach us about the role communication plays in insuring a healthy interdependence with a partner versus an unhealthy codependency?
4. Cathy refers several times to Sternberg's (2006) Triangular Theory of Love. In order to have a consummate (enduring) love, you have to passion, intimacy, and commitment. Which of these three essential elements have been missing for you in past relationships?

REFERENCES

Altman, I., & Taylor, D. A. (1973). *Social penetration: The development of interpersonal relationships.* Oxford: Holt, Rinehart, & Winston.

Brown, B. (2015). *Rising strong: The reckoning. The rumble. The revolution.* New York, NY: Spiegel & Grau.

Buber, M. (1970). *I and thou.* New York, NY: Touchstone.

Ford, D. (1998). *The dark side of the light chasers: Reclaiming your power, creativity, brilliance, and dreams.* New York, NY: Riverhead Books.

Lee, J. A. (1988). Love-styles. In R. J. Sternberg & M. L. Barnes (Eds.), *The psychology of love* (pp. 38–67). New Haven, CT: Yale University Press.

LePoire, B. A., Hallett, J. S., & Giles, H. (1998). Codependence: The paradoxical nature of the functional-afflicted relationship. In B. H. Spitzberg & W. R. Cupach (Eds.), *The dark side of close relationships* (pp. 153–176). Mahwah, NJ: Lawrence Erlbaum Associates.

Lipton, J. (Host). (2003, November 16). *Inside the actors studio.* Burbank, CA: Bravo.

Scott, S. (2002). *Fierce conversations: Achieving success at work & in life one conversation at a time.* New York, NY: The Berkley Publishing Group.

Sternberg, R. J. (2006). A duplex theory of love. In R. J. Sternberg & K. Weis (Eds.), *The new psychology of love* (pp. 184–199). New Haven, CT: Yale University Press.

Whitfield, C. (1991). *Co-dependence: Healing the human condition.* Deerfield Beach, FL: Health Communication, Inc.

THINGS I MUST STILL DO

Keith Berry

Just as there are social practices, or ways of performing, I do not need to enact as a gay man (see Chapter 5), there are also things I *must still* do because I occupy this social location. In this chapter, I convey and explore a wide array of "notes" on these ways of relating and being. Many of these necessities relate to issues of stigmatization. I orient to, and organize, the following notes similarly to the approach I used in Chapter 5. However, the content and tone of these notes are quite different.

1. I must still try to come to terms with this truth: there are usually two worlds concerning sexual orientation: a "LGBQ" world and a "straight" world. When it comes to everyday performances, that which is allowable, encouraged and valorized, or prohibited, discouraged, and shamed, the performances are often different depending on the world in which one lives. Human-made assumptions and expectations work to divide the ways "freedom" should (and should not) be lived. Some of these divisions are noticeable, but many of them dwell outside of everyday awareness. I have heard more discussion about these differences in recent years, and that has felt promising. However, much silence still prevails. No advances in terms of civil rights and social justice have occurred that have sufficiently collapsed this divide; a bifurcation that informs life in nearly every way I can imagine psychologically, emotionally, relationally, and economically.

2. I must still tolerate and resist the "post-Ellen" and "post-marriage" social positions concerning LGBQ cultures, identities, and desires that I hear others communicate. Sometimes those others are allies, and sometimes they are LGBQ. These orientations tend to work off the assumption that because the comedian Ellen DeGeneres is "out" as lesbian and liked and successful in her career, and because marriage equality is legal (for now), major problems no longer exist for LGBQ. We should stop complaining and "move on." These positions are similar to "post-race"

mindsets purporting that racism is no longer an issue following the 2018 election of U.S. President Barack Obama. A closer look at social cultural conditions in the U.S. and elsewhere will reveal that these "post" beliefs are factually inaccurate, and harmful. At times they feel rather delusional.

We must not bury our heads in the sand. As my notes here demonstrate, there is *much* more work to do. This labor includes, but is in no way limited to, the violence committed against LGBQ youth, and youth of difference with respect to other aspects of their identity, such as gender expression, in schools (Berry, 2016, 2018).

3. I must still deal with what it feels like to live with a stigmatized social location. Being gay involves being ascribed a "spoiled" identity (Goffman, 1963). My difference renders me abject "other." This "otherness" is a byproduct of homophobia and heteronormativity, and is common and consequential. Stigmatization may not look and mean the same in every moment of my lived experience, nor am I always aware of it *in situ*. Nonetheless, gay stigma is still always already present, looming with its scrutiny, self-righteousness, and pettiness.

Stigmatization motivates people, including me sometimes, still, to perform or manage my impression (Goffman, 1959) in ways that aim to prevent others from detecting and responding unfavorably to my difference. This entails gay "covering" (i.e., toning down, or making less visible or obtrusive, my difference) and gay "passing" (i.e., hiding difference) (Yoshino, 2007). For instance, I have worked to pass and cover as an out gay professor (see Berry, 2012a). The stakes of this cultural labor are diverse for different bodies and beings. For some people, covering and passing are more fleeting and innocuous. For others, this work is a persistent life-saving practice.

People who stigmatize people like me tend to do so in two ways. First, there are the blatant offenders who seem to feel no compunction about directly calling out and judging my being gay, and performing in ways that work against the rights I have, or deserve. The temerity that fuels this oppression stuns me. Second, some stigmatizing practices are not deliberate, or at least ready to awareness of the offenders. This "othering" is less visible and sometimes obvious. For instance, gay stigmatization occurs through microaggressions, or the "brief and commonplace daily verbal, behavioral, or environmental indignities, whether intentional or unintentional, that communicate hostile, derogatory, or negative slights and insults toward members of oppressed groups" (Nadal, 2013, p. 23). This process is most assuredly communicative: communicators create, and survive, stigma as a linguistic, or verbal, and somatic, or embodied, discursive process comprised of micro- (social interaction, relationships) and macro- (media, government) cultural phenomena.

Stigma also has a curious way of staying around, so to speak, and influencing lives in indirect ways that are not necessarily harmful. I am thinking here of identifying and reckoning with one's stigmatization. For instance, I am grateful to be able to recall many experiences when people (e.g., colleagues, strangers) who are aware I am gay do *not* stigmatize me. In these moments, I remember thinking about how wonderful and refreshing it was that a given person was so accepting and progressive. To be sure, these are good moments. However, that I even had these realizations, those prompted by the absence of othering, still indexes and reiterates this aspect of my life as a gay man.

Noting stigma in these layered ways means coming to terms with its discursive nature. Stigma not only addresses but (re)shapes identities, and in ways that complicate vital relational factors, such as autonomy, authenticity, and intimacy.

4. I must still look out for friends, colleagues, and students who are transgender and LGBQ persons of color. These amazing human beings often face a form of marginalization that is vicious and unrelenting. They need and deserve persistent and heartfelt empathy and advocacy.

5. I must still come to terms with the likelihood that setbacks and defeats regarding LGBQ inclusion and equity will always be recurring characters in my life story's plot line. This entails preparing myself to lose rights, such as with the right to marry, or struggling to understand why some people have rights as citizens of the U.S. that I am not allowed to have. Not everyone in my life appears so open to this reality. Allies will sometimes say, "It'll never happen." "It's harder to take away something from people once it's established." "The longer marriage equality is the 'law of the land,' the harder it will be to take away." I appreciate and need these comments. I also accept that my life could end up being radically different in this regard. However, my lived experience as a gay man has historically required me to prepare myself to have things taken away or kept from me. Thus, being gay has meant needing to anticipate loss. I have learned to feel this anticipation on an instinctive level; indeed, I sometimes foreshadow loss and risk feeling as though experience has embedded them in my Being (Heidegger, 1996/1953). Sometimes the anticipation occurs even when there are no clear and pressing signs of imminent losses.

There are additional consequences to orientating to loss in this way. For instance, I have benefited over the past 25 years from reading, learning about, and practicing mindfulness in everyday life. In addition, I first turned to mindfulness as a way to stay well, and alive, when struggling with my sexuality and coming out of the closet. Looking back at past losses, and to prepare myself for losses that will come in the future, shows a distressing way of relating that prevents me from living mindfully "in the moment." In this sense, the practice functions in ways that create the conditions for rumination, and re-living and forecasting pain and suffering. At the same time, this practice also shows self-preparation, self-protection, and self-acceptance.

This plot line creates the conditions for the possibility of feeling unhappiness, skepticism, and rigidity. It is a formidable opponent to even the strongest among us.

6. I must still face the reality in my professional life that I am usually the only gay man, and often LGBQ, in my university department. This sometimes feels lonely, and scary. However, most of the time I do not even notice this absence. Not noticing tends to scare me even more. Have I accepted this reality as inevitable?

7. I must still reconcile counsel from others, including good friends, loved ones, and colleagues, in which they tell me to "rise above" or "ignore" difficult people and experiences. "Kill enemies with kindness," they tell me. The people who tell me this are usually looking out for me. However, sometimes their encouragement over-simplifies issues and entices me to avoid conflict, and that piece of their care does not settle well with me. Avoidance means silence, and in the LGBQ community silence has equaled death. Sometimes I must rage.

8. I must still resist the temptation to let marginalization consume me. Mindfulness practice usually helps me to stay well and sometimes well enough. Still, the constant pursuit of wellness within the context of societal oppression is fatiguing. "Being the warrior" gets old. It would be easy to let marginalization overcome me. I don't plan to let that happen.

9. I must still deal with the likelihood that some people will feel like the notes I convey in this story are "too negative." Some might think I am exaggerating the hardship LGBQ persons encounter. There are readers who may call me "pessimistic" or "bitter," and perhaps they prefer my notes in the story in Chapter 5. Some of these reactions might even come from LGBQ and allies. I feel like these notes are honest and brave, and

necessarily call attention to tough experiences and realities. I may also be understating the severity of the conditions in these notes.

10. I must still come to terms with the realities of objectification. I can figure this out by turning on the television. For instance, watching cable news immerses me in a process of observing commentators who I do not know debating my existence, talking about who they think I am, what they think I want, and what they think I deserve. Many of the conversations I witness stereotype me, sometimes egregiously. Although there are also more positive stories, and more allies, today than in the past, I sometimes wonder: Do the commentators know I'm watching? Do they care?

11. I must still acknowledge that I am more than my stigmatized gay subjectivity. I mean this idea in at least two ways.

First, communicators are interdependent; thus, our subjectivity is always already a matter of (inter)subjectivities (Schrag, 2003). Yet, my Being transcends what others think of me, or how others orient to me because I am gay. In real and material ways, the ways in which others treat me, e.g., their claim to my being "spoiled," need not mean that I orient to myself in those ways. Their ascriptions don't have to become my avowals. In this way, part of this note speaks to issues of boundaries between "selves" and "others," as well as self-ownership.

Second, I am more than my gay social location. Put differently, my sexual self does not encapsulate or essentialize all of my Being. After all, our social locations are comprised of a diverse *range* of different and interrelated dimensions.

I am not including these ideas to suggest there are not times when I feel as though I am *only* my stigmatized subjectivity. Sometimes I internalize the hate and harshness. Stigma is powerful. I include them to note, and show, a critical reflexivity that compels me to look at this issue in circumspect ways.

12. I must still imagine that it would feel wonderful, and comforting, to occupy a social location that allows one to see these notes as "too negative," and not justified, and maybe less negative than they should be.

13. I must still tolerate others' appraisals of the platonic friendships I maintain with some heterosexual men. You see, the closer the bond I share with the straight friend, the more attractive that friend is, and the more visible our closeness is to others, the better the chances are that someone will question whether or not our relationship is truly platonic. Certainly, we must be hiding something. These appraisals might be

funny if they weren't reckless and cruel. For one thing, they implicate me, the gay one, as potentially having ulterior motives. Certainly, the gay friend wants more than friendship. Such stereotypical judgements usually take the form of gossip and rumors; rarely, if ever, are they communicated directly to one of the friends in the friendship. This happens more often than one might imagine. It is also more hurtful than the appraisers might believe. Setting aside the homophobic predatory insinuation, these assumptions diminish the intimacy and love inherent to these friendships.

14. I must still be hyper-vigilant to my physical surroundings. Although my fear and the attending need to be alert when I am in public, especially at night, has significantly diminished over the years, hate crimes, including murder, continue to be perpetrated against LGBQ (and T) persons. As a result, I stay on guard.

15. I must still hope that people will "unlearn" things concerning LGBQ lives. "Unlearning" is a practice in which persons work to confront the limiting assumptions, expectations, and ways of communicating that they have learned over time. Put differently, to "unlearn" means to learn and practice more inclusive and equitable ways of relating and being. This process is, to me, common in most people's lives and with all types of difference. I've experienced it on multiple fronts with respect to LGBQ issues. For instance, coming to terms with my sexuality entailed unlearning internalized homophobia, self-critique, and shame. In addition, when teaching university classes like queer theory, autoethnography, gender and identity, interpersonal communication, and intercultural communication, I assist students in learning and practicing more socially just ways of knowing, being, valuing, and practicing. I find this pedagogy to be rewarding yet also arduous. Additionally, I have been around or affected by many friends' and family members' efforts to unlearn. The extent to which they (and I) unlearn influences the ways in which we can and cannot relate, and, thus, the closeness we share. On all of these fronts, there have been successes and failures, and most successes have come with relapses. Participating has been challenging and at times risky. Folks who confront themselves directly and honestly, perhaps for the first time in their lives, can make hurtful and violent comments. I've witnessed folks who seemed to genuinely want to do better, and often did better, and those who have talked about wanting to unlearn, but in ways that entailed lip service, or efforts to smooth over moments of internal struggle or relational conflict.

16. I must still marvel at the character of the LGBQ community. In spite of all of the challenges and tragedies we have endured and survived, this community is strong and resilient. Even more, it is one of the most gentle and peaceful communities I know.

17. I must still challenge fellow gay or queer men who feel as though it is acceptable and fun to participate in misogynistic communication, especially when it comes to communicating about, or with, lesbians. Such performances are parodies of clichés. They're hurtful and unnecessary. It's time to return to kindness.

18. I must still work to reject and combat social problems, including ageism, body shaming, racism, hegemonic masculinity, and status (HIV) shaming, which are prevalent among some LGBQ, including many gay men. Take, for example, the social media dating and hookup apps, such as Grindr. Problematic discourse pervades these apps:

    - "Stay away, old men … I'm not going to date my father."
    - "No blacks."
    - "No FATS, no FEMS … straight-acting MEN only."
    - "I'm looking for safe sex … *clean* men only."
    - "No HIVs."
    - "Normal and SANE men only."

    It is a curious thing: Most of the gay men I know have been judged and excluded. We know what it feels like to be othered. Yet, so much judgement and exclusion connected to external issues like age, weight, race, etc., still prevails at the expense of sympathy and empathy, and the embracing of difference more generally.

19. When relating with close family members and friends, I still need to relate with them in terms of my personal safety. These folks are no strangers to the news headlines on violence against LGBQ. They know that investigating LGBQ issues is at the center of my work as a proud and out gay academic. In addition, as someone who is committed to phenomenology and autoethnography, I root most of my work in the unique vantage point of my lived experience. In short, my personal and professional lives expose me intimately and vulnerably. As a result, those who are closest to me are often concerned about me, and sometimes they worry about me. Yet, I do not want them to have to worry. Yet again, maybe they are okay with worrying. Perhaps they would not want me to worry about them. Maybe they do not need my reassurance. Maybe my attempts to reassure them that I am okay, as I am inclined to do,

exacerbate their worries. Maybe I am more worried than they are about me. In these ways, our bonds speak to the "knotty" (Laing, 1972) nature of relationships. We are always already intertwined beings

20. When I tell others about the time in my life when I came out to my parents—in the summer of 1996, when I was twenty-five years old (see Berry, 2012b)—many conversation partners look shocked, or they speak to their belief that I came out "late" in life, especially compared to today's standards. I often respond by telling them that there were no concerts, like Lady Gaga's *Monster Ball* or *Born this Way* tour, or television programs, such as *GLEE* or *Will & Grace*, in my youth that encouraged acceptance and created safer places in which children and youth could dwell and feel okay. There were no safe models for LGBQ. Instead, cultural and interpersonal discourse in my youth was comprised of examples of people ridiculing and joking about LGBQ people, lives, and sex. Needing the "right church" or "right woman," society deemed LGBQ persons as abominations, if we were engaged with at all. Marriage equality was not even fathomable. In these ways, as a gay man I must still recognize and remember that even with ongoing social injustices, life is probably better today for people like me than it was in the past.

    Realizing and remembering our progress may not take away the bad realities conveyed in these notes. However, it does give me hope. At times, our progress amazes me.

21. I must still work through the fraught relationship I have between HIV/AIDS and sex with other men. I first learned about HIV/AIDS in the mid-1980s. Back then, the media was the main source for information on the illness. Television taught me AIDS was the "gay cancer." Bigots on television talk shows told me "only faggots got AIDS." Families, including my own, knew very little and were silent about the illness. Schools did not teach me anything on the issue. In these ways, the silence in relational and cultural discourse was deafening. In turn, then U.S. President Ronald Reagan fueled this toxic culture by remaining silent about the illness, all the while tens of thousands of gay souls were dying from it. Research on the illness was minimal. Meanwhile, a lack of public awareness and education on the topic motivated widespread public fear, and panic. I remember the terrible ways in which his public school system, and the media, spotlighted the story of Ryan White, the teen in Indiana who lived with the disease, and was banned from attending his school, out of fear he would infect others. Little reassurance and hope existed in terms of HIV/AIDS when I grew up,

creating a dismal outlook in terms of what it might mean for LGBQ persons to thrive in their lives.

This outlook, in turn, created a bleak background story that guided my life when I was a young gay man. The death and destruction from AIDS in my earlier life still shapes the ways in which I constitute my lived experience with other men, especially in terms of having sex with them. For instance, when I first started to experiment sexually with other men in the early 1990s, as an undergraduate college student, even the lightest form of sex, like giving or receiving oral sex or hand jobs, led me to feel *certain* I would then contract the illness and soon die. In the mid-late 1990s, I "relaxed" somewhat when having sex with my first committed and long-time boyfriend, Robert. However, even then my paranoia continued. I remember intense arguments he and I had related to sex and his body. Every so often when we were naked together, I would notice a notable mark on his skin. It was a birthmark, but I took it to be a sign of Kaposi sarcoma, the infamous sores I first learned about while trying to watch the film *Philadelphia*. Understandably, my panic led Robert to panic. (The prospect of deadly illness can be a real mood killer.) I recall years later, in the early 2000s during my doctoral program, attempting to have penetrative sex with a man who was thin to the point that I could feel his hip bones and ribs. Although I believed him when he disclosed his HIV-negative status to me, and even though I was ready to use a condom when penetrating him, I could not forget the thought that his boniness was in my fears a sign of his wasting from the complications of HIV/AIDS (Fox, 2007).

My comfort level and ability to have sex with other men, over time, greatly improved with advances in medication that told us that HIV was a treatable condition. Improvement also came as I continued to educate myself on the illness, and as public awareness came to be more informed about the risks that do and do not exist. However, I do not know an existence that does not, at least in part, link my ability to have sex with my health and wellness. I'm sure the same goes for people other than gay men. Sex is one of the most beautiful parts of life I know, and I enjoy meaningful and even exciting sexual activities and relationships today. Still, the potential of acquiring HIV is always present in some way.

22. I must still work to accept the ways in which Pride parades and festivals have turned into extended opportunities for politicians to campaign and businesses (e.g., bars) to pedal their products (usually liquor). This work also entails dealing with the ways in which many progressive,

cis-gendered and (presumably) heterosexual people attend the parades because it is a "great party." I witness so many people today who do not realize the original purpose for these parades: to participate in a political march and protest. The Pride parade is a great party. Actually, it's FABULOUS. Yet, it is always necessarily a march for our civil rights.

23. I must still remind myself that planning for my future is something I need to do. Until I was in my thirties, well after I came out of the closet, I never thought about myself in terms of a long-term future for which I had to plan. Perhaps this absence stems from the outlook I conveyed above regarding HIV/AIDS, because I did not think I would last to be a senior citizen. Or maybe it's due to the heteronormative model that continues to shape and often govern lived experience in the U.S. today. There is no model of the LGBQ senior, at least not one widely conveyed and explored. Regardless of the reason, this absence of a LGBQ senior story is intriguing. I am only beginning to reflect on this note, but it feels important enough to include as a placeholder until I learn more (see Goltz, 2009, 2011).

24. I still need to make lists of things I must still do, lists of things entailing hardship and relational and cultural work needing to be done, because I am gay.

***

The above notes illustrate the social practices and ways of being that are still required of me as a gay man. Similar to Chapter 5, I believe the notes in this chapter can be valuable on their own. Thus, I offer only two reflections to end this chapter.

First, as with Chapter 5, while the ideas I convey here are resonant with my lived experience, I would be shocked if readers cannot identify, at least in part, with many if not all of these ideas. In addition, having the things that lesbians, bisexuals, and transgender folks must still do listed in note form is vital. I suspect that we would find many similarities between our lists, as well as significant differences that call for our consideration.

Second, I do not end this chapter with the same uncertainty about how to move forward from/with this work. The needs demonstrated in this list feel more vital, and the stakes in many ways feel grave. We must identify, acknowledge, and celebrate the progress made to date for gay men, and LGBQ in general. In some situations, that progress has been unexpectedly groundbreaking. At the same time, we must also move forward by fighting for rights we need and deserve.

May we all be energized, well, and successful in the process.

DISCUSSION QUESTIONS

1. What do these notes lead you to think and feel about what it means to be LGBQ? What have you learned from the notes?
2. What personal connections do you have with these notes?
3. What different notes would you add to this list?
4. In terms of your sexuality, what must you still do?
5. What do these notes lead you to think, or feel, about the power of communication (e.g., relational communication, mass communication) in terms of LGBQ identity? In terms of diversity, inclusion, and equity?

REFERENCES

Berry, K. (2012a). (Un)covering the gay interculturalist. In N. Bardhan & M. P. Orbe (Eds.), *Identity research and communication: Intercultural reflections and future directions* (pp. 223–237). Lanham, MD: Lexington Books.

Berry, K. (2012b). Reconciling the relational echoes of addiction: Holding on. *Qualitative Inquiry, 18*, 134–143. https://doi.org/10.1177/1077800411429088

Berry, K. (2016). *Bullied: Tales of torment, identity, and youth.* New York, NY: Routledge.

Berry, K. (2018). LGBT bullying in schools: A troubling relational story. *Communication Education, 67*, 502–513. https://doi.org/10.1080/03634523.2018.1506137

Fox, R. (2007). Skinny bones #126-774-835-29: Thin gay bodies signifying a modern plague. *Text and Performance Quarterly, 27*, 3–19. https://doi.org/10.1080/10462930601045956

Goffman, E. (1959). *The presentation of self in everyday life.* New York, NY: Anchor Books.

Goffman, E. (1963). *Stigma: Notes on the management of spoiled identity.* Englewood Cliffs, NJ: Prentice-Hall.

Heidegger, M. (1996/1953). *Being and time* (J. Stambaugh, Trans.). Albany, NY: State University of New York Press.

Goltz, D. B. (2009). *Queer temporalities in gay male representation: Tragedy, normativity, and futurity.* New York, NY: Routledge.

Goltz, D. B. (2011). *Our legacies: Writings from Chicago's older gay men.* Bloomington, IN: iUniverse.

Laing, R. D. (1972). *Knots.* New York, NY: Vintage.

Nadal, K. L. (2013). *That's so gay! Microaggressions and the lesbian, gay, bisexual, and transgender community.* Washington, DC: American Psychological Association.

Schrag, C. O. (2003). *Communicative practice and the space of subjectivity.* West Lafayette, IN: Purdue University Press.

Yoshino, K. (2006). *Covering: The hidden assault on our civil rights.* New York, NY: Random House.

REFRAIN

Catherine M. Gillotti

Dear Cathy,

You are 31 years old and about to come out to yourself, and I am you 20 years in the future reaching back in time to let you know that you will be okay. You have been through a lot in the last four years: you survived a white water rafting accident; earned your doctorate and 3rd degree brown belt in Kenpo Karate simultaneously; moved from Kentucky to Indiana to start your first full-time job; looked for other jobs in the last two years, and actually turned down two job offers; and now you are coming out. I know your head is swimming in the uncertainty of it all. I know you question every decision. I know you are terrified that the family is going to disown you once they find out you are gay. I know you "worry for your mortal soul" as your mother said. Looking back now, I wish I could erase that uncertainty, pain, confusion, and doubt you're feeling. You made all the right decisions, even if things would have turned out differently for you 20 years in the future had you accepted one of the jobs in the Carolinas, or if you decided to bury your authentic self by living as everyone expected you to live. This meant being married to a man and having children.

Like you do now, in the future, you will still believe that things happen for a reason. There was a reason you almost drowned four years ago. That was a profound experience that still strongly influences the way you move through life. It is still fresh for you at the age of 31, especially given all of the difficulties you are experiencing with coming out and trying to achieve tenure and promotion at Purdue University Northwest. Right now you are living in constant cognitive dissonance as you struggle between the Catholic values you were raised with and the undeniable self-knowledge of who you are. You are not quite ready to believe in yourself, and so I am here to assure you and to explain why it is so important that you stay the course, follow your heart, and accept and love yourself.

What your heart tells you now is that you are terrified to come out, but you also know you cannot return to denying this part of yourself. Many loving

© KONINKLIJKE BRILL NV, LEIDEN, 2020 | DOI:10.1163/9789004418790_016

friends surround you. It is okay to lean on them. Your graduate student and friend, Keith Berry, will become a brother of choice. His loyalty and love are unwavering and will continue in the future. He jokes that you chaired his graduate committee and he chaired your coming out.

Your colleagues and friends, Theresa and Jane, will give you very important advice and support along the way. You may not always want to hear what they have to say, but trust yourself to listen to their words and accept their loving support. There will be one conversation in particular where you grapple with the question of your sexual identity. Theresa will tell you that any of us can sleep with anyone else. The question is, "Who do you want to share your life with?" What a powerful moment that will be when you hear those words, and fully begin to grasp the complex fluidity of sexual orientation and identity.

You will also meet two influential priests who will help you begin to let go of the guilt that suffocates you at the moment. One will tell you "people judge, Jesus doesn't." Another will liberate you from the self-imposed prison where you now reside by stating, "God is the author of your heart, and you give back to God by being who He made you to be" (see Chapter 7). Hearing those words from this priest in the sacrament of reconciliation will be one of your closest moments to God.

All of the nightmares will dissipate, and the hours you spend ruminating about throwing yourself from your third floor apartment balcony, to alleviate your pain and suffering once and for all, will seem like wasted time and energy. We both know that you are not seriously considering suicide. You were spared from drowning in the rafting trip for a reason, and it surely wasn't to take your life four years later because you are gay.

You also will meet an international student from Chile named Pedro, a man who has lived through many hardships. He is a survivor, evidenced from the time he escaped Chile to the point where he had to sell his body in prostitution to live and go to school here. You will experience the loss of a romantic relationship and he will comfort you by saying, "Deja que el tiempo, te de la repuesta" ["Give it to time and time will give you the answer"]. Twenty years later, the business card that he wrote the phrase on still sits on your dresser as a constant reminder that time is an unwavering teacher and healer. Along with other words of wisdom, it will become your refrain; those repeated phrases of comfort.

The Buddhists say that all of life is suffering, and although it is difficult for you to fathom right now, it will only be years later that you will begin to understand how important your current suffering is to who you will become.

It will fortify you for what lies ahead. You will fall in and out of love multiple times, and sometimes find yourself without hope that true love will find you. Because you are coming out at 31, you feel an urgency to find "the one," fearing that you may already have missed your opportunity for love. Unfortunately, this fear motivates you to treat dating like a profession in which goals are set, sometimes met and sometimes not, but you dust yourself off and get back to work finding love. Your friends will notice your *need* to be in a relationship, and will tease you about how you disappear when you get a new girlfriend. What they do not understand is that you are on a quest to find romantic love, and if that means you have to date long-distance you will and do multiple times. In time you will come to realize what really matters, where to put your energy, and how you should share your love and generosity with others and yourself.

January 2016 will mark the beginning of a heart-breaking and treacherous time. The year will be fraught with challenges that at 31 years old you cannot imagine. You will end a four-and-a-half-year relationship; your dad will be assaulted and nearly die from the complications of the attack; and Steve, one of your older brothers, will die from an unexpected diagnosis of Stage IV colon and liver cancer. Fourteen months later, your dad will die of congestive heart failure. Why do I tell this to you? Will it not change the future if you know at 31 that the people you hold most dear are suffering in immeasurable and unthinkable ways? I hope it does. I hope that you will make some different choices about what you value and how you live. If you knew at 31 that you only had 18 years left with your brother, you would have spent more time with him, and all of your family.

Now you revel in the joy of your nephew, Thomas, and your niece, Katie. You have yet to meet the other two beautiful nieces and nephew in your life. Thomas will have a sister named Christina. Katie will have a sister, Maria, and a brother, Dominic. These children will be the light of your life—the kids that you never will have, not that you really want children of your own.

The preciousness of their lives will take on more meaning with each of your passing years. You will love them wholeheartedly (Brown, 2010) like no other humans because while they technically are your brothers' children, you will love them as if they were your own. When Steve dies, your faith will be shaken to its core. The grief will suffocate you. You will miss his sense of humor, his intellect, and pragmatic nature, and even his lovable irritableness. Most of all, you will grieve the loss of his wisdom and kindness. Steve was a great sounding board. He was instrumental in you pursuing your doctorate. You know you can count on him. It will be his and your sister-in-law, Cindy's, love and support during your coming out that will be the lifeline you need to know that, despite your fear of losing your family because of your sexual identity, *it will never happen*. Steve and Cindy's unshakeable support will be the foreshadowing of all your family's support in years to come.

However, at 31 you think that the entire world revolves around your coming out. As a result, you miss other important moments and opportunities to bear witness to friends' and family's joy and pain. You are often in a self-absorbed place, understandably, because you think you might die if you speak your truth. That fear will pass. Unfortunately, your focus will stay on yourself for a number of years as you move from one relationship to another in the endless pursuit of romantic love.

I know you feel the urgency now. I know you know that our time on this earth is temporary. You are still swimming in the security of your near-death experience. You know there is an afterlife. You know that grandma and grandpa are waiting for you on the other side. You sometimes wish you had died in that river, so that you could be spared all of the pain you are experiencing now as you grapple with reconciling what feels like irreconcilable parts of yourself. How can you be Catholic, Jerry and Winnie's kid, *and gay*? Many sleepless nights are ahead of you, and I wish I could tell you that all of that energy and worry are a waste. I wish I could reach back through time and give you the gift of self-love that you will spend the better part of the next 20 years chasing. I wish I could convince you to "just relax, breathe and be."

Those were the words Steve said to you the night you went to dinner with him at a local pub when you decided to pursue your doctorate. When the subject of pursuing the Ph.D. came up, mom asked you if you wanted to be a pauper for another four years. Dad seemed focused on the job offer you had, but was less explicit than mom about his feelings regarding what you should do. Mike was living in Pittsburg and focused on his career. It was Steve who talked to you about what would end up being one of the most important decisions of your life. You remember it well. He said, "Okay, Cathy. Why don't you go to the University of Kentucky for a year, and if you don't like it—quit? It is not like they can take your master's degree away from you. You simply get a job then."

You knew Steve was right about the Ph.D., and you trusted his judgment, which is why in a few weeks you will reach out to him and tell him you are gay. He is going to feel responsible for your sexual orientation at first, as mom did, but he just wants you to be happy. "Mike and I were too hard on you Cathy" is what he initially will say, indicating his perceived culpability in the matter. He is referring to all the rough housing, teasing, and treating you like the tomboy you were growing up. Similarly, mom will think she is responsible because she somehow did not think she socialized you to be feminine enough, mistakenly conflating gender and sexuality. Conversely, dad will think it is everyone else's fault, such as going dancing with Keith at Roscoe's, a favorite gay bar in Chicago.

Eventually all of your family members will come to terms with your sexual orientation and realize that no one controls anyone else's sexual identity. You punctuate this point when you say to them, "I hate to break it to you all, but you don't have that much power. Can anyone you know control your sexual orientation?" Steve will say, "just be Cathy … just be."

You are blessed to have such a loving family, albeit flawed like everyone else's. It may have been Steve who convinced you to pursue your doctorate, but Mike helped as well. It was Mike who sent you money one month when you are running short of cash. Like Steve, he is a big brother you could count on at all times. It was Mike and your sister-in-law, Paula, and their kids, Thomas and Christina, who years later will host you, your partner, and her daughter, entertaining you with a trip to a museum and dinner over a holiday weekend. Also, as you know, once you made the decision to enter a doctoral program, your entire family was behind you. You simply have yourself convinced that these same people are going to abandon you now. They are not.

Steve and dad are both gone now and not a day passes that you do not think of them. At 31, you think about your family, but then your focus shifts to your current anxiety regarding your existential crisis. You think of them only in terms of what they will think about you once you come out. Oh, how I wish I could get you to let all of that go, and to cherish each moment like you did when you emerged from those raging rapids and took your first breath after nearly drowning. It was hard to breathe at first—you remember? Life was almost gone. You were in shock and disbelief. There was even a sadness that overtook you at the thought of what you missed by not dying. You walked around for weeks feeling certain you were not going to die; relieved you did not die and simultaneously feeling like you missed out by not dying. But it is 1998 and while progress has been made, there is a pervasive undercurrent of homophobia still lurking beneath the surface of society, which makes it hard to feel okay about your identity.

It was not your time to die at 28. It is not your time now at 31, no matter how grave things seem to be regarding your sexual identity. Trust that in time, it will be just another part of who you are. At the moment it feels like the only part of your identity that matters, but you will come to see that if our identities were like stained glass windows reflecting the light of our lives, your sexual identity is merely one tiny section of what makes you uniquely you. Also like stained glass, perspective is everything. Up close, we focus on one section, but from a distance we can see the entire picture. In spite of the comforting words the priest told you in the confessional about God being the author of your heart, you are afraid that you will lose your church and your faith in God by being authentic. I wish you knew now that quite the opposite happens. Steve's death propels you into a deeply spiritual journey where you spend time thinking about life's big questions, and how you fit into the answers. You still don't have all the answers, but you are more comfortable with the uncertainty of the journey.

There are and will be very important repeated lessons that you will carry with you over the next 20 years, and to the end of your days when it is time to be reunited with Steve, dad and all of those you loved who have passed. These phrases of consolation—repeated lessons and chorused refrains of love from life's teachers—will offer you comfort in the difficult times.

God is the author of your heart and you give back to God by being who He made you to be.

People judge, Jesus doesn't.

Deja que el tiempo, te da la repuesta. [Give it to time, and time will give you the answer.]

So, close your eyes Cathy, breathe deeply and just be. Just be.

Love always, Cathy

DISCUSSION QUESTIONS

1. What life lessons would you share with your younger self?
2. Of Cathy's refrains, which spoke to you the most and why?
3. What are the refrains that you carry from your life's teachers?

REFERENCE

Brown, B. (2010). *The gifts of imperfection: Let go of who you think you're supposed to be and embrace who you are.* Center City, MN: Hazelden.

RESILIENT YOU

Keith Berry

You are living in a time when school bullying is an omnipresent societal problem that shapes the lives of youth, especially youth of difference. Cultural discourse on bullying is commonplace. News anchors routinely convey dramatic stories about the latest youth who were bullied at school. Also, you hear others who are around you, those whom you know and are strangers to you, interacting about/through bullying issues. These conversations are often deeply emotional ones. Indeed, the corrosive impact bullying has on youth's well-being has rendered this issue a topic *du jour* in communication (Berry, 2016). As a result, it is rare for many days in your lived experience to pass you by when don't hear stories about harsh violence committed against yet another vulnerable body and being.

Your engagement over time with this discourse and these interactions has exposed you to the ways in which bullying is, at least in part, a problem concerning youth identity. A cast of characters comprises the bullying storyline and includes "bullies," "victims," "bystanders," "parents," and "teachers," just to name a few. In addition, attributes assigned to these characters and their actions, especially concerning those who are victimized through bullying, matter to the stories you're hearing and helping to co-construct. "Jocks bullied him because he is gay." "Choir kids bullied her because she stutters." "Cheerleaders bullied her because of the way she looks." These and other appraisals are uttered regularly and often without equivocation, as if they represent unquestionable certainties. In these ways, bullying discourse, much like bullying itself, is infused with loaded labels pertaining to youth's social location or subjectivity.

Your research and teaching at the intersections of relational communication and cultural identity, inquiry that you primarily conduct by using autoethnography, ethnography, and phenomenology, lead you to be keenly interested in the ways this communication frames the youth who are bullied, primarily how it renders them "victims." You notice mediated and interpersonal accounts about bullying most often stressing the pain and

© TAYLOR & FRANCIS, 2019 | DOI:10.1163/9789004418790_17

suffering they endure. They demonstrate how bullying changes youth, and these changes are usually unwanted and harmful. Much of your research and writing on bullying in which you explain this subset of peer aggression as a problem that is decidedly communicative, and rooted in formative processes of identity negotiation (Berry, 2016), has focused on the damaging role bullying plays in constituting and re-constituting (i.e., making and remaking) youth into victimized beings. You have learned that this emphasis is commonplace in much of the research literature you've read on bullying. But this reliance on prioritizing the negative doesn't surprise you. After all, bullying is a concrete instantiation of unethical and socially unjust communication, which, in turn, mindlessly harms youth who are less able to defend themselves. You want your work to help prevent bullying, and shine a light on how destructive this problem really is to youth's ability to live well—openly, freely, and mindfully in the moment.

At the same time your research and teaching has also led you to identify bullying as a cultural issue that, much like cultural issues generally, is performed through canonical storylines (see Berry, 2016; Berry & Adams, 2016). With your current story here in mind, you believe the emphasis on the negative dimensions to bullying represents a *normative* storyline that most often directs people's attention to certain factors when orienting to bullying and bullying prevention, and away from other possible factors. Consequently, you wonder what alternate social locations are being taken for granted through this singular emphasis on harm and the negative, more generally. While this normative orientation, indeed, serves to reveal the darkness that feels, to you, to be inseparable from bullying, your life and work have taught you that it also concomitantly *conceals alternate stories* about what it looks like and means to perform as bullying victims, including stories that speak to more positive and affirming factors of bullying, factors that exist in tandem with youth pain and suffering. With this in heart, you decide to write a chapter that will explore moments of resilience, and even happiness and joy that were part of your experiences with being bullied in your youth. You convey this story because you hope to expand the storyline concerning bullying, communication, and identity, by advocating a re-imagination of the multiple selves possible, and often necessary, in experiencing and enduring bullying. You convey this story because you have come to believe the bullying story is far more complex and layered than many people, including you, sometimes suggest.

***

You were bullied in middle school and high school (see Berry, 2016) in ways that taught you at an early age that identity labels, and identity generally, matter a great deal to you and others. Other kids (boys, mainly) bullied you based on your physical appearance. You were a chubby boy off and on during your youth. Boys honed in on your weight and didn't often miss a chance to use words against you like "blubbo-lard," "fat ass," and other variations of fattist-based humor and aggression. In addition, you moved through the world with a graceful gait; you were more gentle and not as physical than most of the other boys you knew. Also, you spoke with an equally graceful and gentle voice, softer than most of the other boys. These ways of being provided boys with fodder to use when bullying you. To them you were a "fairy," or at the very least you were not "tough." Physical attacks sometimes accompanied the boys' verbal attacks. Although these boys never beat you up in ways that left you black and blue or at the hospital, as they did to other kids like you, they did occasionally find enjoyment in pushing you against lockers, and shoving you in the hallways. Even more, many boys loved to intimidate you with the *threat* of violence. Their promise of hurting you felt real and scary, leading you to be vigilant of your surroundings, and to avoid them at all costs.

To add dis-ease and an ongoing sense of confusion to your experiences with this bullying, you often felt "different" as a kid. These feelings exacerbated your experiences with being bullied, as well made you an attractive target to boys who bullied you. You were different, but you didn't know why you had those thoughts and feelings, and you had a hard time talking through those feelings with parents and friends. Your parents tried valiantly to help you reconcile these feelings. Yet, it wouldn't be until you were in your early twenties when you would realize feeling and being "different" primarily related to being a gay boy, and then a gay teenager, in a heteronormative world that successfully thwarted, to put it gently, your being able to acknowledge and be open and proud of who you are and love. In these ways, your youth in bullying was further confounded by your being in the contested and complicated space of the "closet" (Adams, 2011), a most problematic, even though hidden, dimension to your story.

Yet, while your youth was filled with bullying that at times harmed you, and that produced unwanted and impactful feelings of dis-ease, you also lived with a backstory, so to speak, that was filled with various ways of performing that tended to keep you well, or at least well enough. These were ways of relating, largely with yourself, and being as a boy that you performed outside of the spotlight of the kids at school, and in some cases, even your family.

In this sense, you lived within a "secret apprenticeship" (Garfinkel, 1967), exploring the possibilities for performing the graceful, gentler, and softer you; that is, the you who was abject to others, but instinctive and fluid. It was through this backstage apprenticeship that you learned to be *the resilient you*.

The resilient you came to life when you performed as teacher for some of your friends, boys and girls, in your neighborhood. Your mother, aunt, and one of your grandmothers were teachers, so they were partially responsible for inspiring these performances. However, there was more to these enactments, particularly in terms of the sort of relating with others they entailed. For instance, you often would try to teach Spanish to your friends, even though you were only in your first year of Spanish class in middle school. You put these kids in a circle and had them recite certain Spanish words and phrases: "Hola." "Adios." "Me llamo es … (fill in the blank with their name)." "Me gusta limonada." You adored how they would mimic how you acted and the authority and power demonstrated therein; how you had to correct them from time to time, and their openness to your feedback; how you were helping them to practice a language different than English, one that would help you and them enter into a different and special world; and how their respect for your teaching, even if they didn't really mean it, made you feel respected and like a teacher, someone who had something to give to others, something for which they felt appreciative and happy. As teacher, you were embraced, even if your students didn't like the homework you gave them.

The resilient you also came to life at home and in the washroom. There, under the premise of your needing to urinate, you would sometimes experiment with your mother's makeup. Once you securely locked both of the washroom doors behind you, double checking to make sure they were truly locked, so as to be confident you would not be detected by others, you would play with your favorites—her foundation, powder, and sometimes lipstick. You would start by applying the base and then adding some powder. You didn't hold back either. You figured if you were going to use it, you wanted to really see what it would feel and look like. When you did try lipstick, you usually only applied it to one lip. That way you could see what it looked like on your face without taking things too far. Overall, when playing with her makeup, you felt pretty and fancy. Your skin looked soft and your lips shiny. You felt sophisticated. You loved the way it felt on your skin, too. Restrictive gender roles and rules outside of this room kept you from ever telling someone about how makeup was prevalent within your apprenticeship process. Still, performing in this way allowed you to free yourself, even if just for a few secretive minutes, from paralyzing and exclusionary ways of performing "boy" that dominated your life outside of the apprenticeship and in everyday life. You never felt like you were a girl, and you don't look back at yourself today and wonder if you were transgender. Nonetheless, you felt more comfortable doing these things to/with your body than you did attempting to do the things boys and men needed to do, such as playing sports and hitting on girls.

Yet also, the resilient you came to life when you took a shower each night after dinner. There, you would pretend you were the announcer voice for television commercials. As you stood in the shower, you read the flowery language on the bottle of your mom's soap. Hidden by the loud sounds of the shower water hitting the plastic shower walls, you announced boldly, "This soap offers daily silkiness. It's for noticeably soft skin and contains white peach and orange blossoms. Revel in the feeling of irresistibly soft skin that invites the touch. Silkiness. Elegance. Delicateness. This soap is for you!" There, in the shower you felt more open to utter the consonant "s" in prolonged and exaggerated ways (i.e., effeminate and non-real-boy-like), and to use fabulous words like "silky" "elegance," and "delicateness." There, in the shower with your exposed and unguarded chubby body you performed these words repeatedly, each time trying to accentuate a different letter or word, and with tones that you *wanted to use* rather than those you had to keep from using out of fear of being policed for gender violations. Your parents would at times ask why you were taking such long showers, sometimes expressing their concern about wasting water. However, you showered un-phased. To you the shower performance allowed for a glorious safe space that, even if just for a part of the day, you felt like you could be playful and not have to be vigilant of how you sounded or looked. In that space, you felt free and cleansed from the dirt that you'd accumulated at school that day. You felt free.

The resilient you came to life most frequently when you were in bed each night trying to fall asleep. Then you listened to your favorite songs on cassette tapes, which you played on the double cassette boom-box you received for Christmas one year, a gift that was formative in multiple ways in your gender training (see Berry, 2013, 2016). This musical bedtime resilience entailed your visualization—vivid and detailed imagination work—of you performing on stage. One of your favorite settings had you performing as one of the backup dancers during a concert of The Pointer Sisters, a hit R&B singing group of the 1980s. On stage you knew every word to their songs— "Jump for My Love" and "I'm So Excited" being two of your favorites. You would imagine yourself on stage with the sisters. Although you didn't wear a dress like they would wear in their music videos, you sang every note with them, and moved seductively underneath the covers, mimicking how they moved on stage. You sang through the songs, blasting out with excitement the words to the songs' choruses, sometimes to the point your parents would call into your room and ask you to keep your volume down.

Although the Pointer Sisters were your most common inspirations, you also performed with other singers and groups, including Culture Club, Michael Jackson, and Huey Lewis and the News. Whichever song you sang, you felt happy, and sometimes joyously so, to be able to escape into the imaginative world of these musical performances. During those visualizations you were someone who others in your life would barely be able to recognize, but someone you who you loved to be.

While these practices helped to sustain you, creative visualization also had a partner technique that you developed and came to rely on: visualizing hardship while in bed. You would often visualize yourself in conflict situations in which you lost, ruminating about what you said that would lead to others' harsh attacks. Later in college, you would also visualize yourself "coming out" as gay to the people who were closest to you, only to be scorned for doing so, and at times, jettisoned from their lives. To be sure, imaginations have limits and, while positive in some ways, can take a deep toll in other ways.

***

The above four ways of performing the resilient you may not have allowed you to forget about being bullied, or your dis-ease from feelings of difference generally. But they were definitive moments of your bullying story that demonstrated you being well, thriving, and in some cases feeling at peace and joyful. They were important to your story, too. Granted, you did not feel comfortable enough to share these performances with others, save for your times as a teacher. Also, moments of dis-ease often overshadowed these resilient moments. After all, you were quite good at visualizing the pain and suffering you felt was inevitable to your being rejected for being yourself. Regardless, the resilient you showed creative and resourceful performances of selves that conditioned your existence in real ways that mattered. As such, they demonstrate that multiple modes of being can appear within bullying and its aftermath, not only the ones that entail harm and damage, and, thus, further underscore the complexities of bullying and its impact on youth identity and well-being. As Schrag (1997) writes on the issue of subjectivity,

[W]e are dealing not with a single unitary, sharply defined portrait, but rather with a portrait that is itself curiously diversified. What thus appears to be at issue is a multiplicity of profiles and perspectives through which the human self moves and is able to come into view. (p. 1)

Thus, telling your story here makes you think about the possibilities for learning about, and responding to bullying, and for "doing" bullying research and teaching, that can come into being if others are willing to locate and reflect on similar moments.

You also think about how performances of the resilient you most often occurred in more isolating ways. Save for moments of teaching Spanish to friends, these ways of performing and staying well enough occurred outside of face-to-face interaction. Now it is important to mark that moments of being by yourself are not divorced from the influence and presence of others. Gergen (2009) writes,

[V]irtually all intelligible action is born, sustained, and/or extinguished within the ongoing process of relationship. From this standpoint, there is no isolated self or fully private experience. Rather, we exist in a world of co-constitution. We are always already emerging from relationship; we cannot step out of relationship; even in our most private moments we are never alone. (p. xv)

However, the deep and inevitable intertwinement of human lives doesn't change the fact that you performed these resilient identity practices outside of the presence of others. In the here-and-now this leads you to ask: what would have happened if you made your performative choices more public? For instance, how would the makeup play have been received by others? If negatively, how would that response further shape the dis-ease you felt? Were the shower and makeup practices better left as performances for one, enactments whose main audience was your self-as-other? While you don't regret a single thing about those performances this many years later, you do take pause concerning the ways you felt it necessary to keep these things secret. You cringe when remembering the need for you as a young boy to have to be so vigilant in your apprenticeship. You wonder how life might have been different throughout your youth, how life might be different now, had you felt allowed and free to be open.

You end this story with a mindful awareness and caution about the complexities involved with advocating a more multilayered orientation to the identit*ies* inherent to, and performed within, bullying. Moving forward with this position—that multiple possible selves are present, influential, and need to be talked about concerning bullying, not just the ones speaking to the pain and suffering of being victimized—matters a great deal. The extent to which you emphasize resilience risks de-emphasizing and disregarding the pain and suffering intrinsically connected to, and accentuated by, bullying. In turn, your doing so risks disconfirming the vulnerable youth of difference being bullied. And yet, by circumspectly exploring the identities of bullying, and, thus, by resisting singular and static portrayals of the victims of bullying, as well as all characters who are involved in this corrosive problem (e.g., those who bully, educators), you stay honest to the communicative and constitutive nature to bullying practices, one that assumes bullying, much like communication, to be contextual, contingent, and subject to change and variation.

Whichever ways you use to move forward with understanding bullying's hold on vulnerable youth, and the consequential ways you talk about this problem, you still understand that bullying typically not only involves hardship, but also the admirable task (and achievement!) of having found your way resiliently through harmful interactions and relationships, as well the role of secret performances in helping youth to survive.

DISCUSSION QUESTIONS

1. What were your experiences like with being bullied or bullying someone else in your youth? As an adult? In what ways were you or others resilient? Was it difficult for you or others to be resilient?
2. Thinking of Keith's techniques, what practices did you enact to protect yourself and stay well?
3. This story demonstrates the ways in which people's identities are multilayered. What identities do you perform?

ACKNOWLEDGMENT

This chapter originally appeared as Keith Berry, Voices for visibility: The resilient you, in *The Routledge Handbook of Communication and Bullying* (Routledge, 2019). Reprinted here with permission (permission conveyed through Copyright Clearance Center, Inc.).

REFERENCES

Adams, T. E. (2011). *Narrating the closet: An autoethnography on same-sex attraction.* New York, NY: Routledge.

Berry, K. (2013). Spinning autoethnographic reflexivity, cultural critique, and negotiating selves. In S. Holman Jones, T. E. Adams, & C. Ellis (Eds.), *The handbook of autoethnography* (pp. 209–227). Walnut Creek, CA: Left Coast Press.

Berry, K. (2016). *Bullied: Tales of torment, identity, and youth.* New York, NY: Routledge.

Berry, K., & Adams, T. E. (2016). Family bullies. *Journal of Family Communication, 16,* 51–63. https://doi.org/10.1080/15267431.2015.1111217

Garfinkel, H. (1967). *Studies in ethnomethodology.* Englewood Cliffs, NJ: Prentice-Hall.

Gergen, K. J. (2009). *Relational being: Beyond self and community.* New York, NY: Oxford.

Schrag, C. O. (1997). *The self after postmodernity.* New Haven, CT: Yale University Press.

ESTRANGEMENT ⇔ PRIDE ⇔ FORGIVENESS

Tony E. Adams

I opened my first book, *Narrating the Closet*, by cataloguing difficulties queer persons and persons with same-gender/sex attraction could experience (Adams, 2011, pp. 21–27). I described how friend and familial relationships could be strained or shattered solely by the disclosure of their attraction, and how once-loving others could emotionally and physically harm queer persons, hurt them with their words and actions, and maybe even require them to seek reparative/conversion/ex-gay therapy. I described mundane moments of homophobia and heterosexism, particularly everyday assumptions and ascriptions of heterosexuality placed on queer people, as well as violent hate crimes that queer persons could incur. I described ways queer persons might deal with the residue of hateful discourse, possibly through a lack of self-care, estrangement, or suicide. I noted how queer persons not only have to account for their attractions, but also why they supposedly betrayed others by hiding these attractions for months, years, and decades.

Writing this chapter nearly a decade later, I can still chart many of these same difficulties. Many governments continue to advocate policies and practices that disregard or criminalize same-sex/gender attraction. Within the United States, there are continued debates about whether same-sex marriage is necessary, as well as an ever-present threat of same-sex marriage disappearing with future Supreme Court rulings. In 2016, the Pulse Nightclub massacre happened, the deadliest attack on queer persons in the United States (see Alexander & Weems, 2017). Some businesses refuse queer customers, and reparative/conversion/ex-gay therapy is still allowed in many states and nations. There are suicides, worries about HIV, and the continued mundane use of homophobic language such as "that's so gay," "no homo," and "butthurt." A quick scan of comments on queer-related YouTube videos includes references to same-sex/gender attraction as being sinful, parents preferring heterosexual children more than queer children, and sentiments that queer people should die. Some queer people still fear disclosing their

© KONINKLIJKE BRILL NV, LEIDEN, 2020 | DOI:10.1163/9789004418790_018

attractions, and in many locations, a person can be fired solely because of their LGBQ sexuality.

The everyday slights still happen, too. I still encounter routine avoidances and silences about same-sex attraction among my colleagues, so-called friends, and families (see Chapter 6)—avoidances and silences that are difficult to theorize, and there are many moments when others treat my same-sex relationship as secondary to, or not as important as, their heterosexual relationships.

At a recent dermatology visit, I was told that the (female) doctor had to be accompanied by a witness, another (female) staff member, out of a concern for harassment and assault that might occur within the physician's office. I asked if the need for a witness was a requirement when all doctors meet with patients. I was told that a witness is necessary only when a female doctor meets with a male patient (and not when a male patient meets with a male doctor or when a female patient meet with a female doctor). Similarly, my university has policies against cisgender female and male students rooming together out of concerns that sex, assault, or discomfort might occur solely because of sex/gender differences; the same (heteronormative) concerns do not apply to same-sex/gender roommates.

I am still tangled by hateful religious discourse about the ways I relate and love, such as that made by Timothy Sauppé, a Catholic priest at St. Mary's Church in Westville, Illinois, a town next to my hometown of Danville, Illinois—and a priest of a parish that occupied a prominent part of my childhood and which many friends still attend. In August 2015, in response to the U.S. Supreme Court ruling in support of same-sex marriage, Sauppé mailed a letter to all Westville residents (about 4500). The letter, which, as of this writing (March 2019), is posted prominently on St. Mary's website, espouses many harmful, homophobic assumptions: it praises biological reproduction, celebrates (un-divorced) mothers and fathers; expresses a need for (heterosexual) families to defend themselves against the "homosexual culture war"; and disparages same-sex attraction and relationships. Sauppé also includes links to "Courage," a website with information for anyone who needs "help" dealing with "same-sex attraction," as well as a link to EnCourage ministry, an organization "dedicated to the spiritual needs of parents, siblings, children, and other relatives and friends of persons who have same-sex attractions."[1]

There are articles, chapters, and books describing the myriad harms that happen because of heteronormativity and anti-queer sentiments. We need these texts, and more of them. We also need texts that discuss how to address and remedy these harms, as well as texts that explore how queer people live with heteronormative and anti-queer harms across the lifespan. For instance, how might a queer person deal with heterosexism, homophobia, and the onslaught of negligence and harm? How does one deal with the incessant accumulation of hateful discourse, of being told that you are not worthy, important, able to live a meaningful life? How does one cope with the incessant fear and anxiety of physical attacks and killings, and the subtle and silent neglect promoted by friends, families, churches, schools, governments? I have explored responses to these questions using the concepts of "estrangement," "pride," and "forgiveness."

ESTRANGEMENT

In the essay, "Family Bullies," Keith and I critiqued the assumption that families are "nonvoluntary" relationships (Berry & Adams, 2016).[2] The norm of "obligation" that characterizes familial relationships frames them against and unlike friend relationships in that they cannot be chosen—they are voluntary and, as such, should be maintained regardless of conflict, or the desire to maintain them in the first place. The norm of obligation also can imply that people who emotionally or physically distance themselves from their family—become "estranged" (Agllias, 2013; Carr, Holman, Abetz, Koenig Kellas, & Vagnoni, 2015)—are naïve, deficient, or irresponsible. After all, "blood" is (supposedly) "thicker than water."

We reject the norm of obligation and the notion that family relationships are nonvoluntary. This is especially important when family members harm queer persons and when resistance and activism by these queer persons in familial contexts becomes too exhausting. Instead, we contend all family relationships should be understood as chosen, voluntary, and not obligatory, and we believe it is harmful to refer to families as nonvoluntary relationships as such nonvoluntary-framing complicates the ability for victims of familial heterosexism and homophobia to leave these abusive relationships. Estrangement should be considered "a balanced and appropriate response to an unhealthy situation" (Agllias, 2015, p. 117). LGBQ persons may have to remove themselves, unapologetically, from the family context especially when harm exists, and they should not feel shame or guilt for doing so. Arguing for the appropriateness of family estrangement also can make estrangement less of a "hidden loss," an issue that, as Agllias (2013) writes, is currently "difficult to speak about in public, resulting in social isolation or superficial social relationships" (p. 6).

Keith and I do not suggest that just because harm exists within a family then a person should abandon family relationships. Instead, it is important to challenge and reconsider the canonical, nonvoluntary understanding and social importance of these relationships, especially in extant research and everyday conversation (e.g., asking others about their relationships with family members). In families characterized by physical and emotional violence, continued instances of hurt, and unresolvable conflict, being estranged from specific family members or the general family system may be a necessary and healthy response. People should not be shamed solely for avoiding or abandoning family relationships, e.g., shame as manifest in comments such as "they're your family—you're obligated to them," or by framing the deliberate lack of contact with a family member as a "broken" relationship (Carr et al., 2015, p. 139), or by suggesting the lack of contact is indicative of a lack of love for one's enemy and, as such, a slight against some religious dogma. Conceiving of families as more voluntary and less obligatory also can cultivate different expectations about how certain roles within the family (e.g., "parent," "child," "sibling") can interact. Conceiving of a troubled sibling relationship as more voluntary might encourage siblings to interact in innovative and productive ways, as they are no longer presumed to be beholden to each other.

PRIDE

When homophobic, heterosexist, and anti-LGBQ sentiment exists, so does the need to create spaces and opportunities for feeling content—proud— of who we are. A second response to anti-queer sentiment is to establish contexts of support and pride. When queer people dislike themselves solely because of their sexuality, or feel embarrassed about their desires, then sources and spaces for pride are important, whether they come in the form of bars, parades, churches, non-profit organizations, mass mediated programs, and social media texts that celebrate queerness. With an abundance of homophobic and heterosexist sentiments, queer people need and deserve to find ways to cultivate self-love and self-care.

In many mostly-urban areas of the United States and in other urban parts of the world, same-sex/gender attraction, desire, and communities are welcomed and celebrated. In the U.S., many of these celebrations occur in June, officially designated by some officials as LGBQ pride month and in remembrance of the Stonewall Riots in New York (1969). These celebrations offer opportunities to counter the barrage of heteronormative hate by cultivating self-respect, resilience, and a love for LGBQ communities (see Bruce, 2016).

I have heard criticisms of pride, often from self-identified heterosexuals. The criticism usually takes two forms. First, there are those who ask why queer people need pride, why pride parades exist, or why it is important to be proud about same-sex attraction. I also hear statements such as, "I'm heterosexual and I do not need or expect a parade." These remarks indicate a lack of understanding that heterosexuality is rarely demonized. But heterosexuals typically do not experience neglect by friends, families, and local institutions solely for being heterosexual. They are not fired for being heterosexual, and they are supported systemically by many key social institutions, especially organizations (schools, governments, hospitals, insurance providers) that praise and privilege heterosexual marriage and the importance of (married) "mothers" and "fathers." When same-sex/gender attraction and LGBQ identities become just as celebrated, supported, and reinforced, there may then be no need for pride.

The second criticism stems from often-religious people who criticize pride as one of the seven "deadly sins." One definition of pride is "a cherished person or thing" indicated by "self-respect." A second definition of pride is "an excessively high opinion of one's own worth or importance which gives rise to a feeling or attitude of superiority over others" (*Oxford English Dictionary*, n.d.). In my experience, being "proud" and "pride" events are rooted in the first definition. These events exist to cherish people who are not cherished in other contexts. I am against pride parades that promote feelings of superiority; instead, they should promote self-respect among queers.

There are queer persons who critique pride as well, often for how capitalistic and/or exclusionary pride events have become, e.g., too White, too male, too able-bodied, too transphobic. These concerns are vital. In response, other pride events have emerged—e.g., Black Pride, Trans Pride— with the intent to cultivate self-respect. There may be queer persons who adamantly refuse pride altogether—they may not feel as though they need it, or they may be "self-hating" queers who have absorbed a lifetime of anti-queer sentiment—but these people should recognize that others may need to learn how to love their queer selves, especially in heteronormative contexts that disparage same-sex/gender attraction.

The call for pride is a call to love ourselves more than others might love us, to recognize queer beauty and potential, and to celebrate LGBQ communities. It is a call to celebrate sexual difference, to remind ourselves that we are okay, not deficient, and to seek—demand—just and equal rights and opportunities.

The call for pride may lessen in importance when animosity toward LGBQ persons dissipates. Until then, pride matters.

FORGIVENESS

Throughout this book, we have written about slights we and others have inflicted based on assumptions about, and enactments of, sex, gender, and sexuality. We have described ignorant friends and family members, bullies, and institutions endorsing and advocating heteronormative values and practices. We have written about the harms a LGBQ person may encounter pre- and post-coming out, necessary but incapacitating rumination practices, awkward responses, and moments of intense pain. Yet we have not addressed ways to deal with the troubling residue of the past, and how we live with moments and with others who have inflicted harms primarily because of sexuality.[3]

For instance, how does a child live with a parent who physically or emotionally harms the child for disclosing same-sex/gender attraction? How does a person make room for heterosexist and homophobic acquaintances, friends, and family members who refuse to acknowledge the person's queerness or same-sex/gender relationships and who continue to inflict harm on the person? And how might we live with ourselves for our bullying behaviors or when we too have been complicit in situations in which we learn, via hindsight, that we harmed others? Post-harm, we must consider how to deal with others who have slighted us, must determine how to live with others who have committed slights against us to live with them across the lifespan.

In my recent research, I have explored these questions through the concept of "forgiveness" (Adams, 2016, 2017, 2019; Berry & Adams, 2016). The concept of forgiveness is premised upon three conditions: (1) an offense occurs; (2) there are agents, typically an offender(s) and a victim(s); and (3) there is a need to, or desire for, acknowledging and making amends for the offense. The severity of an offense can be extreme, such as with killing or sexual assault, but also mundane, like when someone refuses to acknowledge another person, makes a disrespectful comment, or wishes that an offender will experience harm themselves—metaphorically, an "eye for an eye." Sometimes an offense can be intentional, such as when someone assaults another person, uses a comment to shame others, or wishes someone ill will; and sometimes an offense can be unintentional, such as when a person is oblivious to the negative consequences of an action or fails to recognize the insulting connotations of a seemingly-pleasant remark.

Forgiveness happens with "a change of heart, a shift in attitude, an alteration of an inner state" (Neu, 2011, p. 134); it occurs when a victim overcomes resentment and contempt toward an entity for committing an offense (Hagberg, 2011). If a change of heart or shift in attitude does not happen, or should resentment and contempt exist, then forgiveness has not occurred. When forgiveness does occur, the offense is no longer the "most salient feature of the offender, just as our own victimhood" is no longer the "most salient feature of ourselves in our relation to the wrongdoer" (Gerrard & McNaughton, 2011, p. 99). With forgiveness, a person does not forget an offense, but rather develops a new relationship to the offense, e.g., recognizing cultural constraints that contributed to the offense; acknowledging their complicity or participation in the offense; believing others acted as best they could under given circumstances.

Forgiveness is important for three reasons. First, being able to forgive others, to overcome resentment and contempt, can improve our relationships. Perpetually resenting an offender leaves little hope for collaboration, improved interaction, and social change or justice. Second, forgiveness can encourage us to consider the ways we, too, have committed offenses and recognize that "we may all need at times to be forgiven" (Neu, 2011, p. 136). As Gerrard and McNaughton (2011) write, even the "worst" humans are not "monsters"—"if they are monsters, then so too are we, at least potentially— there's a recurring streak of evil in the human blueprint" (p. 103). Third, forgiveness can release the burden of a harmful past, as holding onto anxiety and pain can be exhausting and toxic; as Betty Kilby notes, "Hate is like taking poison. The only person you hurt is yourself" (cited in Drash, 2010). Although an offense itself may indeed feel severe, the burden of not forgiving can infuse us with hate, stress, and contempt.

I opened this chapter with a few instances in which heteronormative harm can occur: friends and family members who perpetuate homophobic assumptions; the mundane sexist and heterosexist assumptions of a dermatologist's office and my university's policy against co-ed roommates; and a letter, sent by a priest, to residents of the town next to my hometown. With my anti-LGBQ friends and family members, I do not feel as though I have much resentment and contempt toward them; instead, I choose estrangement. I have been out for nearly two decades, and I am exhausted from trying to address and cede to their incessant heteronormative hate. With the dermatologist and my university, I have less resentment and contempt for those who enforce the policies. I consider the policies institutionalized manifestations of heteronormativity that cannot be attributed to a sole individual/group. I could (and should) challenge the policies, as well as those who reinforce the policies, but I would first have to explain the inherent heteronormative assumptions, and then identify the person/group who can initiate change.

My relationship with Sauppé is more complex, as it involves Sauppé and (former) friends who attend the church. I resent Sauppé and worry about his prominent presence and significant (ab)use of power: In a rural community like Westville, a priest can wield great authority, e.g., by providing supposedly-correct interpretations of Christian scripture; being viewed as a trusted community friend who participates in many life events including baptisms at birth; conducting (heterosexual) marriages; helping people live with/confess their sins; and performing last rites in preparation for death.

In addition to Sauppé, I feel anger toward community members who walk through the church doors every Sunday and, in practice, condone Sauppé's hateful assumptions. Although I recognize homosexuality and same-sex/gender marriage are not the only issues that should concern parishioners, nor do I believe parishioners are cultural dupes who agree with Sauppé's views, parishioners do comprise the church; without them, there would be no need for Sauppé.[4] If a less hateful priest led St. Mary's, I would not have such an adverse reaction.

Although forgiveness cannot be prescribed, I have some ideas about how forgiveness could happen, at least in relation to Sauppé, the agent and wrongdoer of harmful discourse. If he is alive and well, I could first find and inform Sauppé about the ways his discourse has harmed me and inquire about his intentions for creating and perpetuating hateful ideas. I would like to assume that he did not know he was offensive with his discourse. Yet, I also believe Sauppé knew his discourse could offend others and would not agree that is harmful. Why else would he make the discourse public? Further, should he disagree about the offensiveness of the discourse, more harmful discourse might ensue, thereby requiring new instances of forgiveness.

If Sauppé cared about the ways his words harmed me, and others like me, and if he ever sought my forgiveness, I would demand the hateful discourse to be removed from St. Mary's website. I would also want a public apology for his actions, either at mass, in a newsletter, in a local news outlet, or maybe even a letter, like the first, mailed to all Westville residents. Further, I would expect a commitment from him to challenging Catholicism's demonization of same-sex/gender attractions and relationships. I also expect parishioners to refuse to attend St. Mary's Church, especially if Sauppé does not remove and apologize for his hateful letter, as well as commit to challenging Catholicism's demonization of same-sex/gender attractions and relationships. Although I recognize these demands may be untenable or undesired by some, I cannot yet forgive Sauppé or the parishioners who, by their presence, support his leadership. Consequently, I will continue to harbor resentment and contempt toward these entities, and I recognize they may not care.

I might also work to recognize cultural constraints that contributed to the discourse, attempt to understand the conditions of the texts' production, realize that Sauppé's profession practices and celebrates offensive views, and, consequently, that agents acted as best they could under these circumstances. However, understanding may not be enough to forgive the agents. They espoused harmful messages and need to be held accountable for the discourse.

I think about other articles and historical documents that espouse heterosexism and homophobia. I have more understanding/forgiveness toward a homophobic text from 1955 (e.g., Rees & Usill, 1955), less for a text published in 2003 (e.g., McLaurin, 2003), and much less for a 2015 letter written by a priest and still posted on a church's website (2019). I have more understanding/forgiveness toward a person who argued for only cisgender, heterosexual marriage in 1970 than a person making the same argument in 2019. Yet even with the arguments from decades ago, I wonder how I should view the agents who created and perpetuated hate and the homophobic discourse, even though it may have been acceptable at the time. I try to monitor "semantic contagion" (Bochner, 2014; Hacking, 1995)—applying current terminology, meanings, values to past practices—but I struggle.

I want Sauppé to engage in corrective actions for his harmful discourse. Should he not choose to do so, I will merely tolerate him. He does not garner my respect or care, nor will I make time for him, dialogue about the worthiness of my same-sex attraction or marriage. I also will continue to call out his hate. I recognize such a lack of civility might offend Sauppé, yet he should not be shocked, because my reaction shows what can happen when offensive discourse is made public without apology. Further, I do not subscribe carelessly to civility, politeness, and respectability politics, especially when these acts silence criticism and protest (McKerrow, 2001).

Under ideal conditions, people who have committed slights against others would apologize, seek forgiveness, commit to working through homophobia and heterosexism, and pledge to never intentionally harm a person. Yet, I live in contexts where the homophobia, criticism, and thoughts about forgiveness continue every time a family member makes an inappropriate remark, as I move through the heteronormatively structured world, or when I learn about a friend attending St. Mary's Church.

***

Estrangement, pride, and forgiveness are possible responses to homophobic, heterosexist, anti-LGBQ sentiments. Out of a care for self, estrangement may be necessary, especially when a person is tangled in an abusive relationship. There might be a desire for supportive LGBQ spaces and events, ones that allow people to come together to feel less terrible about themselves. There may be a need to have discussions about how to deal with others who have inflicted—and who may continue to inflict—harms on LGBQ persons, as well as discussions about instances when victims should never grant forgiveness. Estrangement, pride, and forgiveness: three interrelated responses for cultivating self-love, overcoming adversity, and becoming resilient, responses against those who believe queerness is not okay, responses to remind LGBQ persons that they too are worthy of love and care.

DISCUSSION QUESTIONS

1. Estrangement, pride, and forgiveness are possible responses to homophobic, heterosexist, anti-LGBQ sentiments. What are your thoughts about each of these responses?
2. What might be additional ways a LGBQ person could respond to past harms? How should a LGBQ person live with others who continue to commit slights against them?
3. In what situations and under what circumstances might a LGBQ person not forgive others, when their resentment and contempt toward offensive others may be healthy and justified?

NOTES

[1]   This paragraph has been revised from Adams (2019).
[2]   This section on estrangement has been revised from Berry and Adams (2016, pp. 60–61)
[3]   This section on forgiveness has been revised from Adams (2019).
[4]   In 2010, St. Mary's school closed because of low enrollment. For that, I am thankful—one less organization espousing homophobic discourse, fewer chances for (queer) children to encounter oppressive religious dogma. Yet I simultaneously feel evil for wishing ill-will knowing the many students, parents, faculty, and staff who can no longer attend a religious school (but one that, in my experience, perpetuates hateful ideologies).

REFERENCES

Adams, T. E. (2011). *Narrating the closet: An autoethnography of same-sex attraction.* Walnut Creek, CA: Left Coast Press.

Adams, T. E. (2016). Sexuality and self-forgiveness. *Women & Language, 39,* 121–125.

Adams, T. E. (2017). Critical autoethnography, education, and a call for forgiveness. *International Journal of Multicultural Education, 19,* 79–88. http://ijme-journal.org/index.php/ijme/article/view/1387

Adams, T. E. (2019). Critical rhetoric, relationality, and temporality: A case for forgiveness. *International Journal of Communication.*

Agllias, K. B. (2013). Family estrangement. In T. Mizrahi & L. E. Davis (Eds.), *Encyclopedia of social work* (20th ed.). New York, NY: National Association of Social Workers and Oxford University Press.

Agllias, K. B. (2015). Difference, choice, and punishment: Parental beliefs and understandings about adult child estrangement. *Australian Social Work, 68,* 115–129. https://doi.org/10.1080/0312407X.2014.927897

Alexander, B. K., & Weems, M. (2017). Special issue: June 12, 2016: Terrorism and hate in Orlando, America—poetic and performative responses. *Qualitative Inquiry, 23,* 483–571.

Berry, K., & Adams, T. E. (2016). Family bullies. *Journal of Family Communication, 16,* 51–63. https://doi.org/10.1080/15267431.2015.1111217

Bochner, A. P. (2014). *Coming to narrative: A personal history of paradigm change in the human sciences.* Walnut Creek, CA: Left Coast Press/Routledge.

Bruce, K. M. (2016). *Pride parades: How a parade changed the world.* New York, NY: New York University Press.

Carr, K., Holman, A., Abetz, J., Koenig Kellas, J., & Vagnoni, E. (2015). Giving voice to the silence of family estrangement: Comparing reasons of estranged parents and adult children in a nonmatched sample. *Journal of Family Communication, 15,* 130–140. https://doi.org/10.1080/15267431.2015.1013106

Drash, W. (2010, May 20). When kin of slaves and owner meet. *CNN.* Retrieved February 28, 2019, from www.cnn.com/2010/LIVING/05/20/slavery.descendants.meet/index.html

Gerrard, E., & McNaughton, D. (2011). Conditional unconditional forgiveness. In C. Fricke (Ed.), *The ethics of forgiveness: A collection of essays* (pp. 97–106). New York, NY: Routledge.

Hacking, I. (1995). *Rewriting the soul: Multiple personality and the sciences of memory.* Princeton, NJ: Princeton University Press.

Hagberg, G. L. (2011). The self rewritten: The case of self-forgiveness. In C. Fricke (Ed.), *The ethics of forgiveness: A collection of essays* (pp. 69–80). New York, NY: Routledge.

McKerrow, R. E. (2001). Coloring outside the lines: The limits of civility. *Vital Speeches of the Day, 67,* 278–81.

McLaurin, S. (2003). Homophobia: An autoethnographic story. *The Qualitative Report, 8,* 481–486. Retrieved from http://nsuworks.nova.edu/tqr/vol8/iss3/8/

Neu, J. (2011). On loving our enemies. In C. Fricke (Ed.), *The ethics of forgiveness* (pp. 130–142). New York, NY: Routledge.

Oxford English Dictionary. (n.d.). *Pride.* Retrieved July 20, 2014, from http://www.oed.com

Rees, J. T., & Usill, H. V. (Eds.). (1955). *They stand apart: A critical survey of the problems of homosexuality.* Melbourne: William Heinemann.

ABOUT THE AUTHORS

Tony E. Adams (Ph.D., University of South Florida) is a Professor and Chair of the Department of Communication at Bradley University. He researches interpersonal and family communication, autoethnography, qualitative research, communication theory, and sex, gender, and sexuality. He is the co-author and co-editor of six books including *Narrating the Closet: An Autoethnography of Same Sex Attraction* (Routledge), *Autoethnography* (Oxford University Press) and the *Handbook of Autoethnography* (Routledge). He is a co-editor of the *Writing Lives: Ethnographic Narratives* book series (Routledge) and founding co-editor of the *Journal of Autoethnography* (University of California Press).

Keith Berry (Ph.D., Southern Illinois University Carbondale) is an Associate Professor of Communication at the University of South Florida. Much of Keith's research has focused on bullying and identity, LGBTQ cultures and identities, and reflexivity in autoethnography. His recent book *Bullied: Tales of Torment, Identity, and Youth* (2016, Routledge) has received several honors, including the 2017 Goodall/Trujillo "It's a Way of Life" Award by the International Congress of Qualitative Inquiry, and 2016 "Best Book" by the Ethnography Division of the National Communication Association (NCA). Keith's research has also appeared in journals such as *Communication Education, Journal of Applied Communication Research,* and *Qualitative Inquiry*, and in books such as the *Handbook of Autoethnography*. Dr. Berry is a member and past Co-Chair of NCA's Anti-Bullying Task Force.

Catherine M. Gillotti (Ph.D., University of Kentucky) is an Associate Professor of Communication in the Department of Communication and Creative Arts, and has been a faculty member at Purdue University Northwest for 23 years. She has held administrative appointments as the Graduate Program Coordinator and the Basic Course Director. Her research agenda primarily focuses on the study of patient-provider interactions and health outcomes. She has published in the *Handbook of Health Communication,* and the journal *Social Science and Medicine.* While the majority of her publications and conference presentations focus on the study of bad news delivery in the health care context, she also has published in the area of gender studies.

www.ingramcontent.com/pod-product-compliance
Lightning Source LLC
Chambersburg PA
CBHW05044328O326
41932CB00013BA/2221

* 9 7 8 9 0 0 4 4 1 8 7 7 6 *